Contemporary Choral Work ~i~~ ~

Silana
Sr.

2019

Contemporary Choral Work with Boys

Martin Ashley

compton
PUBLISHING

This edition first published 2014 © 2014 by Compton Publishing Ltd.

Registered office: Compton Publishing Ltd, 30 St. Giles', Oxford,
OX1 3LE, UK Registered company number: 07831037

Editorial offices: 3 Wrafton Road, Braunton, EX33 2BT, UK
Web: www.comptonpublishing.co.uk

ISBN 978-1-909082-05-2

A catalogue record for this book is available from the British Library.

Cover design by David Siddall Multimedia (www.davidsiddall.com)

Set in Adobe Caslon Pro 10pt by Stuart Brown

Table of Contents

Acknowledgments

This is a book I have wanted to write for some time. It is a book that I think also is needed, so I would like to thank the publisher, Noel McPherson for seeing the need and giving me the opportunity. As is explained in the introduction, though I have received a good number of research grants during my career, this is a book written during the first year of retirement, my pension being my research grant! I have been able, therefore, to research and write whatever I liked without the need to worry about how to please a grant awarding body. Nevertheless, much is owed to Edge Hill University, which has continued to provide the supporting infrastructure that is so often taken for granted but without which it is difficult to function as an academic. In particular I would like to thank Robert Smedley, Pro-vice chancellor and Dean of the education faculty, who has been a most supportive line manager in the years leading up to this book.

I had naively imagined that this would be a book I could just sit down and write. This proved to be far from the case, particularly when venturing outside my academic comfort zone. I would therefore like to thank Professor Gary Butler, consultant paediatrician at University College London for his help with the paediatrics and endocrinology, and Professor David Howard, Head of the Department of Electronics at the University of York for his help with the physiology and acoustics of the singing voice. I owe much also to Dr Ann-Christine Mecke of the Felix Mendelssohn Bartholdy University of Music and Theatre in Leipzig for the German perspective. I would also like to acknowledge the support of Drs Ursula Geisler and Karin Johansson for their supportive work in setting up the European Choir in Focus research network and the happy hours in Sweden and Germany. For historical and archival material, I must thank Stephen Beet whose efforts in this field are legendary and whose willingness to share is most generous. It was a privilege to correspond with Dr John Cooksey before his death, and I would like also to thank Dr Don Collins of the Cambiata Vocal Institute of America for his encouragement.

A number of UK musical colleagues have contributed much to the book and they receive due acknowledgement in the chapters that describe their work, though I would like to thank them all again here for their willingness to contribute. I need to single out Ian Wells from whose choir in Southport a number of the most closely and recently studied boys have been drawn, but who does not have his own chapter section. A good many boys have given me many hours of their time. I would like to thank them for this, the ones named in the interludes have their own memorials, but there have been many others too. I am very grateful to all the boys who have bravely allowed me to measure their growth and development and probe some of the inner secrets of their vocal functioning. In particular I must thank the parents of these boys who have acted as their chaperones, but in many cases going further and further beyond the call of duty – from cups of coffee to a full supper! It has been a privilege to be invited into people's lives in such a way. I really ought particularly to thank Gill Fourie of the Association of British Choral Directors. Not only does Gill hold the undisputed record for provision of supper, her enthusiasm and readiness to put into practice the principles of this book has resulted in many adolescent boys learning what choral singing can do for them.

Finally, this is the third book I have written on boys and singing, as well as many academic papers. Each and every such publication has presented a new aural challenge for my long-suffering wife Jo. Not only has she suffered a house full of loud treble voices being tested to destruction, she has proof read with an eagle eye every result.

This book is dedicated to all who can see the need to inspire and interest boys in choral singing. May their work prosper.

Foreword

'His two elder brothers were choristers at St Paul's.'

These words could have been spoken many times in the past few years. But the young man they referred to was William Byrd, in the mid-sixteenth century. The tradition of boys' singing in the United Kingdom is broad and deep and, in my view, along with the Associated Board, the chief reason for this country's peculiar musical strength.

But traditions need constant reinvention if they are to remain vibrant. Hence recent significant changes in the organisation and recruitment of boy choristers, the founding of secular boy-treble choirs and the attempts to encourage boys to begin what for some will be the source of joy for a lifetime. The introduction of girl choristers, first by Richard Seal to Salisbury Cathedral Choir in addition to the boys, was perceived by some as a threat to the tradition, but with thoughtful organisation, mindful of social gender differences, it has been a great success. For a girl to sing and for a boy to sing are very different matters, socially and physiologically, because the nature of the change that happens to a boy's voice is much more extreme.

Until recently it has been difficult to understand the physical nature of these changes: singing-teaching in general has relied to a certain extent on guesswork and practical experience. But now that we have the benefit of good, clear practical research we can know for certain what happens, and our teaching can be based on solid facts derived from direct observation.

It is important that musicianship develops along with the voice. It is no good just having a good voice and expecting later on that someone will teach you the notes. For this reason, and for general social and vocal development in a singer, it is extremely important to sing well in a good choir. This book helps with all of these processes, and for the first time brings together social, physiological and vocal research to give a wonderfully clear view of the way forward for a young singer.

Ralph Allwood, MBE

Introduction

How and why this book was written and who it is for

This is a book for anybody who wants to understand in some depth the boy choral voice and perhaps begin or improve their work with boys' choirs. It is the third book I have written about boys and singing. My first two were based primarily upon sociological studies of how boys negotiate masculine identity through voice. If you are worried about whether boys do not want to 'sound like girls', if you think boys will only sing in rock bands, or if you want to understand how 'cuteness' is exploited by the big recording companies, you may find those books of interest. This book differs from the first two because it is written unashamedly with one particular population of boys in mind. These are the boys for whom we do not have to make singing 'cool' and to whom we do not have to apologise for choral work. These are the boys who might hear a great choral sound, experience a feeling from deep inside and want to join in. Who can analyse exactly what they feel? I have plenty of research conducted over the years that reliably informs me that whatever these feelings are, they exist in quite young boys. There are perhaps more of these boys than is sometimes imagined. They are waiting for somebody who will open a musical treasure trove for them and unlock the key to something that will fulfil them for the rest of their lives.

In this book, I attempt a blend of different kinds of knowledge. For much of my time as an academic, I wrestled with the difference between theoretical knowledge and professional knowledge, never more so than when trying to explain to prospective postgraduate students the difference between a Ph.D. and an Ed.D. The former has to do with the creation of new knowledge that may be quite esoteric or abstruse, theoretical in the sense of 'blue skies', abstract, or as is sometimes said, 'basic'. The latter has to do with the creation of new knowledge about professional practice, applied knowledge, 'useful' knowledge even. Too often one hears theory decried, usually by relatively indifferent practitioners who would improve their choir work considerably if they understood its theoretical base better. Equally, one comes across brilliant conductors of boys' choirs who with a false modesty confess themselves to be in awe of academic professors with theory. But these brilliant conductors do have ways of working which constitute theory. It is simply a matter of articulating it.

In assembling my material, I have drawn on three principal sources. First, I have looked at the existing body of scientific research into the boy voice. I have interpreted this theory critically in the light of my own experience and my observations of how others put it into practice. I have added to it from the latest research in endocrinology and paediatrics. Second, there is my own, original empirical work on puberty and choral tone. I hope the claim that this does add something new to what is known, challenging legitimately some existing beliefs and practices, is not too immodest. This work has involved many long hours of work with boys who have consented to participate in this study. Over 1 000 boys' voices have been recorded and analysed by my research. A cohort of the sample has been involved in longitudinal assessment over several years. I have got to know these boys and their families well. I have perhaps unique data on their growth and development that is amply supplemented by the conversations I have recorded with them during their assessments. I have also made good quality recordings of their singing. Cameo portraits of some of these boys are included as interludes between the main chapters. They are, after all, the most important participants in contemporary choral work with boys. Finally, I have looked closely at the work of some choir directors I respect, drawing those colleagues into reflective dialogue about the nature of their work. In these ways, I hope I have produced a book that is not full of abstract or rarefied theory, but theory in use. I have attempted to analyse and explain what successful directors of boys' choral work actually do, in the hope that others may incorporate aspects of that understanding into their own work.

If you are looking for a book of hints on repertoire, you will need to look elsewhere. My aim is that the reader him or herself should be able to select repertoire on the basis of the knowledge of boys and their voices that is contained within these pages. Repertoire lists rapidly date and what works for one choir may not work for another. Nevertheless I have asked the choir directors interviewed to provide lists of repertoire that has worked well for them in recent years. These are included as appendices but more usefully on the companion web pages where they can be regularly updated.

Also on the companion web pages, you will find an extensive bibliography for each chapter. Many things are said in the book about boys and their voices and, unless I use an expression such as 'in my opinion' or 'it is my belief', what is said is based on peer-reviewed scientific research or the writings of authoritative and experienced practitioners. The book is not written in an academic style in which the flow of the text is constantly interrupted by referencing and citation, but for those who wish to interrogate in the academic manner, the web bibliography is there. For other readers, I have included reference to the major seminal sources and, at the end of each chapter, recommendations for further reading.

Some lessons from the evolution of the book

Whilst I have my research on masculinity, boyhood and vocal identity to draw on, this book is based on new research specifically into the boy voice in choral singing. This is my real passion and I have been able to write this book beholden to nobody but myself. There is a reason for this. I have reached that stage in my career where I no longer have to obtain research grants, either to find the time to research and write, or to justify my university position. Research grants were never forthcoming for something that was perceived as the preserve of a privileged elite. It was only when I adopted the language of singing as an inclusive activity for young males that the grant money began to flow. One of my larger grants afforded me a whole year out to do nothing but travel the country talking to boys who had recorded commercial CDs and asking young people in schools what they thought of those CDs. The title of the grant application on which it was based was *Young Masculinity and Vocal Performance* (Ashley, 2011). It required me to look at the use of the young male voice in every musical genre. Later, when I received an even larger grant to work with the National Youth Choirs of Great Britain, the official title of the project was *Widening Young Male Participation in Chorus*.

Why all this beating about the bush? Why such care to avoid the words 'choir' or 'choral' at any point? Well, for a very good reason. It has been my experience that the words 'choir' and 'choral' tend to signal a privileged elite that is going to find it very hard to get public money for research. This is particularly so if boys are involved, for the perception is that of an exclusive activity for white boys from the middle and upper classes. This may not be an entirely accurate perception and is certainly not one I endorse or in any way seek to perpetuate. I have nevertheless learned the hard way over many a long year that it reigns in the minds of the gatekeepers of public funding. For all sorts of reasons, this situation seems to have gone largely unchallenged by the guardians of choral singing.

One of the most troublesome words in the musical lexicon for me is 'classical'. I prefer to understand this as the style of the Haydn/Mozart period but this, of course, is not the popular meaning. The popular meaning has much more to do with privilege and exclusion. In the popular imagination there *is* funding available for the promotion of 'classical' music, but only for huge sums that seem to go to London opera houses. There *is* funding available for the social inclusion of disaffected young males through 'music', but not exactly what anybody might call 'classical' music. So is this book about 'classical' music? I prefer to think not. I prefer to think it is about high-quality choral work, though I do have views on what makes for the 'high quality' and the 'choral'.

I will confine my political statements to the assertion that high-quality choral work should be available to all and leave it at that for the time being. This is a book about the boy choral voice. Its content is influenced primarily by my scientific interest in how that sound is produced. I have no particular desire to become embroiled in cultural disputes. I will confess that I seldom read reviews of the latest choir recordings in musical journals. I am far more likely to read and study scientific reports about the acoustics of the vocal tract or, most of all, the impact of puberty on the quality of choral tone. This latter topic has constituted my own particular attempt to add to the sum of human knowledge, as one is required to do as a research professor. I could have written a whole book on the topic of puberty and choral tone, but I wished to write a book that would have wider appeal and more use. My intention has been to provide a text that will serve as the handbook of a workable, practical theory on choral work with boys.

Significant 'health warnings' are nevertheless required at this point. First, it must be plainly stated that we know a great deal less about the boy choral voice than might be imagined. Whilst we have not explored in much depth what lies beyond the frontiers of Jupiter's moons neither have we discovered anything like all there is to be known about the great depths of our own oceans. The same is true of the boy choral voice. A constant feature of my quest for knowledge of the topic has been disappointment at the inability of leading voice coaches and researchers to answer some of my questions. My own understanding has proceeded in fits and starts as I have come to realize the extent to which published texts that sound authoritative owe more to their authors' imaginations than to the thorough process of slow, painstaking scientific advance. This book, therefore, is full of gaps in knowledge. I endeavour to make it clear when a claim is based upon my own belief as opposed to a piece of scientific research that seems to be valid and reliable. When I state that something is uncertain, it is less likely, I hope, because I have failed to 'do my homework' than that I have found flaws in some of the 'homework texts' consulted. All true scientific knowledge is in any case provisional and subject to modification or refutation.

The second health warning concerns perhaps the biggest professional challenge I have faced in a long career of teaching, lecturing and teacher training. Is it possible to distil the art of a great teacher or conductor in a way that its elements can be taught to others? This has certainly been the aim of what has been called the 'technocratic' approach to teacher training that has prevailed in recent decades. Critics of this approach suggest that it de-professionalises teaching, reducing it to a mere technology that can be learned by anyone capable of repeating procedures determined to be 'what works' by other 'experts'. Supporters of the process claim that it results in more consistent outcomes.

The pot of gold at the end of the choral work rainbow is that the postcode lottery which operates with regards to any one boy's chance of coming into contact with a high quality choral conductor might be ended.

I had thus hoped, earlier in my career, through the codification and transmission of relevant knowledge to achieve more consistent outcomes and greater equality of access for boys to good choral work. A level playing field in which any boy joining any choir anywhere will have equality of opportunity with any other remains frustratingly elusive. I am coming to accept it as perhaps inevitable. Not all choirs will ever be equally good and the deciding factor is always the availability of a conductor who is literally 'outstanding'— who stands outside what can be taught by technocratic means. This will not stop me working throughout the book towards a resolution of the art versus science dichotomy. I hope to persuade the reader that there is merit in a creative approach that understands that science has to be practised as much as art.

My own recent learning has been the product of much that is measurable and quantifiable. More things than we might care to admit, indeed, can be measured and quantified. It is possible to measure such straightforward qualities as boys' heights, weights, lung volumes, laryngeal waveforms, acoustic spectra and so on. I have made measurements of over 1 000 boys and derived tremendous insights as a result. The creative synthesis of such basic quantities can and has led to huge advances in the understanding of something that might otherwise be regarded as an inaccessible, mystical art. Nevertheless, I have borrowed from Dylan Wiliam the term 'black box' to describe those many elements of choral work with boys that retain for the present either a mystical dimension, or an area where scientific illumination remains far from adequate.

I hope to convey as much of what can be known and understood as possible, but scientific insights too cannot be reduced to words and numbers on a page. One has to do the measuring oneself to understand in depth what it means and gain the 'feel' for the practical relevance of the knowledge. I have produced, with my colleague David Howard, a smartphone app which should make the process much more accessible and I will refer to this app at various points throughout the text.

Ultimately though, I have never been able to capture, distil and codify the mystique of what is added by an outstanding conductor when he or she brings this together in a way that defies reduction and codification. There is then the further complication of working with boys! It might be thought that the proliferation of IT-driven aids to singing, particularly endoscopic imagery of the larynx, would motivate boys who belong to the generation known as 'digital natives'. I certainly thought this once, but experience has taught me otherwise. Boys certainly do not learn to sing through instruction in a set of codified principles. Most boys just want to get on with the singing and what appeals to them most is the choir director who has the practical art of being inspirational, funny, able to retain control in spite of this, musically demanding and well-paced in rehearsal (i.e. singing not talking!). So the challenge is to get the best out of boys through skilful interpretation of theoretical knowledge in a practical context. No small ask!

Out of these considerations, I have evolved the following general theory of contemporary choral work with boys. I will explain, justify and elaborate on this theory as the pages of the book unfold.

1. Boys learn to sing through being in choirs. Their becoming proficient musicians is a particularly useful by-product of this process.
2. Successful choral work with boys begins with a search for the right boys—musical boys who can readily access their 'head voice'.
3. These boys then learn to sing in choirs through imitation. They need to be surrounded by good musicianship and good vocal role models.
4. No one will get anywhere in choral work with boys unless they are passionate about success with boys and also able to discipline them whilst earning their respect, trust and loyalty.
5. Anyone undertaking choral work with boys needs, in addition to all the other knowledge bases of the choral director, a good understanding of adolescence, puberty and the voice. This is necessary to avoid damage either to boys' future careers as adult singers or to the sensibilities of listeners.

One does not, in an empirical work, simply pontificate about one's beliefs—one seeks the evidence to test, refine or discard them. What has pleased me most during the researching and writing of this book is the feeling that I have been able to evolve the above general theory through collaboration with people who do actually obtain inspirational choral performances from boys. It has been my unique privilege to articulate in a book the knowledge that these experts carry about in their daily work. I hope I am successful in demonstrating how theory and practice are not mutually exclusive but intimately intertwined in the best choral work with boys.

Further reading

Durrant, C. (2003). *Choral Conducting: Philosophy and Practice*. London: Routledge.

Chapter 1: Into the choral black box

This chapter is all about the underlying rationale for choral singing. Each section begins with a 'W': What is choral singing? Who are the boys who do it? Where can and does it take place? Perhaps most important of all, why do we do it?

1.1   What is choral singing?

What is choral singing? I am going to avoid discussion of whether it is in any way a 'classical' form of music-making and adopt an acoustic definition. According to Sten Ternström (2003), the minimum number of singers that can constitute a vocal chorus is three to a part. This is because the chorus effect of conflicting intonation, attack and delay is first heard when the number of voices is more than two. Thus, for the performance of four-part vocal music, the smallest number of singers possible to count as a choir is twelve. Eight singers would be a double octet, acoustically different to a choir. This assumes that a choir is also a chorus. Choir singing, therefore, is an activity, the nature of which is tied up with acoustic (and social) factors that require at least twelve performers. Something called a 'chorus effect' differentiates choral work from 'singing'.

Jim Daugherty (2003) offers us this definition. The 'chorus effect', he states:

> occurs when many voices and their reflections create a quasi-random sound of such complexity that the normal mechanisms of auditory localization and fusion are disrupted; in effect, [the chorus effect] dissociates sound from its sources and endows it with an 'independent' existence.

Nowhere more than in work with boys does this dissociation of the sound from its sources matter. For literally thousands of years, the sound of boys' voices in chorus has been regarded as the sound of 'angels'. The boys' choral sound is not the sound of wannabe stars on Whatever Country's Got Talent. It is the disembodied, ethereal sound that belongs, not to the singer, but if one is inclined to the poetic metaphor, to the angelic hosts far beyond the skies. This is the principal reason that boys' voices have been thought so suitable for use in Christian worship over millennia. Even in what is, to all intents and purposes, a post-Christian age for most people, it is no bad thing for small boys to learn that they are not divas around whose vainglorious hopes for fleeting and vacuous celebrity status the universe revolves.

Returning, however to my strictly scientific brief, there are all sorts of acoustic considerations that bring angel voices into existence. A key word that unites theorists and practitioners is blend. More readily understood by boys is the notion of teamwork. As one conductor we shall meet later in the book said, on the football field a boy can pause to do up his bootlace. In the choir, one boy who drops out of the team effort for even a split second ruins the whole chord. Boys need absolutely to understand this and to be wholly committed to the concept. 'Understand' for boys means a complete focus on the task, which is the product of absolute discipline. I shall have a lot more to say about how this is achieved in a positive way by the power of a conductor who wins boys' respect out of admiration and loyalty, not tyranny and fear.

Blend is more than just teamwork, however, and something of a Holy Grail in choral singing. Many choir directors worry that individual voices will stand out in the chorus, particularly if some members of the choir are also solo singers. For the subdued adult singer, this can lead to choral singing that is less resonant than solo singing. We shall need to develop an understanding during the book of what this means. There has been a fair amount of research into how adult solo singers adapt their behaviours when singing in chorus. Some cut back on the higher resonant frequencies, particularly those that peak as the 'singer's formant'. They emphasise the fundamental tones more than the upper harmonics. Voices blend as a result into a whole that is favoured by some choir directors though often a cause of frustration to singing teachers. We shall return shortly and several times later to this very important topic.

The process differs somewhat with regard to boys. It is an area in which I am currently conducting research (see Chapter 10) and I am some way from a definitive answer. Colin Baldy (2010) believes that choir directors are wrong to request singers to subdue their voices. A choir composed of singers singing as soloists will always, he argues, sound better than one in which voices are compromised in order to 'blend'. Blend will occur automatically, he argues, when voices are used properly. Boys should certainly 'sing out'. This does not mean force the tone through raising sub-glottal pressure. Boys may do this if you just request more volume from them or they interpret 'sing out' in this way. 'Sing out' means use the whole voice with its fully developed resonances and it takes boys time to learn this.

I have heard it said that boys' voices blend easily because they lack individual character. In acoustic terms, this is a claim that the spectrum is simple and the wave form sinusoidal. This is patently false. I have solid evidence that shows how every boy's voice in a choir is entirely unique and easily recognizable to anybody who knows the boy. There have been a few boy trebles over the years that have had astonishing and memorable voices. I will name James Rainbird as one voice that haunts me. A whole choir of James Rainbirds would certainly blend. Take most individual boys out of a fine sounding choir, though, and the result is usually less impressive than the sound of the whole choir. With good adult singers, it can be the other way round.

This is not though because boys' treble voices lack complexity or harmonic interest. There has been some interesting work recently on the phenomenon of 'ring'. 'Ring' is a set of formant frequencies which allow a child's treble voice to carry powerfully above the bigger sound of men's voices, organs or orchestras. It is ring that creates the spine tingle of a great boy choral sound in the resonant acoustic of a big cathedral. Other research has shown that not only ring frequencies but most other interesting formant clusters disappear from the young male voice towards the end of puberty. There are perfectly objective scientific demonstrations of the fact that boys' treble voices are special, whilst the voices of older adolescents are dull, uninteresting and weak. I use the term 'schoolboy bass' for this period of waiting for the resonance or harmonic interest to return in the mature adult voice.

I am going to use from time to time the metaphor of the 'black box' to describe the current state of scientific insight into the acoustic blending of boy treble voices. However, my attempts to capture and codify the 'theory in use' of choral professionals have met with greater success. All agree that choral singing differs from other kinds of singing by virtue of the fact that it is highly disciplined. In the words of one respondent, boys in a choir are not 'just singing'. Choral singing must provide boys with a challenge that takes them beyond singing together the songs they might in any case sing along with on their iPods. Choral work with boys is the process of teaching them as a team demanding music that is unfamiliar. It is this stretching and occasional excursion beyond the comfort zone that generates the process of achieving absolute unanimity. All good directors of boys' choral work stress unanimity in vowel production, breathing, intonation, consonant placing and articulation, attack, decay, and just about any other common action of the choir. These are the elements they concentrate on in their rehearsals. These, and the way a particular conductor likes them done, seem to be the things that create both the blend and the distinctive sound of the individual choir.

This is not a matter of 'classical' music only. The same disciplined focus on challenge and unanimity makes any genre of music choral. Boys can sometimes respond well to actions and choreography and I have seen some thrilling performances where these too are achieved with fantastic unanimity and discipline. You should have no doubt that plenty of boys are up for the kind of effort involved. One thing my own research and observations have taught me over the years is that one of the major reasons boys turn against singing in schools is low expectations and lack of challenge. So you should not be afraid to challenge your boys—though with an important caveat I address in the section 1.2 . I am often told by conductors and teachers who work with both boys' and girls' choirs that boys are usually less likely than girls to hold grudges. I have seen and experienced this for myself. This is not an excuse for treating them badly, but I have learned over the years that boys in choirs tend to be quite robust. If they are boys who are going to enjoy choral work, they will rise to your challenges and demands. They will most likely shrug off your occasional frustration in much the same way as they might shrug off the occasional fight with a peer. If they are not suited to your choir, they will leave and such attrition has to be accepted as part of the process of maintaining a boys' choir.

Returning to the metaphor of the black box, there is just so much that we do not know that remains a subject for scientific curiosity. For example, there is a growing body of research that seems to show how our conscious mind follows behind actions taken much more quickly by the subconscious. This applies to the way in which some voices lead and some follow within the choral blend. There have been interesting studies that have simultane-ously recorded independently all the voices of a choral blend and mapped out in milliseconds where each one is in relation to the others. These studies have made me aware of how, when singing in a choir myself, I can mis-pitch an interval I would normally get right if another singer next to me gets it wrong. I am aware that this has happened before I notice consciously the other singer's error and it is then too late for conscious remediation. Precisely when a singer comes in is likely to be a function of the subconscious, even if the conscious is under the illusion it has played a part in the process. Even following a conductor may be partly illusory. I have sat through demonstra-tions in which choirs have sung with and without conductors whilst under close scientific scrutiny. These show that there are certainly many cues other than the conductor's obvious gestures which singers follow. It may be that attention to the conductor's gestures is not as much part of the elusive choral blend as is sometimes thought. Conductors, particularly of boys' choirs, have many tasks other than arm-waving to perform.

Perhaps the greatest of all the choral black box mysteries is that of how boys actually learn to sing. One thing I have come to appreciate only relatively recently is the extent to which so many of the muscles used in singing have no conscious nerve feedback to the brain. Perhaps most significant of all is the elusive diaphragm muscle. There was a time when breathing from the diaphragm was the 'in thing'. Boys would be exhorted to 'support the tone' as though the diaphragm would gently push up an air column. This is complete nonsense as an elementary knowledge of anatomy and physiology ought to confirm. Muscles only operate on one direction by contraction and in the case of the diaphragm this is downwards to expand the chest cavity and cause inhalation. An expanding 'tummy' might confirm that this is happening and is to be preferred to raised shoulders, a sure sign of both tension that will compress the larynx and clavicular breathing that will not fully inflate the lungs or give 'support'.

Tell your boys to 'expand their tummies' though and some of them may do just that—push their stomachs out with little in the way of effective inhalation. With many boys, even experienced cathedral choristers, the battle is simply to get them to breathe at all. It is no use asking your boys to sense the muscular action of the diaphragm because it has no nerves conveying sensation to the brain. All it can do is relax whilst a host of other muscles control the exhalation process. To attempt to explain these complex muscles to a choir of boys would run the risk of boring them to death. Any that survived might then fall victim to the highly counterproductive 'frog and centipede' syndrome. The old story of the centipede that could walk perfectly well until the frog asked it how it managed to coordinate all its legs in the right order is a way of communicating the idea of involuntary muscular action to boys.

The answer is more likely to be regular reminders to the whole choir about good posture (head, bottom, feet in a line) and the need for relaxation (floppy shoulders, knees unlocked). Approaches to rehearsal that induce relaxation and allow the involuntary reflexes to do their work will help maintain correct posture once it is established. Enjoyment and fun are vital parts of a boys' choir rehearsal—partly because most boys are fun-loving but mainly because this is how you create the necessary relaxation. Most of the faults you are likely to encounter in your boys' technique are the result of poor posture and tension. For example, a locked jaw or jutting chin, indicative of all the wrong sorts of pressure on the larynx, are very common. These faults may well increase as puberty progresses and register breaks become more pronounced. Many singers testify to the benefits of the Alexander technique. Teachers of choristers use it with younger boys and I have received very positive feedback from older boys to whom I have recommended Alexander technique lessons.

If you have difficulty in getting your boys to remember the importance of breathing, I have found that recording the choir, and particularly individual members, can sometimes work wonders. Boys who previously ignored everything that was said to them can be quite shocked to hear how the end of their phrase collapses because of insufficient breath control. The boy will then take ownership of the problem and this may be all that is necessary. Choral work should teach boys the skill of critical listening and attention to those parts of their bodies used in singing. They need to know what running out of air feels like and sounds like.

Boys are, I believe, by their nature first and foremost choral rather than solo singers. They can produce a fine choral sound without the faintest understanding of what a vowel formant might be. They will blend the actions of different laryngeal muscle groups without even, in many cases, knowing in a propositional sense that they possess a larynx. They do this because they have an amazing capacity to learn complex skills by imitation. Boys are not taught in the best choirs by technical instruction. They absorb art. A good boys' choir is a place where a boy, more than anything else, learns through imitation. They absorb the musicianship that will serve them for the rest of their lives. The job of the boys' choir director, I would summarise, is to surround the boy with the art to imitate, whilst at the same time knowing enough about singing and the pubertal male larynx to do no harm to his voice or future vocal technique.

There are many adult singers who have learned almost all that they know about singing through membership of a choir. The question inevitably arises as to whether this is sufficient. In an earlier book (*Teaching Singing to Boys and Teenagers*, 2008), I interviewed Roy Massey. I hope he will forgive me if I describe him as one of the 'old school' of English cathedral organists. Here, once again, are his words:

> I always produced the sound I wanted to hear and half the time it was just the way I liked it really, there's no more theory than that . . . It's a great shame it all started getting bogged down with theories really and people were brought in as voice coaches. We have voice coaches these days, they worry me . . . [b]ecause I'm sure there's some very good voice coaching going on but are they producing a sound of the choirmaster's creation or are they producing the sound of the voice coach? I wouldn't have wanted anyone near my boys because they might spoil it, they might alter what I want to hear.
>
> (Ashley, 2008, p.103)

If readers become 'bogged down' with theory, I will have failed. The theory I am seeking to describe I hope will be a liberating one that will enrich practice. There is a difference between an obsession with theory and having enough knowledge about what one is actually doing to avoid harm or unintended consequences. I have spoken to, observed and interviewed various singing teachers and voice coaches over the years. They no more attempt to fill boys' heads with 'theory' in their teaching than does the good choir director. The focus of a boy's voice coaching session is every bit as practical. Some voice coaches I have spoken to, though, have been quite uncomplimentary and uncharitable about choir directors. If they are to be believed, choirs are places where boys actually learn a number of bad habits and poor technique that need correction if the boy wishes to take singing seriously as an adult. It is important to remember that a boy does not actually belong to a choir director. Boys are not bought and disposed of in the way musical instruments are.

Happily, all of the coaches interviewed for this book reported a good working relationship with their conductors. The conductors too reported very positively on what they themselves had learned about singing and on the advantages of having somebody able to give boys the individual attention that is not possible in choir rehearsal. Good singing teachers who work in partnership with the choir director are not attempting to turn boys into miniature adult singers. They are more likely to be participating in the process of constant drip-feed that reminds boys of the necessity for very basic things, such as actually remembering to breathe. A choir is a place where great sounds are created but also where many individual faults are hidden. There is no need, in my view, to fear that a voice coach will take away the 'choirmaster's sound'. I do not think this is possible, and neither do the voice coaches! Boys spend far more time with their choir directors than they do with their voice coaches. They learn so much more through the repertoire they sing, and by imitation of the sounds and actions around them in choir, than they do by any form of coaching that the conductor who is able to achieve discipline and focus has nothing to fear.

1.2   Who are these boys?

I adopted an acoustic definition of choir. I am also going to adopt an acoustic definition of boy. Previously, I have explored the meaning of 'boy' through social constructivism. 'Boy' as a social construction could refer to a newborn baby, as in 'It's a boy!' It could refer to a 25-year-old hotel porter, as in 'The boys will bring your bags up'. A bio-medical definition related to adolescence and puberty will take us nearer the kind of definition we need for this book, but to hit the nail right on the head, we need an acoustic definition. My acoustic definition of 'boy' is a young male with a fundamental voice pitch frequency in the range of about 200–250 Hz, a rich acoustic spectrum with ring frequencies in the regions of 1.5–5 and 7.5–10 kHz. Translating this scientific definition into more familiar terms, we might arrive at the word soprano, or treble.

We shall see in later chapters (especially Chapters 3 and 5) that this acoustic definition will serve very well and there are extremely solid grounds for employing it. It enables us to differentiate between boys and girls, between boys and 'young children' (even if male), and it enables us to differentiate between the boy 'treble' sound that is commonly accepted and other high male voices such as boy sopranos or adult male sopranists (castrati now being extinct). These matters will need to be explored in greater depth. Finally, it enables us to differentiate between what I am going to call 'boys' and what I am going to call 'young men'. The word 'young man', when considered as a social construction, can be at least as abstruse and ambiguous as 'boy'. Examples might include 'Now look here, young man' when addressing a seven-year-old who has perhaps done something requiring firm correction, or 'the young men in Year 8' when it is desired to inspire a sense of maturity. My acoustic definition of 'young man' is a young male with a fundamental voice pitch frequency in the range of about 130–190 Hz, a limited acoustic spectrum and absence of either singer's formant or ring. Readers may recognise such a voice as a rather dull one.

These acoustic definitions, rather than everyday language or actual chronological age, are what really count. They do, however, come with inevitable complications. First, there is probably the greatest paradox in choral singing. A boy of twelve can perform to an exciting professional standard in a choir that can charge strangers expensive ticket prices for a concert. Add two years' 'seniority', however, and that same heroic twelve-year-old is reduced to a mere 'youth' whose voice, if of interest at all, is of interest only to parents, teachers and family friends. Perhaps, by then, if the young man has worked sufficiently hard, his maturing mastery of any musical instruments he may have been learning may begin to compensate for the loss of his choral ability. In terms of choral performance, however, progress can appear to run in reverse for males aged anywhere between about twelve or thirteen and fifteen or sixteen. The whole process of developing a singing voice that strangers will pay to hear begins again at around seventeen years of age and can take at least as long to develop as the treble voice it replaced. Nature can be neither retarded nor hurried.

The acoustic definition unfortunately cannot be entirely hived off from chronological age or bio-medical definitions of boy. Here there are two immense challenges. The first is that chronological age does not synchronise with biological age. Much of this book is about male puberty, a topic of towering importance in choral work with boys. Puberty is no respecter of chronological age. For some boys it comes early and for others late. There is a critical period in the young male lifecycle when boys of similar age may be at quite different stages of puberty and consequently differ from their peers with regard to the acoustic definition of boy. It is not only perfectly possible but an everyday occurrence in this way for a twelve-year-old to be a 'young man' and a fourteen-year-old to be a 'boy'. The question arises, therefore, as to whether a book about choral work with boys ought to include young men at all. On balance I think it should, and this one will. However, there is an important caveat that a distinction needs to be made between pushing boys' voices to the highest standards of choral performance and maintaining the interest of young men in choral singing during that period in their lives when their voices are changing from those of boys to those of mature men.

These voice changes can make it difficult for boys to cope socially but they can present impossible challenges when faced with the way schooling is organised. Put simply, a boys' choir cannot exist within most schools. All sorts of reasons are put forward to explain the great exodus of boys from singing at age eleven, but this most fundamental reason of all is often overlooked. Throughout these pages I will be reiterating constantly the theme that boys learn choral singing by imitation. Rather like a termite colony, the boys' choir is like a single organism made up of individuals acting in mystical unison. Split off the eight- to eleven-year-old individuals from the twelve- to fourteen-year-old individuals and you have killed the organism. It is actually as simple as that. It is less of a problem when schooling is organised with junior to senior transfer at age thirteen, as in UK independent schools. You might scrape by in Scotland or most US states where transfer is at age twelve. Transfer at age eleven, however, means near certain death. Boys' choirs can and do exist successfully in independent schools. They can and do exist successfully as community ventures outside schools, but they are rarer than hen's teeth in school systems organised around transfer at age eleven.

Another thing that struck me in the research for this book was the extent to which selecting the right boys in the first place was reported to be part of the process of creating the choral sound. In some cases, this could refer to a search for boys with a particular kind of vocal quality, but in most cases, just a search for boys who could readily access a 'head voice' and pitch notes with some accuracy. The large majority of boys like to sing, in some way. For many, this is something like singing along with their iPod or singing in the bathroom when they think they cannot be heard. Choral singing, as we heard in section 1.1, differs from 'just singing' by the level of challenge, discipline and commitment. This extract from an interview with some twelve-year-old boys should be carefully noted:

> MA: Can you tell me about anything that's actually put you off? Maybe from primary school?
> Boy 3: Yeah, I didn't like the singing teachers. They go mad if you go wrong.
> Boy 2: An' they say it takes loads of commitment. They make it [seem] like a job or a chore.

According to Paul Freer (2012), many boys turn away from choral music precisely because of pressure from their conductors never to withdraw. In Freer's research, boys suggested that teachers shift away from an emphasis on continuous participation in choral music and focus more on musical skills they can see the value of. In other words, they had experienced choir conductors who make it like 'a job or a chore'. You are doing something fundamentally wrong here if you end up like this. You have failed to distinguish between pedagogy and performance. This is so important that I have made it a key theme of the book and I shall elaborate in the section 1.3 . For a very small number of boys, choral singing is a job, and one they greatly enjoy. We shall meet some such boys in Chapter 10. Not every boy, however, wants to be a plasterer, a paramedic or a lawyer. Neither does every boy want to be a professional choral singer.

You have to find the boys who will share with you your aim of achieving performance standards in choral music, even if they will only ever do so as good amateurs. This requires that all sorts of searching, screening and perhaps auditioning processes be set in motion. Auditioning, though, we shall see is a controversial issue and some of the best boys' choirs do not in fact audition their singers. Finding boys who will be loyal to a choir is absolutely not a process for the faint-hearted. In the second part of the book we shall look in some detail at the various strategies for this employed by successful directors. I think it quite sad if boys give the demand for commitment as a reason for rejecting choral singing. Something in a boy's life has to teach him the value of loyalty and commitment. We have to find the boys for whom choral singing is the right activity to serve this purpose. Part of this is another 'black box'. It has to do with boys' spirituality.

By 'spirituality' I do not necessarily mean religious belief. I mean more the capacity 'to fill an existentialist vacuum' with a 'sense of vocation for music making' and to feel an 'ontological thirst for the non-material' . This is an area in which I have in the past conducted detailed research. I continue to be motivated by the findings of this research that such boys exist. I cannot explain why I became completely smitten by choral music when I first walked into Rochester Cathedral over fifty years ago. What I can state is that my research has revealed that there are boys alive today who experience similar profound feelings. Boys seldom discuss their deepest feelings because our society conditions them to believe that this is not a masculine thing to do. Set up the right conditions for a serious and candid conversation with boys, though, and you will be amazed at what you find.

Unfortunately, the same social hegemonies that proscribe male reflection on the spiritual largely also proscribe male participation in choral work. This social conditioning is the main source of 'uncool' and you will be fighting against it. Your principal allies in this fight, perhaps surprisingly, will be the boys who also resist hegemonic versions of masculinity and 'cool'. This is what a large body of research tells us about boys in general and my own research about boys in choirs in particular. It is necessary, though, to apply much thought and effort to how a viable number of boys who resist narrow and culturally limiting definitions of masculinity are to be found and assembled for choral music-making. This is going to focus attention on whether the non-auditioned community singing group can also be a choir.

16

I shall be providing illustrations of various ways in which these questions have been answered in practice in Chapters 5–10 . For the present, I wish to introduce my own theorisation of the issue. On the one hand, the definition of choral work I have given is one that almost requires auditions. Choral singing, we have seen, requires complete unanimity of intonation. That will clearly not happen without a process to exclude boys with poor pitch-matching skills. Choral singing requires a complete focus on the task. This will not happen without a process to exclude boys who cannot accept the necessary discipline. Closely associated with this is a process to screen out boys' parents who cannot accept the necessary commitment.

Taken to the highest level in the best cathedral choirs, choral singing is neither a chore nor a job but a profession. No one enters a profession without screening, selection and training followed by commitment. On the other hand, one cannot apply the same rules and procedures to boys as one can to adults. I say this not out of being soft on boys, but out of the very pragmatic consideration that many young boys will never have had the opportunity to develop pitch-matching skills. Neither will they have had the opportunity to discover that they might enjoy choral work. We look at the consequences of this in Chapter 8 where we consider the relative position of boys and girls in children's choirs of primary school age.

If you are in the fortunate position of directing a good professional choir with an attached choir school, you may well be able to ignore this. You may be able to advertise a voice trial and receive six or more applications for every place. Most directors of boys' choral work however are inevitably cast sometimes in the role of remedial music teacher. You are going to have to spend a lot of time sifting, searching and nurturing. If young boys are written off too soon, there is a high chance of future able choral singers being lost forever before they have even sung a note in tune. This brings me to the central theme of this chapter: why would anybody want to do this?

1.3   Why are we doing it?

I think I have by now established my position that boys learn to sing and become proficient musicians through being in choirs. I happen to believe that singing in a choir is far and away the best foundation for any young person's future musical proficiency, though some may see that as a partisan view. In order to make full sense, however, of the range of possible approaches to choral work with boys I think we need to step back and take a broad view of what we are doing and why. Without such a pause for reflection, there is a danger that our choral work with boys will become little more than a personal indulgence. It will become all about the 'me' as the conductor and much less about the boys who come to our choirs as children learning to sing. As we shall see later, 'me-mania' in a conductor is something that can (and does) sometimes cause major problems.

Let me therefore place on record my own answer to the question of why we are doing it. This is why I have spent much of a lifetime involved in one way and another in choral work with boys.

1. I think, first and foremost, that boys are important. They represent the juvenile proportion of half the world's population. They grow up into men, by no means all of who are emotionally literate or capable of sustained empathy with fellow human beings. It is from the population of men lacking emotional sensibility and empathetic capacity that the majority of the world's violent crimes from war to rape emanate. I am passionately against war, rape and all other crimes that arise from a lack of empathy. Boys should participate in activities that develop emotions and empathy.

2. I think singing is one of these activities and an important one. Music has always been profoundly important in my life. Music has a unique power to give meaning to human lives. As I have matured and experienced life, my interests have shifted from the simplistic mechanics of how musical instruments work to the mystical realms of the human voice and the contact with boys' souls that is uniquely possible through choral singing.

3. When points 1 and 2 come together, something overwhelmingly sublime happens. I do not know whether to call it 'magical' or to call it 'spiritual'. Whatever it is, it cannot be reduced to psychological test results.

A result of choral work with boys, then, can be sublime music-making. For me, though, that is more the means. The end itself is the boys who have grown up able to appreciate and contribute to the spiritual power of music.

I am going to define two different kinds of possible choir: the pedagogic choir and the performance choir. A pedagogically orientated choir is one that exists primarily to teach people, usually children, to sing. It may achieve commendably high performance standards, but its primary goal is the teaching of musical skills, the inculcation of a love for music and the development of future adult singers. It may attract a considerable following if it is good, but its primary audience will always be parents, teachers, choir family and well-wishers of the children concerned. A performance-orientated choir exists primarily to satisfy discriminating audiences who expect technical high standards and insightful interpretation of a demanding repertoire. It may attract friends and family of the singers to its concerts and its members may increase in musicianship and vocal virtuosity through their work, but its primary audience will be strangers who have paid often-expensive ticket money to hear it.

Is this distinction between pedagogic and performance orientation a meaningful one? Early on in my research, I put the question to the director of a choir I felt might particularly straddle the performance–pedagogy continuum. It was a choir of trebles belonging to a specialist music school in the English Midlands. The boys' performance venues ranged from cathedrals to a rugby ground. Their eclectic repertoire raged from Magnificats (which several of the boys said they liked the best) to music theatre. The director had little hesitation in responding as follows:

> To answer your question, unequivocally pedagogic. The beautiful performances are certainly important but are a by-product. Yes, the aim is to inculcate a love of singing, teach sight-singing and reading to a high level and generate scores of choral scholars in the future as part of a wider programme to create a centre of musical excellence that can challenge both choir schools and the specialist music schools.

I have subsequently put the same question to the conductor of each choir featured in the book. The process has invariably opened up meaningful dialogue and reflection that will be reported in later chapters . In sum for now, the responses received are not dissimilar to the one above. There is a broad consensus that in all but the most professional of choirs, pedagogy precedes performance in choral work with boys. If you are only interested in the best possible performances, why bother with boys? Why not just hire the best adult sopranos you can afford? Working with boys can and indeed should still mean striving for high choral standards, but in the pedagogic situation the trumping priority is the welfare and development of the singers. This is so much about relationships that the whole of Chapter 7 is devoted to that topic.

Once we are clear that we have significant pedagogical and pastoral obligations to the boys in our choirs, we can consider the performance dimension. I have always been interested in children as performers. It fascinates me the way a child who would find difficulty in writing a novel is able to act out complex emotional scenes in a filmed dramatization of a novel written by an adult. Equally, I have long been fascinated by the way children are able to join with professional adult singers in some of our best choral work. When confronted with a musical instrument, even highly able twelve-year-olds are usually discernible as children. Freed from the constraints of technical mastery of the instrument boys can truly perform, often surpassing many adults who would struggle to reach the standard to audition for choirs of the necessary calibre. This is another place in the mysterious black box.

No boys' choir can be wholly pedagogical any more than it can be wholly performance-based by virtue of the fact that we have defined choral work as more than 'just singing'. As one of my interviewees pointed out, boys will begin to drift away from the choir with a 'What's the point?' attitude if there is no performance event to work towards. The performance event needs to put the boys under pressure otherwise they won't see their choir work as much different from routine school work. As Paul Freer's work seems to suggest, if the only person worked up about a forthcoming performance is the conductor, the enterprise will fail. A problem of this nature arises from failing to think through where the activity lies on the pedagogy-performance continuum and recruit the right boys to it.

The boys too need to feel the pressure and respond positively to it as they would if they were in a sports team preparing for a match. Many people say that boys need frequent short-term goals to work towards and I have no reason to doubt this. An important part of choral work with boys is therefore planning and arranging an interesting programme of concerts, events and perhaps festivals. It is second nature to most boys that sports teams play in matches, competitions and tournaments, sometimes winning, sometimes losing. The choral programme needs its equivalent fixture list of routine challenges and seasonal highlights, some 'won', some 'lost'.

The performance venue and the audience are also important. Is it the village field or Wembley Stadium? Formal research, however, is always full of surprises and the results are often counter-intuitive. A good example recently was the finding that, when asked who they would be most pleased to see in the audience for a concert they were performing in, the most frequently given answer was 'my Mum', followed by 'my Gran'. This reminds us that we are dealing with children. The nurturing adults closest to them are ultimately more important than the unknown, anonymous, paying audience of the true performance choir. The counter-intuitive element, however, is the wish for mums. I have reported this research at several conferences. I have in each case asked members of the audience to suggest whom they thought the boys most wished for. The (wrong) answer each time has been their Dad. It is the old chestnut of 'common sense' and 'role models'. This particular boy's response, I think, is highly revealing:

INTERVIEWER: Who would it please you most to see in the audience?
BOY: I expect my close family to come. More distant family would mean more, it would show they care.
INTERVIEWER: Who particularly from your close family?
BOY: My Dad. My Mum goes to see me all the time. My Mum was there every night. My Dad so that he could understand it more.

'My Dad so that he could understand it more'. A significant majority of the boys questioned recognized that it was their Mum who first introduced them to music, their Mum who dealt with their emotional ups and downs and their Mum who pushed them to do well in their music. Only the boy quoted above appeared to possess some inkling of insight into the inequity of this gendered division of labour, and the lack of adult male engagement with boys' choral work. This is emphatically not an argument for more male conductors, as we shall see in Chapter 6. There is, I believe, a case for more male interest from parents, relatives and friends. This is a topic I intend to research on a larger scale in the future.

I have been acutely aware of this issue ever since the *Young Masculinity and Vocal Performance* (Ashley, 2011) research when boys consistently mentioned 'grannies' and 'mothers' as the audiences for their singing. In that project, boys identified the lack of male engagement with their choral singing by omission. They just never referred to males in the audience. Of the twelve solo boy artists studied for *Young Masculinity and Vocal Performance*, eleven were accessed via the female parents who were clearly the ones nurturing and backing their careers. Another negative was that the only time adult males featured as significantly and pro-actively engaged was in connection with the commercial exploitation of the boys. This was almost invariably through the manufacture of 'cute' images and repertoire that could be described as pop–classical crossover fodder for female audiences.

Now I have new evidence that the boys' perceptions of adult male disengagement may be largely correct. Pilot surveys have shown that females outnumber males in the audiences for boys' choral concerts and boys positively identify female adults as the main supportive force behind their choral singing. There is a need to plan and execute a comprehensive, in-depth study of this phenomenon and that is what I am doing at the time of writing, February 2014. My intuition is that the pedagogical function somehow needs to extend to attracting higher levels of engagement by the boys' fathers and educating these men about the adolescent male voice and choral singing. I cannot yet report further than this as it is only a research proposal, but I think there are good grounds to recommend that pedagogical initiatives and efforts be directed at male parents as well as boys.

1.4   Where does choral work with boys take place?

My final, brief 'W' in the overview concerns the Where. Boys' choral work obviously needs a 'home' and a venue for rehearsal and performance. Equally if not more importantly, it also needs to happen within some kind of institutional framework that offers the necessary underpinning infrastructure. This will include a respectable identity for the choir as well as such vital practical matters as financial underwriting, insurance, child protection policies, places to store music and a backroom staff willing to do anything from organise transport to bake cakes. Schools and churches are probably the two homes that most readily spring to mind and usually have individuals in some kind of position who will undertake such duties as child protection. Also significant are choirs operated in conjunction with county music services or hubs. The boys' sections of the national youth choirs are perhaps the apex of a network of county and regional choirs. Arts centres, stage schools and suchlike may occasionally promote or offer a home for a boys' choral venture. A few boys' choirs operate more independently in the community, though often in loose association with a church or school through hire of premises. I become progressively less enthusiastic in proportion to the extent I see choral work with boys developed around the cult of an individual outside any recognised organisation. I do not endorse such ventures in this book.

There is little doubt that some of the finest boys' choral singing in the world takes place in the cathedrals and collegiate chapels of England. In spite of many odds against it, the tradition continues to thrive. It would be hard to deny that the standard for boy treble sound is set by the professional choirs of the best of these establishments. They are examined in Chapter 10 of this book. As was stated at the outset of this chapter, the ethereal, other-worldly sound of boys' choral voices is uniquely well-suited to cathedral worship. One thing that these establishments undoubtedly offer is continuity. This is in marked contrast to the singing projects that flare up with the brief intensity of a project grant, only to wither with equal haste to oblivion. Really good choral work with boys does require continuity and security of tenure. It takes three to four years to train a good boy treble and as much as 100 years to evolve the secure choral tradition that is a necessary part of that boy's training. There is a message here that politicians, economists, and funders of the arts have traditionally been slow to grasp. A steady but reliable trickle of funding is far more likely to achieve worthwhile results than flash-in-the pan funding.

References

Ashley, M. (2008). *Teaching Singing to Boys and Teenagers: The Young Male Voice and the Problem of Masculinity*. Lampeter: Mellen.

Baldy, C. (2010). *The Student Voice: An Introduction to Developing the Singing Voice*. Edinburgh: Dunedin.

Daugherty, J. (2003). 'Choir spacing and formation: choral sound preferences in random, synergistic, and gender-specific chamber choir placements', *International Journal of Research in Choral Singing*, 1(1):48–59.

Ternström, S. (2003). 'Choir acoustics: an overview of research published to date', *International Journal of Research in Choral Singing*, 1(1):3–12.

Further reading

Ashley, M. (2009). *How High Should Boys Sing? Gender, Authenticity and Credibility in the Young Male Voice*. Aldershot: Ashgate.

Neall, L. (2002). *Bringing the Best Out in Boys: Communication Strategies for Teachers*. Stroud: Hawthorn Press.

Chapter 2: Understanding the instrument

No good composer or arranger would attempt to write a clarinet part for a wind quintet unless they understood thoroughly the tonal characteristics and techniques of playing the clarinet and the limitations and strengths of its compass and range. The same, of course, is true for choral writing. The boy's voice needs to be understood in similar detail by those who would write for it or realize such writing in performance. This chapter is about such detail. I am going to look at how the voice works across its range, at what it can and cannot do, and at what it does best. I am going to advance some key arguments, always with our pedagogical and pastoral obligations to boys in mind:

- Boys learn to sing by imitation.
- Good choral singing requires use of the whole voice.
- The repertoire conditions the voice.

The first of these will be familiar from the Chapter 1. It is a point well worth reiterating. In this chapter, I will go into quite a lot of detail about how the boy voice works and how it differs from the adult voice. Boys will not, however, sing well through being instructed in the technical details of this chapter. They will sing well if the conductors and arrangers of their music understand the principles in such a way that good musical tones and sound techniques are available for them to imitate. There is an underlying pedagogic principle here. Practical competence precedes propositional understanding. Younger boys first absorb and reproduce what they hear and see. As they begin to develop increasing cognitive capacity for abstract reasoning, technical explanations of what is happening can begin to be supplied—but never to the extent of inducing boredom!

The central part of this chapter is about what the whole voice is and why it might be used. However, I return to the learning by imitation theme when I suggest that it is repertoire, above all, that conditions the boy's voice. It should not be hard to appreciate that no boy will learn to use his whole voice if he sings only a limited range that does not require the whole voice. Once the mechanics of the whole voice are appreciated alongside the learning by imitation principle, the reader will, I hope, come to see just how much the chosen repertoire contributes to how boys learn by imitation to use their voices.

2.1   What is the whole voice?

Use of the whole voice is one of the key differences between choral singing and 'just singing'. The boy treble who sings regularly has a range of at least two and a half octaves when at the height of his powers. The A_3 (just below middle C) is most commonly given as the bottom, though there is considerable individual variation with regard to this. C_6 (a fourth above 'top G') can be reached by most boys at some stage in their career, though again there can be quite wide variation. This is considerably more than the maximum of a tenth specified by Graham Welch (2006) for pre-pubescent voices not engaged in intensive choral singing. C_6 is also considerably higher also than the rather conservative 'at least F_5' specified by John Cooksey (1999), whose work we shall look at a little later. Moreover, as the boy choral singer enters puberty, his range has the potential not to contract, but actually to expand to at least three octaves. None of this is possible without the use of the whole voice, and an understanding of how the whole voice works will help the boy who has begun puberty. Fortunately, nature has been kind and supplied a design of boy in which mental capacity to understand what is happening expands at the same time as puberty changes the voice.

The statement 'none of this is possible without the use of the whole voice' is absolutely fundamental to a full appreciation of this chapter. My own understanding was held back for many years by some of the theories that have been advanced in the past concerning how good choral tone is produced. A whole raft of misconceptions now exists because of layers of writings by theorists that predate a good scientific understanding of how the voice works. Also complicating the picture are changes in fashion and the operation of taste. There is no definitive 'boy sound'. Such is the overlap in possible choral tone between one choir and another that some enthusiasts who were almost ready to lay down their lives in defence of all-male choirs were embarrassed by their inability to tell apart a boys' choir from a girls' choir. Girls can imitate sounds expected of boys quite effectively, but boys can also imitate sounds expected of girls at least as effectively. In extreme cases, boys can even be mistaken for older women. An awful lot is down to taste and what we want boys (and girls) to sound like. These matters in turn are operationalized by the extent to which boys use and blend together the different registers of their voices and the ages at which they do so.

Since almost time immemorial, the singing community has talked about 'head voice' and 'chest voice'. These terms, however, are pre-scientific. They have been used by singing teachers and conductors in an attempt to generate some kind of shared language about different sensations that might be experienced in singing. To be fair, they seem to have served that purpose fairly well. There is a shared understanding—of something. When we move into the province of the 'hard' sciences, the measurement and analysis of how singing tone is generated by the vibration of the vocal folds and acoustically shaped by the resonances of the vocal tract, 'head voice' and 'chest voice' can be quite misleading terms. As long ago as 1935, one writer identified the kind of problem that can arise from unscientific terminology:

> Some of the confusion is no doubt due to the capacity which unimagina-
> tive (or perhaps over-imaginative) people have for taking metaphorical
> phrases literally. There was a time when the use of the terms 'chest-voice'
> and 'head-voice' caused a good many people to suppose that the sound
> was actually manufactured in or came from the chest or the head.

There are probably few in the choral world today that would embrace such a naively literalistic interpretation. Nevertheless it is still difficult to cast off entirely any lingering suspicion that the actual location of the resonance somehow shifts from the chest towards the head. My most important point here is that we should be careful about what we say to boys. Boys, by virtue of their youth and limited knowledge, may well be amongst the people who have a capacity for taking metaphorical phrases literally. Boys need to be clear about where their voice is. They need to place two fingers around the laryngeal shield and recognise this as contact with the voice source. This understanding is needed because so many singing faults arise from tension that compresses or distorts the larynx and its position relative to the vocal tract. Boys need to understand why good posture and 'floppy shoulders' are necessary. If you use 'head voice' terminology, you may perpetuate misconceptions that young minds will one day have to put right for themselves. This cannot be regarded as good pedagogical practice. However, I have found myself losing my earlier missionary zeal for the abolition of the terms 'head' and 'chest' much in the way I have almost lost heart in the battle for correcting people when they say the voice 'breaks'. Perhaps it is just an interesting conversation to have with a boy singing pupil—when you have the time.

The end of the nineteenth century was a prolific period for the production of texts on good choral tone in boys' voices. There are, I believe, reasons for this. This was a time when compulsory elementary education for all was on the agenda. Some minds therefore turned to the important question of school singing and how this should be done well. The period was also the time of a renaissance in cathedral singing. Alan Mould's excellent text (*The English Chorister: A History*, 2007) should be consulted for an appreciation of the depths to which this art had sunk during the pre-Victorian nadir.

One thing that the nineteenth-century texts agree on is that the head voice and only the head voice should be used in boys' singing. This is a strange piece of advice as it eliminates any robust tone or even phonation from the bottom part of the treble range. So strongly did the nineteenth-century writers hold this belief, however, that it behoves us to attempt to understand their reasoning and its consequences. *The Child-Voice in Singing: Treated from a*

Physiological and a Practical Standpoint and Especially Adapted to Schools and Boy Choirs by Francis Howard (1895) contains detailed descriptions of vocal anatomy written with seeming authority. One must assume that Howard was acquainted with anatomical texts of his day that reported such matters as the dissection of the vocal apparatus of cadavers. Some pages are devoted to an account of what had been learned through Manuel Garcia's newly invented mirror laryngoscope. The term 'thick voice' and 'thin voice' are accordingly employed to refer to the mechanisms of 'chest' and 'head' voice, so there is no suggestion that resonance shifts from the chest to the head.

Howard's main argument, however, is simply that the 'thick voice' should never be used. He describes tones resulting from its use as 'barbaric'.

> Anyone who has noted the contrast between the harsh quality of tone emitted from childish throats when using the chest-voice, and the pure, flute-like sound produced when the head-tones are sung will agree that the last is music and the first noise, or at any rate very noisy, barbaric music.

Other texts of the time confirm that there was a general acceptance that choirboys who produced beautiful tone did so through exclusive use of the head voice only. The rough, strident utterances of street children were explained by the 'chest voice'. Benkhe and Brown in *The Child's Voice* (circa 1885) quote a Mr Turpin in their collection of opinions on the use of register:

> Rough play in noisy streets, attended by loud shouting, I find to be, though forcing the tones of the lower register, the most frequent cause of failure in training boys' voices; so boys of superior classes make the best singers.

Neither Howard nor Benkhe and Brown, in spite of the latter's positions as lecturer on vocal physiology, and senior throat surgeon respectively, conducted systematic observation and measurement in the empirical tradition. Their understanding of vocal mechanisms, particularly tract resonance, was clearly quite limited by today's standards. Their methods, rather than scientific, were what we might call those of pre-scientific 'natural philosophy'. In other words, they synthesised the prevailing opinions of their time. In this way, they did much to bequeath us with the legacy that boys should stop singing when the voice 'breaks'. They received replies from 190 experts of the day of whom they asked the question 'Do you consider it safe for a boy to continue singing whilst his voice is breaking?' Of these 190 replies, only two stated that it was completely safe whilst 158 stated that it was decidedly not safe for a boy to sing whilst his voice was breaking.

Very few people who work with and understand boys' voices today would advocate that they stop singing when their voice 'breaks'. The so-called 'breaking' of the voice is now much better understood. A present day understanding of 'break' would see it as the needless result of faulty technique, bad planning and poor advice. We understand much better how voices gradually change over several years and how to manage this process. Few choir directors or voice coaches would now expect boys to continue singing treble until the point that their voice breaks down traumatically. Much of this understanding has developed in parallel with a growth in understanding of puberty in boys. I devote Chapter 3 to this vital topic.

The notion of 'barbaric' tone resulting from the use of the 'chest voice' or 'thick register', however, is less easily dismissed. I have in my archives a recording I made of a primary school boys' choir performing the well-known Queen number 'We Will Rock You'. It seems a shame to dismiss the efforts of a teacher who at least got her boys together to form a choir, but Francis Howard would undoubtedly describe the resultant sound as 'barbaric'. The reason is not at all hard to understand. The song is pitched at the bottom of the boys' range and the boys are encouraged to sing loudly. The result is that only the 'thick mechanism' or 'chest voice' is used, and used with tension and force. Intonation is consequently inaccurate, blend is poor and the singing sounds not choral, but 'like a primary school'.

There is no need for boys to sound like this. This is where choral singing parts company with more popular styles of singing. Leaving aside the frequent use of falsetto by male rock singers, many popular vocalists make little use of the whole voice. They employ in their singing only the vocal mechanism used in speech. In other words, they employ only the so-called 'chest voice'. The choral singer, as I have suggested, needs to use the whole voice, equally avoiding going to the other extreme, which is to use only the so-called 'head voice' as advocated by the nineteenth-century writers. The 'head voice' will still dominate in the singing of boy trebles simply because that is where their repertoire is predominantly pitched. The choral director, though, needs to understand how and when to get boys to use their whole voice.

It is not sufficiently appreciated, in my view, that singing is absolutely a muscular activity. This is, however, an easy conversation to have with boys who are often likely to be concerned with how much muscle they have and how skilfully they can control their muscles in sport. The first thing I explain to boys is that if they were to start weight-training, I would not give them weights equal to the absolute maximum they could lift. I would give them much lighter weights and a training regime that required them to use these weights frequently. It is the same with singing. If, as far too many primary school teachers do, you exhort boys who are not practised singers to sing louder, perhaps to 'beat the girls', you are doing the equivalent of giving them very heavy weights to lift, just to prove they can do it. No sports coach would endorse such a practice. Boys develop their singing muscles by frequent use, not forced use. The volume will come if they sing often enough and remain in the choir long enough to grow from inconsequential eight-year-olds to sturdy thirteen-year-olds.

The second key point to appreciate is that there are fundamentally two sets of muscles whose use must be understood. The first is sometimes referred to as the 'vocalis'. This is the muscular tissue that actually comprises one of two interior muscular layers of the vocal folds. Please use the term 'folds' rather than 'cords', and certainly not 'chords'! 'Folds' correctly describes the threefold laminate structure that we need to appreciate in order to understand changes at puberty. I will return to the topic in the next chapter. 'Vocalis' is the popular term, commonly applied to both sets of thyroarytenoids . The correct medical term is thyroarytenoid internis. Boys can respond well to metaphors such as the 'muscle like a slug'. Imagine how a slug contracts its body into a thick, fat shape when you poke it. This is one way of actually describing very nicely why 'chest voice' is sometimes called 'thick mechanism'. It can also have the effect of encouraging boys to use their other singing muscles!

The other key muscle group, as far as boys are concerned, is the 'hinge and tilt muscles' or the 'choiry muscles'. The correct medical term is cricothyroid. These groups of muscles surround the larynx and act externally to the folds. When the cricothyroids contract, the two main cartilages of the larynx (cricoid and thyroid) are pulled together and this has the effect of stretching the vocal folds. The vocal folds are pulled by their ends into a longer, thinner shape—hence the term 'thin mechanism' or 'head voice' if you will. The degree to which the ligament has developed is a critical factor in a boy's ability to achieve the laryngeal tilt of classical singing during this action.

Stretched in this way, the folds tend to vibrate more at their edges and the sound is more delicate and flute-like. Boys recognise this sound as, in their own apt words, 'more choiry'. Introduce a 'slug' to your singing and you have contact across most of the depth of the folds and a richer, darker sound at the bottom of the voice. The art of the whole voice is to use both types of production, but it is not a matter of laryngeal muscular action only. The mucosal waveform of the vibrating vocal folds is modified by the ever-changing shape of the vocal tract and the system has to be understood as a whole. I shall say more about resonance in section 2.2 .

Upward vocalisation is likely to cause the larynx to rise. As I know only too well from my attempts at capturing many boys' larynges between two electrodes, this happens very readily in boys. The consequence is inhibition of tilting and shortening of the available length of tract for resonance. A result can be a horizontal larynx that simply bursts into belt mode. With careful downward vocalisation, the bottom register need not result in the 'barbaric' out of tune singing of untrained primary children. I have long believed the lowest part of the boy voice to be a very beautiful sound, but you are only likely to obtain it if boys have equal facility across the entire possible range.

In my experience, the problem of transition from cricothyroid to thyroarytenoid is seldom a major issue for boys with unchanged voices. Indeed, I have many recordings made by skilled boy choristers asked to glide through their whole voice that appear to suggest that there is little or no perceptible register change (an ideal which many adult singers strive for). The spectral lines denoting resonance continue from top to bottom of the voice without the very obvious disruption or lift point that is seen in older voices. In the majority of boys' unchanged voices an upper passagio around E5 to F5 is often discernible to the ear, but this is almost certainly a shift in resonance, not an abrupt adjustment in cricothyroid/thyroarytenoid balance. Boys in pre- or early puberty are seldom troubled much by the lower passagio.

It is not strictly necessary for boys to know what is going on here in order to sing well. Colin Baldy (2010) goes so far as to suggest that younger boys may be better off not knowing and I am inclined to agree with him. Premature instruction in vocal registration, Baldy suggests, risks breaking the voice into sections at an early age. More likely than this, it will just bore boys who want to get on with things. I have known people use colours, or even types of dog ('woof woof' for low register, 'ruff, ruff' for middle register and 'yip yip' for upper register is actually remarkably effective!). When the time comes for boys to need to know, they are quite capable of using correct vocabulary. There is a school of educational thought that stresses that correct vocabulary should be taught—when it is necessary. At least 'doggy voices' are fun and clearly metaphorical, whereas 'head voice' is just plain wrong. It may be as well, though, to leave things alone until some time into puberty when the boy is going to have to understand something about registration in order to make sense of what is happening to his voice (see section 2.2). It is what boys do with their voices rather than what boys are told about their voices. Choir rehearsal is the time for singing, not lecturing, and the reader may well tire of my repeating that boys learn to sing by imitation!

The adults who teach boys do need to understand that the lower boys go into their range, the more likely they are to be using the thyroarytenoids, and the higher, the more likely the cricothyroids. There is almost no doubt that once a boy becomes a chorister, his dominant method of production is cricothyroid. There is still debate, however, about what happens in the middle of the range and whether there is a 'voix mixte'. At one extreme I have seen the rather extraordinary assertion that in a boy's voice (any boy's apparently), the two sets of muscles are likely to be roughly in balance around middle F$\sharp$. This is almost certainly wishful thinking by a mind that likes to order things into neat logical categories, bypassing empirical investigation of the messiness that exists in reality. At the other extreme I have read a research report that claims that only one or the other sets of muscles are used at any one time. The writers of that report attempted to explain transitional registers as solely the product of resonance change. Those who work with singers regularly will know that some manage to cover the 'clunk' better than others. An obvious clunk is usually understood as denoting an abrupt change in muscular action where more skilful singers probably have learned some blending of the two muscular actions, a process that is almost certainly assisted by simultaneous resonance manipulation.

All this reaches its practical relevance when the question of how far down the range a boy should carry his upper register or 'head voice'. Very few of the more respected practitioners today would wish to create the kind of choral tone that results from carrying the upper register as low as possible. Perhaps the last exponent of this old technique was David Wilcox, renowned for the soft 'King's College coo'. The preference today has long been for a brighter and harder sound. It is probable that many choristers begin to blend in some thyroarytenoid action as they reach the lower regions of their voices to produce this. Younger boys seem able to do this without any fuss and do not struggle with the lower passagio as do boys some way into puberty. I shall address this extremely important question in section 2.5 of this chapter. Before doing so, however, some further words on resonance are necessary. Older texts have neglected this topic in favour of discussion of vocal fold thickness, but I believe that the exciting discoveries and developments of the future are going to be more in the field of how we understand resonance and the working of the vocal tract.

2.2   The importance of resonance

One thing that was mentioned by almost every experienced choral director interviewed for the second part of the book was the importance of meticulous work on vowels. Vowels have to be carefully and accurately formed and a high degree of unanimity in vowel production amongst the boys was often a key aim. There is a good reason for this. Vowel production and resonance are intimately connected. Vowels are actually the result of manipulating the vocal tract so that the peaks of resonance known as formants move around. This cannot be achieved in a musical instrument made of wood or metal whose resonances are fixed. For this reason, the first two formants are sometimes referred to as the vowel formants and solo singers will learn to optimise their voices by a process known as formant tuning. This is not simply a matter of imitating speech vowels.

The vocal folds alone produce a sound that is little more than a buzz. Optimally beautiful tone as well as ease of singing is achieved when the sound pressure feedback from the tract is matched with the mucosal waveform of the folds. This will require the actual vowel sound to be carefully matched to the pitch of the note. The vowel sound is not constant throughout the singer's range and an attempt to sing throughout the range with the same mouth shape will lead to mistuning of the formants. Intelligibility of diction is more dependent upon careful articulation of consonants, particularly for boys in their upper voices. Generally speaking, the higher up the register, the more similar the vowels sound.

Good resonant tone is often destroyed by choir directors who attempt to achieve clarity of diction through insisting that the boys produce the same mouth shape irrespective of the note they are singing. Moreover, there may be little good choral tone to destroy in the first place if there is significant mis-tuning of the vowel formants of one boy relative to another. This is likely to occur if the boys have received little instruction aimed at unanimity of vowel sound. The first steps in producing good choral tone as well as good singing from individuals have therefore to be taken through getting the boys to imitate accurately good vowel sounds, but this can go wrong if the choir director has no knowledge of formant tuning. It is a complex art, the importance of which has only recently begun to be fully appreciated in the choral world. There is much to be said for choir directors working closely with singing teachers, as is increasingly the practice in the best boys' choirs. Teachers willing to experiment with technology have found that visual display of formant positioning by systems such as Voce Vista can enlighten and enhance the process of formant tuning, but I do not know of any attempts yet to extend this into choral work with boys.

How do you make a boys' choir sound the way you want? Individual choirs undoubtedly have their particular sounds. One very important contributory factor is the acoustics of the regular performance and rehearsal venue. It hardly bears repeating that the resonance of a big cathedral can contribute a remarkably large proportion of the total choral experience. Beyond this, though, it is very difficult to explain why particular choirs sound the way they do. Given the extent to which boys learn to sing by imitation, it is not hard to see a 'chicken and egg' situation. The younger boys copy the older ones, but how did the older ones come to have the sound from the very beginning? The most plausible explanation I have heard is somewhat akin to Darwinian selection. A choir director will praise the boys who happen to sound the way he wants. These will be the ones the younger ones copy and over the years or decades the whole choir sound evolves, if not by natural selection then by a form of selective breeding.

The more I study how tone is produced in a boys' choir, the more I come to realise the extent to which I am grasping for purchase within a black box of potentially infinite size. Most of what has been said so far in his chapter can be read up elsewhere. There are good texts I recommend for further reading if you want to know more about such essential matters as good posture. In the remainder of this chapter and Chapter 3, I am going to move into related areas where I have made particular studies and perhaps a small but original contribution to knowledge.

2.3   Puberty

We began this chapter with an account of the nineteenth-century theorists and their insistence upon the use of the 'head voice' only. A text from our own times is that of Kenneth Phillips (2013). Phillips does not hold 'English choirboys' in particularly high esteem. He appears to believe that contemporary English choirboys do sing only in the 'head voice'. Whilst he recognises that this can result in an upper register of some beauty, he does not advocate the method as leading to good singing or proper training of the boy voice. His exact words to describe the 'English choirboy' are:

> English choirboys sing only one vocal part—treble. Because most of them are not permitted to use even a mixture of chest and head voice, the head voice sound is extended below pitch C_2 as low as possible.
>
> (Phillips, 2013, p.92)

He is, of course, correct to state that in most professional English choirs, the boys do sing only the one vocal part most of the time. Quite how he arrives at the conclusion that they are 'not permitted to use even a mixture of chest and head voice', however, requires some investigation. At one level, he is just plain wrong, for none of the English choir directors or vocal coaches I have spoken to agree that they 'do not permit' boys to use 'chest' or 'mixed' voice. There are pieces in the repertoire that would sound very weak, assuming they could be sung at all if boys succeeded in obeying an instruction to remain only in their 'head voice'. None of the many boys known to me has received this kind of instruction, nor should they.

Perhaps Phillips bases his observations on choral practices that have long since fallen out of favour in England. He is careful to employ the term 'head voice sound' rather than to assert categorically that cricothyroid action is being carried as low as middle C. He would be on dangerous ground to make such an assertion for it is probable that a good many boys would be unable to phonate at all were they consciously to employ cricothyroid action at this pitch. Another error is to generalise and homogenise as though all boys were the same. In any given choir, some boys will be stronger in the lower part of the range than others and, depending on where the music is pitched at any given times, different boys may be contributing more or less to the overall blend.

Perhaps fortunately, boys do not think about whether this is happening. Their muscles will work in the way that is needed to produce the sound they are trying to imitate. All this changes at puberty, often quite spectacularly. So important is the impact of puberty on choral work with boys that I have devoted the whole of Chapter 3 to my research into the topic, and references to it are frequent in the remainder of the book.

2.4　　Changes in taste and fashion

A term that is sometimes employed by commentators on boys' choral sound is 'continental tone'. 'Continental tone' I believe refers to a sound that might be described as bright, cutting, hard, incisive, clear, full-bodied or any other such terms that denote something that is not the light, fluty, effervescent, effeminate sound of English boys who are presumed not to be 'continental'. To call such tone 'continental' is something of a hostage to fortune for it is quite possible to go to the 'continent' (i.e. mainland Europe) and hear boys who do not necessarily sound like this. There is considerable variation across German choirs from the light tone of the Dresden Kreuzchor to the hard, robust sound of the Tölzer. More particularly, I have been struck by the extent to which English boys said to be 'continental' can lack the degree of robustness in the lower register that I have heard in the Tölzer tradition. It is possible that these German boys may be using an artificially depressed larynx to increase the effective length of the pharynx and thereby manipulate resonance. Not all vocal coaches would consider this good practice.

'Continental tone' is said to be suitable for the performance of polyphonic music that requires the independent vocal lines to be heard with clarity. This is certainly a 'continental' influence for it denotes a shifting in taste from the classic English diet of Victorian to Edwardian style　floating legato to the crystal clarity required in each part for the great continental polyphonists of the fifteenth and sixteenth century. Vowel production, and hence resonance, is an absolutely crucial part of this process. The influence of Latin and Italian with its pure vowels (as opposed to English diphthongs) may have a surprisingly significant influence on tone. One choir director above all others has been credited for a revolution that popularised this approach in English choirs. This was George Malcolm, who was appointed to Westminster Cathedral in 1947. Malcolm had strong views, not only on repertoire, but particularly on how boys should sing. He gave a candid account of his work in the 1962 Aldeburgh Festival Programme . In it, he states:

> it used to be widely held that the Cathedral Tone consisted primarily in the almost exclusive use of the 'head voice'; yet very few of the choirmasters concerned would now accept this definition, either as to fact or terminology. Indeed, a great show is made at the present day of rejecting the 'old method' altogether, and of training boys on a more rational system.
>
> (Malcolm, 1962)

In rejecting the 'old method', Malcolm turned on its head the accepted wisdom handed down by writers such as Benkhe and Brown and their adherents. Again, according to Malcolm:

> Boys will be boys!—and in most parts of the world this applies to boy choristers too. When they sing, they are expected to sound like boys, and are not taught to produce an uncharacteristic quality of tone, remotely unlike that of the voices with which they talk, or laugh, or cheer at a football match.
>
> (Malcolm, 1967)

One can only imagine the horror with which this would have been received by Francis Howard! Here, we have a prominent musician actually advocating that boys should sound 'barbaric'! Malcolm was highly influential. Benjamin Britten is said to have thought the sound authentic for boys and to have been enthused by it when writing the *Missa Brevis in D* for the Westminster boys' SSA voices. Britten's works often do use the whole voice, requiring boys to sing right down into what is more often seen as alto territory. Many writers make a direct link between Malcolm's work at Westminster and George Guest's equally influential work at St John's College, Cambridge. Malcolm's view—that boys should use for singing their 'shouting and cheering voice'—has done much to displace the old idea that boys should imitate the woman's voice. A new sound, uniquely boyish, came to be regarded as 'treble' and the old boy soprano fell out of favour.

It is sometimes said that Malcolm produced this sound by excessive or even exclusive use of the 'chest voice'. This is no more possible than Phillips' idea that only the 'head voice' is ever used. It is possible for boys to carry thyroarytenoid action quite high. Younger boys who lack the restraining influence of a mature vocal ligament (see Chapter 3) may get some way above C_5 (treble C) but older boys who have commenced puberty simply cannot do this. They begin to sound painfully strained and out of tune in the region between G_4 and C_5 and I have plenty of recordings to prove it. Cathedral choristers, many of whom have begun puberty, simply do not sing like this. They have to use their whole voice. No boy of any description could soar between G_5 and C_6 in thyroarytenoid action.

The 'rational system' that Malcolm called for is simply the dismissal of the dogma that only the 'head voice' should be used and the recognition that, in order to become part of the sound of the choir of which the boy is a member, the boy should use his whole voice as appropriate. This, however, is only part of the explanation. Malcolm also railed against the poor vowel production of Edwardian-style English choirs. The vowel sound 'oo' was considered an aid to the process of 'bringing down the head voice', which indeed it is. 'Oo' sounds will sustain phonation when other vowels might result in a 'crack'. A number of writers describe choirs with systematic vowel distortion such that 'Amen' was invariably heard as 'Oomoon'. Limitation of resonance to the 'oo' formants in this way will inevitably affect choral tone.

The bright, incisive treble sound almost certainly owes much to careful attention to a range of vowels that are produced accurately and sung with absolute unanimity by the whole choir. Control of the voice in its lower register requires a judicious balance of formant tuning and control of fold tension and thickness. Boys will simply do this if they are given the right sounds and mouth shapes to copy. So we are back to good discipline and the ability of the choir director to model accurately the vowel sounds he or she wishes the boys to produce at different pitches. Careful study of the International Phonetic Alphabet should pay dividends.

For many years I grappled with the impossible proposition that boy trebles producing 'continental tone' used only their 'chest voice' and boy sopranos producing traditional English 'cathedral tone' used only their 'head voice'. An understanding of how boys produce their voices during puberty has been the key to moving beyond this position. Before we tackle this in depth, we need to understand a final piece of the jigsaw—the significance of the repertoire that is regularly performed.

2.5   Repertoire

Fundamentally, repertoire conditions the voice. Much of the repertoire published for children in recent decades cannot be described as choral simply by virtue of the fact that it is pitched too low to develop the whole voice. So the first, and indeed last, rule for getting boys to use their whole voice is to choose appropriate repertoire that is not pitched too low. This does not have to mean 'classical'. Music of any genre written by composers and arrangers who understand children's voices can be 'choral'. This is a controversial area and I have been embroiled in the past in arguments between those who believe that 'quality' in children's singing means nothing but inclusion and everybody joining in, and those who believe that it means, in effect, the application of knowledge that would change the tone from barbaric to beautiful, or even 'angelic'. Let me stick with my scientific brief and press on with that knowledge.

We have seen that many children sing only music that is pitched at the bottom of the range for the child voice with the consequence that crico-thyroid production and laryngeal tilt are never learned. Thus, the action of merely choosing repertoire that has a higher pitch centre will contribute to the process of boys learning to use their whole voice. By pitch centre, I mean the average frequency of all the notes in the vocal line. Though finding this out is an academic exercise that will probably bore the more performance orientated choir director, it is a very revealing way of analysing which muscles boys are being required to use. I conducted a pitch centre analysis of one song promoted by a large organisation that ought to know better for Key Stage 1 (i.e. age 5–7+) children. It was 284 Hz. It was a miracle that children could sing it at all. Perhaps they couldn't. Perhaps all that is heard is the voice on the backing track and a general tunelessness from the children.

There is some debate as to whether every boy can access cricothyroid action, or indeed will want to. I have a fair number of interviews with experi-enced choristers who are able to articulate that they happily use 'head voice' in choir but would rather use only 'chest voice' ('tummy voice' in one case!) when performing in front of non-chorister peers. You can read a lot more about the kind of abuse and grief they face in my previous book, *How High Should Boys Sing?* (2009). I also have interviews with choir directors who claim that part of their audition process is to weed out boys who cannot readily access their 'head voice'. These may be those directors who are in the fortunate position of being able to weed out boys at audition. The majority who are just grate-ful to get any boy who might want to sing are going to have to teach boys how to reach this part of their voice, a process that may take some time with a good many of them. My position on this is that there is a general deficit in boys' singing experience at primary school level such that the ability in boys is under-developed relative to girls. We address this in depth and I hope con-vincingly in Chapter 8.

There are plenty of other texts available that describe the kinds of fun vocal exercise that will assist. Whooping sounds, sirens, glides, witch noises, hums, shrieks, doggy and lion noises, nee–naw ambulances. I have space only to recommend the best of those texts. I wish to use my remaining space to draw attention to something I have come only recently to appreciate since I began undertaking pitch centre analysis. Whilst there is a depressingly large range of published material that will never properly develop children's voices, it is also the case that much of the music sung by boys in church and even cathedral choirs does not actually extend the voice to its full compass either.

If the choir is an English-style ecclesiastical one, by far the greater percentage of time will be spent singing in the range E_4–G_5. Boys learning to sing by imitation a typically middle-of-the road piece such as Sumsion's *Magnificat in A* will not actually have to use thyroarytenoid action. Weakness and insipience of the lower register may be the result when the boys are occasionally required to sing a note below E_4.

Compare such a piece with Britten's *Missa Brevis in D* which really does exploit the entire compass of the boy voice. Britten is often thought of as a composer par excellence for boys' choral music. Writing such as the *Missa Brevis* for me confirms that the reputation is justified. If your boys can sing this, they will be able to use their whole voice. If there is substance in what Phillips claims about 'head voice only', it is not that boys are forbidden to use other parts of their voice; it is that they are given repertoire that does not require the use of other parts of the voice. There are two solutions to this. First, whatever the genre of the choir, search for a balanced repertoire that will have boys singing from A_3 or lower—C_6 . This is going to be a far more practical proposition if your boys sing regularly in three parts, first, second and third treble or alto (as in the *Missa Brevis*). The amount of time you spend rehearsing in the various ranges of these pieces will be the amount of time the boys spend developing their different vocal muscles and learning to produce resonances in the frequencies that best enhance those muscle actions.

Second, there is of course the warm-up. This is often the best chance to exercise regularly the whole voice in a way that is perhaps more systematic than is possible through the actual music to be sung. Warm-ups I have seen range from the cursory arpeggio to winding the boys up to a psychic frenzy about rubber chickens. Not every choir even bothers with a warm-up, though they have generally become more popular much in the way that warm-ups in children's sport have become more popular. I remain unconvinced that such routines are vital for warming a child's muscles in the same way as an adult's, though much earnest writing assures us that this is so. What the warm-up does offer you is a chance to calm the boys and get them attentively relaxed and focused. It offers you the chance to remind them (if they need it) why they have come to rehearsal, and then about posture and breathing. It offers you the chance to practice vowel sounds and increases boys' awareness of the articulators (tongue, teeth, hard palate, lips). This is an area in which direct instruction can sometimes succeed. Boys, after all, can feel their tongue and lips. Finally it offers you the opportunity to use every part of the voice and ensure that your older boys are covering their passagio regions.

References

Baldy, C. (2010). *The Student Voice: An Introduction to Developing the Singing Voice.* Edinburgh: Dunedin.

Benkhe, E. & Browne, L. (undated, circa 1885). *The Child's Voice: Its Treatment with Regard to After Development.* Boston, MA: Oliver Ditson & Co.

Cooksey, J. (1999). *Working With Adolescent Voices.* St Louis, MO: Concordia.

Howard, F. (1895). *The Child-Voice in Singing: Treated from a Physiological and a Practical Standpoint and Especially Adapted to Schools and Boy Choirs.* New York, NY: H.W. Gray/Novello.

Malcolm, G. (1967). Boys' Voices. *English Church Music,* 24–7.

Mould, A. (2007). *The English Chorister.* London: Hambledon/Continuum.

Phillips, K. (1996). *Teaching Kids to Sing.* New York, NY: Schirmer Books.

Welch, G. (2006). Singing and vocal development. In G. McPherson (ed.), *The Child as Musician: A Handbook of Musical Development* (pp. 311–29). Oxford: Oxford University Press.

Further reading

Howard, F. (1895). *The Child-Voice in Singing: Treated from a Physiological and a Practical Standpoint and Especially Adapted to Schools and Boy Choirs.* New York, NY: H.W. Gray/Novello. Available at <http://www.gutenberg.org.ebooks/22581>.

Miller, D. (2008). *Resonance in Singing: Voice Building through Acoustic Feedback.* Princetown, NJ: Inside View Press.

Phillips, K. (2014). *Teaching Kids to Sing* (2nd edn.). Boston, MA: Schirmer.

Interlude 1: Max

As I write these words, Max is ten years and eight months old. He is in Year 6 (US Grade 5) of his local primary school and is a member of what has become in recent decades quite a rare entity, an all-male parish church choir. Holy Trinity Church Southport is a cavernous, red-brick space consecrated in 1912 and has maintained since its consecration a strong musical tradition. It has a four manual organ (sadly, out of financial necessity, 'digitised' for the last thirty years) and is one of the very few parish churches that sing a regular weekday choral evensong.

Max first came to my attention as one of a group of three small boys who had recently been recruited to the choir as probationers. I was asked to 'take the probationers' one morning and was immediately struck by a difference in musicality and intelligence. Max shone in a way the other two boys did not. His eyes sparkled with something inside that said 'musical intelligence'. This is of some significance for the other two boys have subsequently left the choir, whist Max has remained and is on course to become one of its future 'stars'. This is not to disparage the other two boys. I am sure they have other talents, but Max is one of those boys I described in the introduction: 'There are perhaps more of these boys than is sometimes imagined. They are waiting for somebody who will open a musical treasure trove for them and unlock the key to something that will fulfil the rest of their lives'.

There are indeed more of these boys than is imagined, but one has to devote considerable effort to going out to find them. Max's case illustrates that if you want a good choir of twenty boys, you probably need to interest at least sixty boys in trying the choir out—a sobering thought. Even more sobering, though, is that without this effort, the musical treasure trove would never be opened. Boys such as Max might just be part of the myth that boys do not and cannot sing—or sing only in a 'barbaric chest voice'. Later in the book I describe some of the issues of creating places for boys such as Max and how one might deal with primary schools and even music 'hubs' lacking any interest in, knowledge of, or insight into choral work with boys.

My inclusion of Max as an 'interlude' is partly to illustrate this, but more because I wanted a case study of a pure, pre-pubertal treble. I will confess to a certain ambition for Max when I asked him to take part in this project. In an earlier book, I had written about Joseph McManners. Joe, who had been for a brief period a probationer in Canterbury Cathedral Choir, had recorded an album for Sony BMG in what a number of reviewers described as 'the pure, unspoiled voice of a child'. I was interested in a 'pure, unspoiled voice' that I could be reasonably confident would be pre-pubertal and which I could assess, measure and analyse. Max and his mother agreed to a rigorous regime of fortnightly measurement—far more frequent than any of the other boys in my longitudinal study or indeed to my knowledge that of any other researcher. I felt this necessary to test out the real stability of measurements assumed by other researchers to be consistent from one week to another, and establish what would be an optimum sampling frequency for the app.

I did not want to clone Joseph McManners, but at our first sessions together, Max and I listened to Joe's album and we together selected Panis Angelicus as a piece that Max would record 'like Joe'. My reasoning was that boys learn by imitation and I wanted Max to imitate a pure, unchanged treble voice rather than some of the ageing falsettists that are common in church choirs. Max took to this project like a duck to water. The result was not an exact imitation, but it was what I wanted, a pure young treble that I was able to analyse in detail. So much did Max and I enjoy our sessions that we have continued to record a repertoire of other pieces, exploring together other choirs and boy voice sounds as well as working on Max's own unique, authentic voice. We will hopefully be able to redub Panis Angelicus as Max develops through puberty, hearing how the treble voice changes and matures. By the time Max ceases to be a treble, we should have a 'choir' of three or four different aged Maxes!

What, then, is the young treble voice? I discovered some interesting features. First, for a reason neither of us understands, Max speaks habitually almost at the bottom of his voice. This would not be noticed under normal circumstances, but the recorded speaking fundamental frequency (SF_0) has fluctuated around the 195–199 Hz mark, just below the 200 Hz indicative of a 'slightly deepening voice' for most boys. Yet the lowest note Max is able to phonate clearly with good tone has been the 220 Hz A or just below, making him a clear treble. The oft-quoted rule that the bottom of the singing voice is about four semitones below the habitual speaking pitch is thus not validated in Max's case. Having been alerted to this by Max, I have started looking more carefully at other boys and it does appear that there may perhaps be a tendency, almost certainly cultural, for the habitual speaking voice to be pitched nearer to the bottom of the voice than the quoted norms. This is yet another observation that needs full and proper investigation.

I suspect also that some of the data on which these norms may be based may also not be that reliable. In a study of one cathedral choir, a colleague and I used two different instruments to measure SF_0 (laryngograph and Voce Vista) and a variety of different protocols (counting backwards, reading the phonetic passage 'Arthur the Rat' and casual conversation). No significant difference was found between the two measuring instruments, but there was a significant difference between the protocols. Counting backwards gave a significantly lower mean SF_0. Too many research studies do not describe accurately the task the boys were given or admit discussion of such possible difference. The figures for Max (as is the case for all boys in my studies) are based on counting backwards, the voice being actually sampled between the numbers twelve and five.

One of the tests in the battery I give to boys is to sing the words 'You owe me five pounds' to the tune of 'Happy Birthday'. No starting note is given, the purpose of the test being to determine where the boy instinctively pitches his tessitura. Most choristers instinctively pitch some way up the treble register, even if this means falsetto. Max, however, pitched it down in his bottom register ('chest voice'). When a higher starting note and a sample of a cathedral chorister performing the same task was given, he pitched perfectly happily in the treble register, singing the difficult intervals of the fifth and octave with complete ease and accuracy. The unusual reluctance to do this without a pitching note is interesting. In conversation, Max has expressed worry or insecurity about his 'head register' but in actually singing he employs it with complete comfort and beauty. Again, having been alerted to the phenomenon by Max, I have re-examined my data and found that there is indeed a tendency amongst parish church choirboys to do this that I have never found in cathedral choristers.

Unlike the recordings of Joe McManners, there are perceptible register breaks in Max's voice and they do occur in the places specified by several texts that deal with the matter. They are barely visible on the electroglottograph (EGG) spectrum but they can be heard by the ear. They vary from week to week. Some weeks when he performs glides, scales and vocalises, they are more perceptible than others. Who can say whether this is Max's voice or my ear? They do not cause Max any problems with his singing and there is no need even to discuss them with him. In that sense, Max has given me exactly what I hoped for. I have a young boy with a first class ear who has learned beautiful singing almost entirely by careful imitation but topped up by specific points of correction. For Max at age 10, instruction in the identification and management of registration is unnecessary and possibly counter-productive. On this point, I am in agreement with Colin Baldy (see Chapter 5). The case should be compared with that of fourteen-year-old William, the next interlude in the book.

Max also listens carefully to criticism. In our sessions he is able readily to modify a vowel sound on instruction (though he cannot roll his rs!). He has worked hard on a difficult interval (down a sixth in bar 19 of *Panis*). Elsewhere, I have learned how easily one boy's fault in judging an interval is hidden by the mystical choral 'blend' (see Chapter 10). Max is learning to be more accurately critical of the sound he produces. It is, I believe, essential that opportunities are created for boys to listen. Too many choir rehearsals, in my view, proceed with one set of instructions after another when, if only the boys heard what they were doing wrong, they would grasp the point quickly. Over the months, his critique has developed from a generalised 'it wasn't very good' to a more specific identification of, for example, a pitch instability attributable to a breathing fault. He will work hard and enjoys the challenge. He has convinced me that individual lessons for boys in a choir are a good thing. They do not change the tone of the choir, but they do increase the accuracy and the boys' understanding and awareness.

Some weeks he may be a little reluctant and wish to set a time limit, only to exceed this as he becomes lost in the music and the technical points we are trying to put right. Indeed, Max's sessions have really taken off since we have focused on achieving a musical result, with the odd bit of instruction on what a bar line means thrown in for relief. Max enjoys being measured, particularly growth measurements such as height, weight and neck circumference. We have discovered that he has a huge pair of lungs for one so young. His performance on the peak air flow meter literally does make boys two or three years his senior jealous (many become highly competitive at demonstrating lung volume!). Interestingly, this has not (yet) translated into any above-average ability to sustain lengthy phrases. We are working on this, as well as a certain irregularly occurring breathiness of tone. The simple business of teaching him to sing a song accurately and beautifully, though, has taken over for me from the scientific interest in growth. I want to get on with the music and that, perhaps, says it all.

One thing that Max has taught me is a scepticism I did not previously have for published means. Above all, I have become wary of the expectation that any given boy will somehow fit within these means, or that the life course for a boy can be predicted from these means. It cannot. Max had an amazing spurt in height growth that looked like puberty but was not. For three months he grew by around 1 cm each month, then for two months, he did not grow at all. There was no relationship between this and the voice. These things are missed when measurements are only termly and there is a temptation to assume that any growth must have happened evenly during the intervening period. There is no general rule that says all boys with x SF_0 and y LTP (lowest terminal pitch of singing range) must be at z stage of development and therefore allocated to this or that section of the choir. It does not work like that. Every boy must be treated as an individual and monitored regularly for healthy singing habits.

Chapter 3: The significance of puberty and its impact on the voice

In Chapter 2 we devoted some space to disagreements about the extent to which only the 'head voice' is or should be used in boys' choral work. We have considered the fact that males of twelve, thirteen or fourteen years of age could, by acoustic definition, be 'boys' or 'young men' with all the attendant social implications. We have not yet considered the vexed question of falsetto voice in boys, nor attempted to explore differences between 'head voice', 'head tone' or falsetto voice. We have not considered the fact that in choral work, thirteen-year-old boys may be singing a high part, whilst in 'just singing' boys of the same age may be singing in a significantly lower range. We have not addressed a commonly encountered belief that boys' voices 'break' earlier now than in the past. All these important issues arise because the entire business of choral work with boys is inextricably entwined with the process of puberty. My aim in this chapter is to give the reader confidence in challenging popular misconceptions about puberty, and to help the reader manage better the boy choral voice. Puberty plays a major part in this.

There are things that boys need to know and certainly things that choir directors and teachers need to know. I rarely meet an eleven- or twelve-year-old who is unable to tell me that the three things that affect the pitch of a guitar string are its length, its mass (or thickness) and its tension. The guitar string metaphor is helpful up to a point, but can be misleading. Vocal sound is produced by the 'chopping up' of an air stream as the folds open and close. This is more like the action of a reed instrument than a string instrument where air is pushed into pulses by the backwards and forwards movement of the string. It is not difficult for boys to understand that the length and mass of their vocal folds in resting state will increase rapidly during puberty. This will result in a deeper and deeper speaking voice. It is useful for boys to know that the bottom of their singing voice is close to the pitch at which they habitually speak. Boys can also see without much difficulty that it is not they but nature that has control over the length and mass of their folds. It is at the point that boys may begin to realise that they have potentially a lot of control (or not) of the tension and shape of their folds as well as the position and orientation of their larynx that the hard part begins.

It was once thought, quite simply, that the voice 'breaks' when a boy 'hits' puberty. In this simple scheme of things, boy trebles had not reached puberty and boys with 'broken' voices had. This is very far from the case. What needs to be appreciated is the extent to which a good many boy trebles have already reached puberty. The choral world abounds with misconceptions, urban myths and downright falsehoods about the topic. Whilst the pre-pubertal boy is able to sing with his whole voice with little need to understand register breaks, this is not so for the boy who has reached puberty. I believe that a lack of understanding of what goes on here has contributed in particular (a) to the claim by American children's voice expert Kenneth Phillips (1996) that English choirboys use only the 'head voice' (see Chapter 2) and (b) a widespread but erroneous belief that puberty came much later in the past than it does now. These things are going to take quite a lot of explaining. Let me begin with the bio-medical facts.

3.1 Puberty in boys

3.1.1 Defining male puberty

This is a topic of which I have made a detailed study. I pondered long and hard in preparing this book over how much bio-medical detail to give. In the end, I settled for what I believe those engaged in choral work need to understand in order to deal with the misinformation they are likely to encounter in everyday talk and the popular press. The medical terminology is restrained so that the chapter will be accessible to people who work with choirs rather than medical doctors, but proper medical terms are used where necessary. I have also been influenced by the work I do with boys on this topic. I have given many talks up and down the country to classes of twelve- and thirteen-year-olds and have gained a pretty good feel for what they know, what they want to know and what they need to know.

Almost everybody knows that puberty is the time of sexual maturation. What is perhaps less widely appreciated about this, but important to understand, is that this event is significantly easier to determine for girls than it is for boys. The age of menarche (first menstruation) in girls is easy to assess. Girls experience their first period and in most enlightened cultures are usually well prepared for this. It is possible to conduct studies when girls report the time of their first period and the average age of menarche in a given culture at a given time is thus relatively easy to establish. Numerous such studies over the years have pointed towards what is called a secular trend. Readers of this book can be forgiven if they are confused by this term and imagine it to mean a drift of young people away from the church and church choirs. Such a 'secularisation' trend undoubtedly does exist, but a secular trend is an epidemiological term meaning a slow gradual drift in a population statistic. The secular trends that concern us are those to greater stature and earlier puberty in boys.

A secular trend in stature is easy to establish and has been demonstrated. Finding a secular trend in puberty is much harder to accomplish for boys than with girls for two reasons. First, the boy equivalent of menarche, which is variously termed either spermarche or semenarche, is rather indeterminate. Various studies have shown the presence of sperm in urine samples at quite early ages, but the studies have also shown that boys themselves are seldom aware of this at the age it occurs. Most boys, according to these studies, do not fully understand the difference between urine and semen until some years after spermarche has actually happened to them.

The second reason is that, partly because of the difficulty in determining whether spermarche has occurred, and partly because menarche is of significant interest for what it tells about the reproductive health of populations, medical researchers are generally less interested in spermarche than they are in menarche. We cannot as a result state with any certainty whether there has been an equivalent secular trend in spermarche. This point will emerge during the book as particularly significant because so many claims about 'earlier voice break' are made on the basis of studies of menarche in girls. As we shall see, the claims may not be justified. The leap from the time a girl becomes of child-bearing age to the time a boy might cease to be a treble chorister assumes perhaps rather more than is justified.

When giving talks to boys, I usually have a slide taken from one of the *Boys Keep Singing* films. The slide has a close-up of a thirteen-year-old who just happens to have acne. I have become wise to the fact that if I ask the boys to look closely and tell me what they notice, one will invariably say 'He's got spots'. This invites me to ask the next question, 'Why?' to which I usually get the response 'Because he's in puberty'. The ensuing dialogue will usually establish that boys understand this to be a time when they start to smell, get hair under their arms and in unmentionable places, get moody and unpredictable, row with their parents, get bigger and stronger and, very often, a deepening voice. This last point is fascinating because I have found boys more likely to use terms such as 'deepening' or 'changing' than 'breaking'. In other words, most average boys in a secondary school have a better understanding than those choir directors who will persist in saying the voice 'breaks'. All I can say is, take note!

A term popular in boys' vernacular is 'balls drop'. This too is not that far from the key medical point that needs to be understood. It should not be confused with the not uncommon medical conditions of undescended and retractile testis. The testes commence their life inside the body and usually descend into the scrotum in early infancy immediately before or soon after birth. Sometimes this does not happen and the condition may go undetected for some time. It can be corrected by a small operation and the occasional younger chorister may mysteriously disappear to hospital for a 'little operation' which is 'embarrassing'. 'Balls dropping' is a different phenomenon. It refers to the fact that during puberty the testes increase greatly in size. Testicular volume is important because it is currently the most definitive medical indicator of a boy's pubertal status and offers the strongest positive correlation with the pitch of his speaking voice. In the pre-pubertal boy, the testicular volume is less than 3 ml. Puberty is officially classed as beginning when a volume of 3 ml is attained.

By the time a boy completes puberty, his testes may have increased to a volume of 16 ml or more and be still growing towards a possible adult volume of up to 25 ml. The growth during puberty is an eightfold increase. At this size, the testes will clearly and visibly hang down, hence the term 'balls dropping'. It is most visible to boys after a hot shower when the scrotal skin relaxes as nature fights to preserve the temperature difference between testes and the rest of the body that is so essential to fertility (it is normal for one to hang lower than the other). To illustrate the point of relative growth, the increase in height during puberty would be from 136 cm to 175 cm for a boy of the fiftieth centile. This is an increase of about 0.3 of the immediately pre-pubertal height. The testes growth described above is in comparison a factor of 8. This tremendous growth in testicular volume enables the testosterone production that revolutionizes the voice and is thus entirely fundamental to our work.

3.1.2   The measurement of puberty

Paediatricians have in their armoury an instrument of fearsome torture for boys with suspected problems at puberty. This is the Prader Orchidometer, a collection of testicle-shaped beads of varying size on a string. The doctor will test this out by 'palpation', that is to say he or she will pull the unfortunate boy's private parts about in an effort to match his testicle size to the nearest bead size on the orchidometer. Needless to say, this is unpleasant and acutely embarrassing. Most boys who have had to face the ordeal report varying degrees of distress and will do all they can to avoid a second visit to the surgery.

There is an alternative to orchidometry known as Tanner staging (1976). J.M. Tanner was a leading paediatrician of the mid twentieth century who conducted a major study of the children at the Harpenden Children's Home. He established five 'stages' of puberty through the production of a series of reference photographs. These depict the amount of pubic hair that has grown and the extent to which the genitalia have increased in size and changed in shape and colour. This method is often used in medical research. However, examining boys in order to match their development to the Tanner photographs is only marginally less intrusive than orchidometry and suffers from the fact that it is somewhat less accurate. The process is both arbitrary and subjective. Studies have shown that, whilst experienced paediatricians made reasonably reliable judgements, general practitioners who do not examine boys on a daily basis were surprisingly unreliable when using the Tanner method.

The point of all this is that it is another reason for why we do not actually know that much about the timing of puberty in boys. Studies that are intrusive, embarrassing and in need of the highest levels of ethical scrutiny are unlikely to be undertaken. A small number of important studies, however, have attempted to correlate vocal qualities with key pubertal indicators such as testicular volume, testosterone concentration and Tanner staging. That by M. Harries et al (1997) is by some margin the most frequently cited. What we have learned from these studies appears to be that the most consistent and reliable positive correlation appears to be between testicular volume and the pitch of the speaking voice (of which more detail in section 3.2). In other words, boys are right about 'balls dropping', though the notion that trebles in choirs have 'their balls screwed up' is somewhat wider of the mark.

The whole notion of stages is one that needs to be treated with some circumspection. Testicular volume and speaking voice pitch are both continuous variables, as is a boy's height. The more we know about the growth patterns of individuals as compared with averaged growth patterns of whole populations, the less trust we are likely to place in arbitrary processes which attempt to make fixed stages out of continuously variable phenomena. For this reason, there has been a move away from five 'stages' in boys' puberty to a more flexible approach based on three phases of 'pre-puberty', 'in-puberty' and 'completing puberty'. This is true in general paediatrics and I have become increasingly convinced that it should apply in voice work also. Much misinformation abounds as a result of misunderstandings about how children grow. A common misconception is that growth spurts occur only during puberty, whereas they may occur anytime for reasons not yet understood.

If you have a choir comprising boys aged between about nine and thirteen, the majority of them will have a testicular volume greater than 3ml. This statement is made, not on the basis of measuring testicular volume, but on the basis of measuring speaking voice pitch and trusting in the generalizability of the few correlational studies that have been conducted. I shall summarise the study I made of seven English cathedral choirs on which this claim is largely based in Chapter 4. The implications are profound. It means that the boy choral sound is created by a majority of boys who are either 'in puberty' or 'completing puberty' according to the definitions of these terms given in the new UK national standards for adolescent growth. This is a long way from the tabloid press understanding that 'puberty begins when the voice breaks'.

3.2   Vocal changes at puberty

I hope I have covered enough of the general medical position to be useful. There is a lot more that could have been said, but I hope I have selected the material that is going to be most useful to those engaged in choral work with boys who need to understand the topic better than the average lay person. To recapitulate the most important points so far:

- The definitive indicator of puberty in boys is testicular volume. This has a close association with testosterone production and hence other bodily changes including those to larynx, vocal tract and lungs.
- The intrusive nature of this indicator makes puberty in boys hard to measure. Whilst a lot is known about the biology of individuals at puberty, surprisingly little is known about the distribution of puberty stages across populations.
- A mixture of boys who have not begun puberty or are some way through it produces the choral sound of young males, acoustically defined as 'boys'. Some boys in the mix may be near to completing puberty.

The choir director does not really need to know the intimate details of individuals and may feel uncomfortable about doing so, but he or she certainly does need to know what is happening to their voices. It has been known for many years that the pitch of the speaking voice falls during growth, but particularly rapidly during the pubertal growth spurt after a period of relative stability in the immediate pre-pubertal years. As well as a fall in pitch, the speaking voice also changes in actual quality and timbre once puberty commences. It is important to state clearly that we are here dealing only with the speaking voice. The singing voice presents such enormous additional complications that we must leave it to the next chapter.

The reason this happens was touched on briefly in Chapter 2. The vocal folds increase in length and mass (or thickness). This should be no surprise. Most other muscles of the body do too. As we have said, caution must be exercised in comparing the voice with a stringed instrument but the analogy can be helpful as an introduction to pubertal change. If you double the length of a string, you halve the pitch. This is largely what happens between the beginning and end of puberty. In fact the entire larynx increases significantly in size. It is here that there is an important dimorphism between boys and girls. The larynx is made up of three main cartilages, the cricoid, which is a ring-shaped cartilage at the base of the larynx; the thyroid, which is the larger shield-shaped cartilage to which the folds are attached at their front end; and the arytenoids, which I referred to in the Chapter 2 as the two small, hinged 'catapult stretching' cartilages.

In boys only, for reasons not fully understood, the thyroid cartilage changes its shape to become more elongated. This accommodates the great increase in length of the folds, typically from 8–10 mm in the pre-pubertal boy to 14–16 mm in the boy completing puberty and as much 17–21 mm in the mature adult. The metamorphosis of the thyroid cartilage results in the protrusion popularly known as the 'Adam's apple', or more properly, the laryngeal prominence. The boys I talk to often do seem quite ignorant at this point. Many call the entire larynx the 'Adam's apple'. When shown an endoscopic photograph of the vocal folds, quite a few boys guess (wrongly) that it is the 'Adam's apple'. If they are in Year 9 in particular (i.e. aged thirteen or fourteen), they may think the photograph is of a particular part of the female anatomy, so be warned. I have learned to use this as an aid to light relief in my talks.

It is very useful to be able to point out to boys that the Adam's apple bobs up and down, which is evidence that the entire larynx moves up and down, a matter of great importance in the attainment of resonant tone. Get the boys to place two fingers around where they think their Adam's apple is. Get them to feel the shield shape of the cartilage, to hum and feel it vibrate, and to swallow and feel it go up and down. Larynx position affects the effective length of the vocal tract, which in turn affects the kind of resonance that is produced. As well as growth in laryngeal size, there is another process that has been ongoing since birth, that of larynx descent with consequent lengthening of the pharynx (the tube above the larynx that forms the first part of the vocal tract).

It is not just small vocal folds that are responsible for a child-like tone. It is at least equally a relatively short vocal tract. The newborn infant has a very high larynx position and consequently almost no length of tract. This assists with suckling and also loud crying. In fact, close proximity of the soft palate and epiglottis enables the small infant to both breathe and eat at the same time. I know a few choristers who might like to do this, but it ceases to be possible for some time before a boy is old enough to join a choir!

Larynx descent and growth in volume of the vocal tract continues for some time after fold growth has taken the voice down an octave. The mature male has somewhat greater overall tract volume than the 'young man' who is completing puberty. This hugely affects resonance and is a large part of the explanation of the fact that the voices of 'young men' are light and dull (lacking rich upper partials) relative to the voices either of boys or mature men. Larynx growth and tract growth are not totally in step.

Finally, we need to be aware of some changes to the vocal folds themselves at puberty. The fully mature vocal folds consist of three distinct and mechanically decoupled layers. This gives rise to complex and subtle air turbulence not found in a simple buzzer sometimes used to demonstrate the sound made by the folds themselves. The innermost fold layer is the thyroarytenoid muscle itself. The middle layer consists of a ligament, itself made of three further subdivisions known as the superficial, intermediate and deep *lamina propria*. The outermost layer, or epithileum, is composed of mucosal (secretion-forming) tissue (as are most outer layers of the body). In marked contrast, the folds of a newborn infant consist of one layer only. This develops into three layers during early childhood. The age of seven is usually considered a landmark stage by which time children will have three-layered folds. It is possibly the youngest age at which a boy might be introduced to choral work.

However, the middle layer, or ligament, of the seven- to twelve-year-old is still immature. Full maturity of the ligament is not generally achieved before the age of thirteen years. By this age the mature ligament shows a hypocellular superficial layer with the middle layer predominantly elastin fibre, and the deep layer collagen fibre. The overall result is that toward maturity there is a stiffening of the folds, increased tensile strength and greater elasticity. This crucial maturational stage occurs towards the end of the treble career and is associated with the first appearance of falsetto style phonation, a matter of considerable significance when the treble voice is maintained through puberty.

3.2.1 Measurement of pubertal vocal status

These are the mechanics and constitute the deeper anatomical theory. Practical theory for those concerned with choral work has to do with measuring pubertal vocal status and acting upon the results. First, as we have seen in the previous section , the two areas of testicular volume and voice pitch are positively correlated. In other words, if you can know from observation and measurement about the state of one, you can infer with a reasonable degree of accuracy the state of the other. If, therefore, we have a means of measuring voices, we also have a means of measuring the pubertal status of boys. This is an area in which I have undertaken and continue to undertake a considerable amount of work. In collaboration with my colleague David Howard, I have produced a smartphone app that I am going to describe in this section.

The motives for the app have largely been twofold. A medical version has been designed for use with the new UK national adolescent growth standards. These are based on charts of height and weight growth and map onto these the normal limits of precocious and delayed puberty. If a measurement of voice can be used to indicate whether boys with suspected precocious or delayed puberty are progressing satisfactorily, enormous amounts of embarrassment and distress can be spared. There is also a means of screening large populations easily and hence answering better questions about secular trends. For choir directors, a simple tool to assess boys' pubertal status can assist greatly with the demographic management of the choir (see Chapter 7) and the development of healthy voice use. I shall now describe the principles behind the app and thereby the principles that underlie the most obvious changes to the voice at puberty.

The app measures the habitual pitch of the speaking voice. The term for speaking voice pitch most commonly used today is SF_0. This is an abbreviation for 'speaking fundamental frequency'. You are probably sufficiently familiar with acoustics to appreciate that any musical sound has a fundamental frequency and a number of harmonics or overtones. The harmonic series is always the same mathematical sequence (octave, fifth, major third, etc.) but the relative strength of each harmonic gives the instrument its distinctive timbre. Uniquely amongst musical instruments, the human vocal tract can alter its resonant frequencies, recognisable principally as different vowel sounds. Movable peaks of resonant frequencies are known as formants. What matters immediately is that the frequency of the fundamental (harmonic number zero) gives the perceived pitch. In the human voice this is the same as the frequency with which the vocal folds collide.

During speech, there is of course fluctuation in pitch due to the speaker's tendency to add expressive inflexion. For this reason, we normally give boys a deliberately boring task, such as counting backwards from twenty. Between the numbers twelve and five, the voice is usually settled at the nearest approximation to a true SF_0 as is possible. Most texts quote this as being between three and six semitones above the lowest note that can be sung, though this may be changing slightly (see Interlude 1: Max). The LTP and its relationship to the habitual speaking pitch is a crucial point we shall return to later. Importantly, I have found consistent and significant differences in my research between counting SF_0 and SF_0 obtained by other methods such as reading or conversation. For this reason, we have to be careful and consistent, and should state how SF_0 was obtained. Many research studies are weak because they do not.

Singing teachers who work with boys will often ask their pupil to count backwards from twenty and pitch-match to the keyboard. This can be a fair approximation, but the app will give a much more reliable result. The standard protocol for using it is to ask the boy to begin counting, then to press the sample function on the app as he reaches twelve and the stop function at five, though the boy continues to zero. It is of very limited use, however, just making one measurement of this. This will not tell you whether the boy has reached puberty or how fast he is progressing through it. Boys of the same age vary greatly in height across a population. Equally they can vary greatly in voice pitch, irrespective of where they are in puberty. You will only achieve a meaningful result if you hear the boy regularly, record changes and analyse the rate of change. Ideally, a boy should have his voice sample immediately on recruitment to the choir. This will tell you whether his voice is naturally high or low. It is perfectly possible for a pre-pubertal nine-year-old to have a lower SF_0 than an in-puberty twelve-year-old.

This regular periodic sampling against a baseline is known as a longitudinal approach. It is likely to be a much more reliable guide than a one-off assessment. Boys increase their height at a rate of about 1cm every three months when not undergoing a growth spurt. This rate can almost treble during a periodic spurt, most often but not necessarily during puberty. If you are associated with a robed choir, a sudden large gap between cassock hem and floor is a sure sign that this is happening. Most texts state that height is quite well-correlated with voice pitch during growth, though less directly once maturity is achieved. I know plenty of tall tenors and short basses. Between the ages of eight and twelve the mean SF_0 of a whole population may fall by as much as 50 Hz, though it does so with less regularity than height growth. Importantly, though, such a mean does not allow you to derive a norm for any given boy. My own current study that is using more frequent sampling than most previous studies is also calling into question relationships between height increase and fall in SF_0 assumed from studies with less frequent sampling.

During puberty it is quite clear that SF_0 will begin to fall faster and very rapidly during the pubertal climax when the rate of voice change far exceeds the rate of change in height. Longitudinal records will enable you to see how this maps out for each individual boy and alert you to the sudden changes that might signal a need for reassessment of his position in the choir. An individualised, change-tracking process really is essential because of the degree of individual variation in both absolute values and rates of change. The app is designed to make this time-consuming process of hearing a boy regularly and noting changes as simple as possible. It will allow you to create a record for each boy you wish to monitor. The boy counts into the app that then displays his current SF_0 and a cartoon figure to indicate whether this is within the SF_0 range for 'pre-puberty', 'in-puberty' or 'completing puberty' (see Table 1). The app will also calculate the rate of change since the previous measurement, displaying this as a traffic light. Green means no significant change, whilst orange means a change from one stage to the next is likely to be in progress. Red means time to leave the treble section!

You may think this needlessly complicated, but it is in fact a very powerful tool that reveals just how often boys can be placed in the wrong sections of their choirs. There is a growing awareness of how often boys remain in the treble section beyond the point that might be considered safe and healthy voice use. Over-caution with regard to this, however, can also lead to boys leaving treble sections too soon. This is an area of recent controversy that we shall need to examine in the next chapter when we look at the different types of singing voice production during the years of puberty. Careful monitoring of individuals really is important in the professionally run choir.

Shirt colour	Meaning
Light blue	This boy's voice is classified as 'high'. It is within the agreed range of SF_0 for pre-pubertal boys.
Dark blue/light green	This boy's voice is classified as 'slightly deepened'. It is within the agreed SF_0 range for boys who are 'in-puberty'.
Dark green/black	This boy's voice is classified as 'fully changed'. It is within the agreed SF_0 range for boys who are 'completing puberty'.

Table 1: SF_0 and the corresponding stages of puberty

3.2.2 Further complications and the Visual Analogue Scale

Before leaving the topic of speaking voice, there are further complications that we need to be aware of. First, there will be changes to the quality and timbre of the speaking voice as well as its habitual pitch. These need to be noted once pubertal changes set in. The human voice is not made of metal or wood. Flesh and nerve can never produce a completely steady tone on a sustained vowel. Although we might say in theory that the vocal folds are colliding 220 times every second for the note A_3, this is really only an average. Each individual cycle may be slightly longer or shorter than the one before it. This variation is known as 'jitter' and it increases once the rapid growth of puberty begins. A similar short-term fluctuation in amplitude (loudness) is known as 'shimmer'. The combined effects of jitter and shimmer can be heard by the ear as a 'roughness' that was not present before puberty.

This is likely to affect our 'light green shirt'—it can be noticeable in the speaking voices of older boys still singing treble. There is an important study by the German phoniatrician Michael Fuchs et al (2007) that needs to be known. Fuchs and his colleagues employed a computer algorithm that was able to compute 'roughness' in the voices of boys at early stages of puberty through the detection of jitter and shimmer. The algorithm was known as the Goettingen Hoarsenes Diagram (GHD). Fuchs looked at the famous Thomanerchor of Leipzig (J.S. Bach's choir). He divided the boys into three stages: the pre-mutation, the mutation as a specific period of obvious vocal instability, and the post-mutation. This is in accordance with German practice and the pre-mutation phase corresponds to the dark blue and light green shirt cartoons displayed by the app (see Table 1). German boys may move to second or third treble or alto during this stage.

Fuchs studied longitudinally twenty-one boys aged between nine and fifteen who were heard reading a verse of the hymn *Jesu Meine Freude* at regular intervals. This study demonstrated clearly that measurable changes in speaking voice quality occur before they are perceived aurally. There was a significant rise in jitter and shimmer during pre-mutation, generally occurring some six months before the onset of the high mutation phase. The authors claimed that the GHD could be used in professional choirs to predict the time boys should withdraw from the soprano/alto section and advised the making of individual plans for every boy's voice in the choir through regular GHD assessment. At the present stage of technology, the GHD remains a research tool rather than an everyday part of the rehearsal room. I cannot state it with certainty, but I suspect that a lot of English trebles might finish their careers sooner than has been conventionally the case were regular GHD assessment to be carried out on speaking voices.

There are plans for a second-generation version of the app that may function through a bio-computing principle in which the software 'learns' the sound of voices at different stages and detects ones that do not fit its model for a particular stage. The bio-computing network would learn amongst other things to recognise jitter and shimmer. This goal is some way distant at present and before it can be achieved a further and almost certainly better known phenomenon needs much more study.

This is the more familiar phenomenon of 'cracking'. The German mutation stage approximates the dark green shirt stage. During this time, German boys in professional choirs such as Thomanerchor may stop singing before being invited back into the choir as young tenors or basses (i.e. black shirt). Boys at this dark green shirt stage are the most likely to experience 'cracking' in their speaking voices. This is a sure sign of mutational climax and often a source of embarrassment to boys. I never fail to raise a laugh when I demonstrate how, if a boy gets excited in class and calls out 'Miss!', the voice will jump between a squeak and its more regular lower pitch. If jitter and shimmer do not stop the boy from singing treble, 'cracking' may well do.

The phenomenon of 'cracking' is not that well understood. Some texts appear to regard it simply as an inevitable part of the process of change, others more as a form of pathology. Not every boy experiences 'cracking', so it is perhaps not an inevitable feature of change. Once the boy approaches the danger zone for cracking, the modal voice will have already extended downwards in pitch due to an increase in the length of the vocal folds. The boy has a continuously expanding range of pitches to control and must do so with muscles that are also increasing in mass. He is also experiencing maturation of the ligament. Some authors suggest that this process happens with such rapidity that the brain has difficulty in keeping up with its mental map of how to exert fine control. Rapid pubertal growth is said to lead sometimes to adolescent clumsiness and a temporary set-back in fine motor control during sport. It has been proposed that the cracking voice is the speech equivalent of this. Asymmetric growth of the folds has also been cited as a contributory factor. If such explanations are true, it may also be plausible that the brain 'expects' to hear a voice that is higher than the new fold length would otherwise dictate. Hence a momentary flip from weakly controlled 'chest voice' to out-of-control 'head voice'.

One authoritative source has suggested that the thyroarytenoid is relatively flaccid and the crycoarytenoid over-used in boys whose voices crack. Why this should be remains a matter of interest, given that most adolescent boys at least in theory wish to achieve a consistently lower voice. Boys at the green shirt stages are usually surprisingly light in weight relative to their rapidly increasing height, and one important reason for this is that muscle mass has yet to increase. The thyroarytenoid may therefore at this stage lack mass in relation to its length and this may contribute to its under-use. Whether or not this is part of the explanation remains to be demonstrated by research.

If 'cracking' is the result of faulty voice use rather than a biological inevitability for every boy, it ought to be possible to help boys go through change without cracking. Development of the emerging modal singing voice may help. One thing we may be reasonably certain about: treble voices should not suddenly 'crack' during a vital solo, as is commonly reported of Benjamin Britten's young star, David Hemmings, during a notorious production of *Turn of the Screw*. It is the choir director's business to avoid such occurrences. A treble voice that 'cracks' at a vital moment is not, as was once thought, 'breaking'. It is a fairly sure sign that the pubertal development and vocal health of the boy has not been adequately monitored.

I have, in my own research, had some success with a tool much simpler than the app that requires nothing more expensive than photocopied sheets and ruler. This is the Visual Analogue Scale (VAS). The VAS is most commonly used in the clinical assessment of pain. It allows the patient to indicate where the sensation they feel lies on a continuous line from no pain at one end to completely unbearable pain at the other. The patient makes a mark on the line and the exact position of this can later be measured. It has been shown to be effective with children as young as five. Some researchers, myself included, have used it as a tool for boys to express the 'pain' they feel with their voice. I have used a VAS for speaking voice in which one end of the line is marked 'my speaking voice is absolutely fine' and the other end 'my speaking voice keeps cracking and sometimes embarrasses me'.

Boys' satisfaction with the singing voice is similarly assessed between the extremes of 'my singing voice is pure and the high notes are easy' and 'I struggle to get the high notes and my voice sounds rough'. What has been quite uncanny in some of my longitudinal case studies is that some boys measured at three-monthly intervals have placed their marks in almost the same place on the lines each time until objective measurements of voice pitch showed them comfortably into puberty. (The boys do not see the marks they made previously.) The boys then moved their mark down the line, before they experienced 'cracking' and whilst still singing treble. It seems, then, that at least some boys have an awareness of an emerging roughness in their voices, and that their subjective judgements are surprisingly good and reliable. This is perhaps evidence, if you need it, that boys should be involved in decisions about their vocal health and progress in the choir.

3.3   From speaking voice to singing voice

Regular documentation of changes in the speaking voice can thus tell us a great deal about whether a boy has commenced puberty and how far he has progressed through it. There is also an important relationship between the habitual speaking voice pitch and the bottom of the singing range. Almost every person pitches their speaking voice towards the bottom of their singing range. A good many texts of recent years have attempted to specify an actual value such as four semitones between the SF0 and the LTP. This is another practice that needs to be questioned. First it does not capture the large range of individual variation and raises questions about individuals whose SF0 and LTP are not four semitones apart when no such questions need be raised. Second, I have increasingly noted a tendency for boys I am seeing to pitch their habitual SF0 lower in their total voice range than the expected norm (see Interlude 1: Max). Pitching of the speaking voice seems to be a cultural variable that is independent of the biological variable of larynx growth.

There is a distressing condition known as puberphonia. I had only read about this in textbooks until real cases were brought to my attention as a result of public talks I had given on boys' voices. Puberphonia occurs when a boy goes through a normal puberty but continues to speak in a high voice. The boy will develop all the expected secondary sex characteristics. He will have the height, weight and appearance of any boy who has completed puberty, but his speaking voice will sound at the pitch of a typical twelve-year-old. This is not due to absence of normal laryngeal growth. It is almost certainly a psychological condition related to undisclosed anxiety and needs specialist help. The boy may need to see a psychiatric counsellor to address the anxiety and a good speech therapist who will know how to teach him to access his new voice. It is a genuine condition and it needs to be taken seriously. It does not, I believe, result from boys who sing treble for too long as is sometimes said. I have known boys with puberphonia who have never been singers and I know plenty of boys who sing a falsetto treble into their mid-teens with no symptom of puberphonia in their speaking voices, or indeed the baritone singing voices that are possessed in addition to the falsetto treble.

The most reliable assessment that can be made in normal cases is the very simple one of finding the bottom of a boy's singing voice. This means using an element of subjective judgement to find the lowest note that clearly phonates with a good resonant tone. Notes that begin to lose tone or are produced with obvious larynx depression as the boy grimaces and attempts to show off manly growls need to be discounted. There is still something to be said for starting on the pitch of the speaking voice (readily determined by the app) and keyboard-matching down in semitones. It is probably even more important though that regular longitudinal records are kept of LTP than SF_0. There is a very considerable degree of natural individual variation with regard to LTP that is entirely normal. Some pre-pubertal boys can comfortably reach lower than G_3 whilst older boys cannot get much below B_3 even though their SF_0 has begun to fall as a result of puberty. Carefully maintained knowledge of individual boys should always be taken into account when one-off assessments are made, for example, at the beginning of a one-week singing course. The latter will almost invariably produce less reliable information about a boy's capability and needs than well-maintained longitudinal choir records.

Finding the bottom of the singing range is nevertheless still relatively straightforward. Patently, however, this procedure does not tell us how high the boy can sing. To find this out, we have to test the boy's singing voice to identify his current tessitura and see what happens when he is pushed to the extreme limits of his potential range. In other words, we need to look at how the boy manages the different laryngeal mechanisms and associated resonances. The You owe me five pounds test (see Chapter 2) can be very revealing, most particularly when a boy whose voice has changed sings up an octave in falsetto because he is a chorister, and that is where choristers sing! This takes us into another area where quite complex professional judgements have to be made, not about the relatively objective question of how high the boy can sing, but the much more subjective one about how high he should sing. We are now ready to consider the impact of puberty upon the singing voice and demographic management if the choir.

References

Fuchs, M., Froehlich, M., Hentschel, B., Stuermer, I., Kruse, E. & Knauft, D. (2007). Predicting mutational change in the speaking voice of boys. *Journal of Voice*, 21(2): 169–78. doi:10.1016/j.jvoice.2005.10.008

Harries, M., Walker, J., Williams, D., Hawkins, S. & Hughes, A. (1997). Changes in the male voice at puberty. *Archives of Disease in Childhood*, 77(5):445–47. doi:10.1136/adc.77.5.445

Phillips, K. (1996). *Teaching Kids to Sing.* New York, NY: Schirmer Books.

Tanner, J. & Whitehouse, R. (1976). Clinical longitudinal standards for height, weight, height velocity, weight velocity, and stages of puberty. *Archives of Disease in Childhood*, 51(3):170–79. doi:10.1136/adc.51.3.170

Further reading

Pedersen, M. (2008). *Normal Development of Voice in Children: Advances in Evidence-Based Standards.* Heidelberg, Germany: Springer.

Madaras, L. (2007). *The 'What's Happening to my Body?' Book for Boys.* New York, NY: Newmarket.

Chapter 4: Singing range and the tightrope of pubertal timing

There is one reason above all others why puberty is such a vital topic in choral work with boys. Choral work we have defined as more than 'just singing'. The best boys' choirs, though inevitably retaining a pedagogical function, achieve standards of choral performance well beyond many amateur adult choirs. Such standards are not going to be accomplished by small children struggling to read the words, let alone the notes. They are not going to be achieved by small children who lack any form of developed musicianship or intellectual capacity to understand something of the music they are to perform.

Puberty is a time not only of physical maturation but also of cognitive or mental maturation. It is the time when a serious capacity for abstract reasoning begins to develop in most boys. The two developments, though each good separately, do not go comfortably together. Just as a boy begins to develop the cognitive ability to perform to a mature standard in the treble voice, he begins to lose the physical ability to do so. Choral work with boys has always occupied that very brief period when cognitive and physical maturity are in the right kind of balance for ripe performance by treble voices. This inevitably means that the boy choral voice is extended for some time beyond the lifespan that might otherwise be expected of an unchanged voice.

In this chapter, I aim to explore this process, looking at different ways it has been done in the past and might continue to be done. This will inevitably lead us to consider the critical topic of the timing of puberty and the secular trend (see Chapter 3 for definition). This is the area in which I have conducted my most substantial recent research project and is in many ways the central theme of the whole book. My exploration is from the point of view of choral singing rather than individual vocal tuition. Choral singing with boys is a process of inevitable compromise. One cannot specify singing ranges and vocal regimes for every boy in a choir as though the choir's work were synchronous with individual vocal tuition.

4.1   Normative expectations

In the Chapter 3 we reviewed the very direct correspondence between pubertal status and the pitch and quality of the speaking voice. We looked at the relationship between the bottom of a boy's singing range and the habitual pitch of his speaking voice. We considered that the bottom of a boy's singing range would gradually descend in pitch as it follows the descent in the pitch of his speaking voice. This process is driven by puberty and begins earlier than many people imagine. The popular misconception about puberty that we dismissed in Chapter 3 was that 'the voice breaks when puberty begins'. In this chapter we need to understand that puberty begins for most boys at around the age of eleven, though with a huge range of individual variation that boys have to come to terms with. In the early stages, it will be hard to detect puberty for endocrinal changes are at first completely invisible. The first visible sign is testicular enlargement. This usually occurs before any pubic hair appears and will obviously not be seen by the vast majority of observers and quite possibly not even noticed by the boy himself. Detectable voice changes do begin, however, very soon after this happens.

A voice that is beginning to change in this way does not mean that a boy's position in a choir also begins to change. Most boys have at least two years ahead of them as trebles once the speaking pitch begins to fall in step with testicular enlargement. It could not be otherwise, for choral singing with boys as we know it would become largely impossible. There have been attempts to move boys from the treble line as soon as voice analysis suggests pubertal onset but I am confident that these, though well-meaning, are misconceived. A proper understanding of the process and how it impacts upon choral singing as opposed to individual vocal tuition is one that knows how to maintain a treble singing range without damage to vocal health during the early years of puberty.

Boys are hugely sensitive to their voices and instinctively understand something of what their speech and singing tells the world about emerging (or not) manhood. We need to understand at this point that there is a massive divide between boys who are involved in choral work and boys who are not. Many boys who are not involved in choral work will attempt to speak (or sing if they ever do) in the lowest voice they can as soon as they are able. This may involve a depression of the larynx that would alarm singing teachers, but since the boys do not have singing lessons, nobody much worries about it. The boys who are involved in choral work, however, may well resort to a number of techniques designed to achieve the opfposite effect. Research, including my own, has shown that boy choral singers not infrequently adopt two voices—a 'normal' school speaking voice and a 'high' choir singing voice (often not revealed to school peers). The latter is absolutely our concern.

We have stated that a good boy treble will have a range of a little under two and a half octaves. This is most likely to be from G or A_3 to C_6 in its extremities, though more likely from D or E_4 to G_5 in everyday use. If the bottom of the range begins to fall gradually towards E_3 and the range remains about two octaves, the top note will be E_5, which will put some of the treble repertoire beyond his reach. In practice, this is not what actually happens to the top of the range. The boy may keep his G_5 or higher, whilst gaining new notes at the bottom of his range. The range therefore expands during puberty. Alternatively, the boy may lose notes at the top of his range more quickly than he gains new notes at the bottom. The range therefore contracts during puberty. What actually happens will depend principally on the unique growth pattern of the boy during puberty, but also in part on how the boy is trained and taught and on what he wants to do with his voice. There do also seem to be other factors not well understood that dictate different courses of singing voice development for boys whose speaking voice development is on near identical trajectory.

It is necessary to reiterate here that we are talking about boys involved in choral singing. Since these are a relatively small minority of the total boy population it behoves us to understand first what is normal for the majority of boys, and probably also normal for the 'non-choir' voices of our choral singers too. This is a topic that has been much examined by researchers of adolescent voices. The work of John Cooksey (1977) is amongst the most thorough and remains definitive for many people at the time of writing. Everybody who works in contemporary choral work with boys should be familiar with Cooksey's publications. Table 2 is one I have synthesised from his publications and refer to regularly in my own work. I have added the app 'shirt colours'.

Stage	Shirt colour	Mean SF0	Tessitura	Full range	Quality
0	Light blue	259	D_4–C_5	A_3–>F_5	Full, rich soprano. The 'pinnacle of development'
1	Dark blue	226	B_3–G_4	A_3–D_5	Breathy, strained upper range; little resonance or 'body' in lower range
2	Light green	210	A_3–F_4	E_3–C_5	Loss of agility, falsetto emerges, uniquely beautiful and rich if in range
3	Dark green	186	F_3–D_4	D_3–A_4	Evolution of modal register into baritone range, retention of stage 2 quality
4	Dark green/ black	151	D_3–A_3	$A\sharp_2$–$D\sharp_4$	Light and husky, approximating mid-baritone, difficulties with 4ths and 5ths
5	Black	120	C_3–B_3	<A_2–D_4	Body, resonance and power increase, agility recovered, adult qualities emerge

Table 2: Summary of Cooksey's vocal stages for male adolescents.

Many researchers and voice coaches who work with boys would agree with the statement that 'Cooksey had it nailed'. I have become increasingly less confident over the years that this is entirely so, developing a healthy scepticism for some of the practices that have arisen as a consequence of Cooksey's work. Certainly, I have found most if not all of the features Cooksey describes in my own measurements of boys. However, there are undoubtedly a number of additional considerations that concern boys involved in regular choral work as well as other matters that have come to light since Cooksey's death.

I would first question the use of stages as a means of determining what any individual might be capable of. Statistical procedures more advanced than those Cooksey was able to employ are now available, telling a slightly different story. It is a misunderstanding of the way in which patterns in large populations evolve out of the many idiosyncratic patterns of individuals to imagine that one can predict from a normative chart how a boy will actually develop. Stages are retrospective descriptions of populations, not predictive charts for individuals. In my experience, a dogmatic approach to stages can lead to some spectacularly unintelligent interpretations of Cooksey's work. There is a well-known precedent for this in the psychologist Jean Piaget's five 'stages' of cognitive development. These were once interpreted in educational theory with similar dogmatism, the result being a near-catastrophic pigeon-holing of children intellectually that has subsequently been discredited.

The recently revised UK standards for adolescent growth now similarly shy away from Tanner's five 'stages' of puberty. Instead, they recognise three broad categories of 'pre-puberty', 'in-puberty' and 'completing puberty'. This is all that is needed to track healthy growth and, in my view, it is also all that is needed to accommodate the choral singing voice. The app (see Chapter 3) accordingly displays just the light blue shirt cartoon for 'pre-puberty', the dark blue and light green shirts together for 'in puberty' and the dark green and black together for 'completing puberty'. These, however, are only indicative of the broad SF_0 bands for whole populations. That is why the app also displays an individualised vocal history for each boy programmed into it. This tracks actual changes in an individual's voice, and these are what count the most.

Such an approach allows for significantly greater leeway and professional judgement, which is absolutely necessary if boys' choral singing is not to be subjected to pointless limitations. Cooksey describes, after all, six voice stages and the reductio ad absurdum is that choral music for boys must be in six parts, one to correspond to each voice stage. This was never intended by Cooksey, though we shall return to the topic in Chapter 7 when we consider whether it is necessary to have differently ranged parts for adolescent boys to the normal soprano, alto, tenor, bass (SATB).

The second critical point to note is that Cooksey suggests that the 'pinnacle of development' for the 'full rich soprano' happens at Stage 0, the pre-puberty stage. His description of the first puberty stage is singularly unflattering—'breathy', 'strained', 'little resonance or body'. The range he gives for boys at this stage is also hopeless. What use to the choral director is a boy who can only sing from A_3–D_5? This is fine for school classroom singing, but if followed dogmatically, it can result in the early dismissal from choirs of boy trebles who may have two or so years' useful life left. These are precisely the two years when the boy has attained the social, intellectual and musical maturity to become a leader and really valuable member of the choir.

A dogmatic stage approach has, in my view, led to misconceptions about how puberty affects choral singing as misleading as the 'puberty begins when the voice breaks' misconception. It has also led to a dismissal of the falsetto register in boys that is not justified by practice. Many choristers at the in-puberty stage develop a falsetto register that can be quite beautiful and the majority of vocal coaches I have consulted see no harm in their using it. It is time to look at the secular trend and the impact of changing fashions in boys' choral tone.

4.2   The secular trend

I have read some highly alarmist claims about the future of contemporary choral work with boys on the grounds that the age at which boys reach and progress through puberty is becoming younger. Certain sections of the press love doomed choirboy stories, as I found to my cost when my own research was misreported. A certain broadsheet newspaper, rather than the more usual tabloid suspects, was the guiltiest and made up some completely fictitious 'quotes'. This is worrying for anyone concerned with accurate public understanding of science—or indeed most other topics reported by the press. However, I also once read in a respected journal of singing that it is 'no longer possible' for most boys to provide reliable treble lines for choirs as the 'average age of onset of voice change is twelve and a half'.

At the same time, one reads intriguing stories claiming that during the 1920s and 1930s boys did not reach puberty until the age of sixteen or so and, even more improbably, that in the time of J. S. Bach, boys did not reach puberty until eighteen (see Chapter 5). If these claims were taken as true at face value, we would have a secular trend of about six years from 1750 to the present day. Nobody acquainted with the way such trends operate could regard this as at all likely, so closer attention to what lies behind these stories is demanded. My own quite extensive investigation of the topic, carried out in collaboration with my colleague Dr Ann-Christine Mecke from Leipzig, revealed that the age of fourteen has been remarkably consistent for over two thousand years as the time 'boyes are apt to change theere voices'. Readers are referred to our paper of that title (Ashley and Mecke, 2013) for the full story. In essence, our conclusion was that it is impossible to make a reliable deduction because nearly all the evidence available is either anecdotal or based on quite seriously flawed research. When every available study is reviewed, only a very small regression pattern is revealed and the distribution of outliers is so wide that little trust can be placed in many of the studies.

It was possible, on the other hand, to provide a much more plausible account of the phenomenon by looking at changes in taste with regard to boys' singing, changes in choir-training techniques and a significantly enhanced concern with vocal health and child welfare. These will be the main topics of this section of the chapter. First, however, I would like to look at some evidence that there has been a small secular trend in the last fifty years, albeit a much lesser one than the alarmist reports have suggested.

An obvious need in a study of trends is for a baseline. This is the main difficulty. It has been all but impossible to find a reliable and trustworthy baseline of puberty and voice measurements from sufficiently far back in the past. After a lot of searching, I have paid some attention to the UK National Birth Cohort study that has followed a large sample born in 1946 from birth to old age. School doctors working within thus study were asked in 1961 to assess the male cohort at the age of fourteen. They assessed the appearance of the genitals as 'infantile', 'early' or 'advanced' and pubic hair as 'none', 'yes, sparse' or 'yes profuse'. They were also asked to rate voice-breaking status as 'no', 'starting to break' or 'completely broken' as a further means of supporting these judgements. The categories are broad and similar to the 'pre-puberty', 'in-puberty' and 'completing puberty' of the present-day standards.

How these medical staff might have distinguished between these three categories has been the subject of a further study of present day medical staff that I have undertaken myself. Unlike the 1946 study, intrusive inspections were not undertaken. The process, at the time of writing, has been dependent upon the correlation between voice stage and genital stage shown by other studies. However, the three voice categories were more carefully determined by a perceptual test. Medical staff were asked to match ten progressively lower voices of known SF_0 to the criteria employed in the 2012 adolescent growth standards of 'high voice', 'slightly deepened voice' and 'fully changed voice'. Their judgements were compared with those of a sample of choral directors and a good degree of internal consistency obtained. 'High voices' were considered to be those of 200 Hz or above, and 'slightly deepened' those ranging from 165 Hz to 199 Hz.

Allowing for the potential margins of error inherent within such a process, Table 3 below is fairly conclusive. The 1962 assessments are those made of

	1962	2012
Pre-puberty	26.8%	0%
In puberty	37.1%	36%
Completing puberty	36.0%	64%

Table 3. Changes in the timing of puberty
in fourteen-year-old boys.

the 1946 birth cohort. The 2012 assessments are those of all the fourteen year olds in my own 1000 voices database classified according to the results of the perceptual test.

It is clear here that there has very likely been some advance in pubertal timing. The number of boys with typical 'in-puberty' voices (i.e. at the dark blue/light green shirt level) is almost the same. This is deceptive, though, because relatively speaking it is not the same segment of the total population. In 1962, a little over a quarter of fourteen-year-old boys had not begun puberty at all, whereas in 2012 every fourteen-year-old had at least commenced puberty. In 2012, not that far short of twice as many fourteen-year-olds had completed puberty compared with 1962.

Let us suppose we had a boys' choir in 1962 and that in that choir at the beginning of the year, there were eight fourteen-year-olds. Two of these boys would remain as clear, unchanged treble voices throughout the year. Of the remaining six, perhaps three would remain in the choir as trebles to the end of the year, though with voices beginning to change. The final three would almost certainly need to leave the treble section before the end of the year. Now, for the same choir in 2012, three out of eight fourteen-year-olds might survive the year as mature trebles, the remaining six would all very likely be lost as trebles during the year.

I think this is a fair reflection of the actual reality and it does match quite well the study I carried out of seven English cathedral choirs between 2011 and 2012. This study classified the boys according to the Cooksey scheme. Assessments were made of SF_0, comfortable singing tessitura and extreme range using a comprehensive battery of tests covering all the criteria of voice pitch and quality shown in Table 3 . The final results (see Figure 1) were expressed as 'pre-puberty' (boys singing a true treble without difficulty) 'in-puberty' (boys continuing to singing treble, but with contracting range and/or changing technique) and 'completing puberty' (boys able to sing treble only in a strained falsetto and remaining in the choir through miming missing notes).

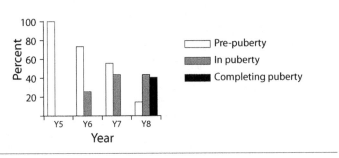

Figure 1. Pubertal vocal stage of boy trebles in seven English cathedral choirs.

In this study, all Year 5 (nine- to ten-year-olds) had pre-pubertal unchanged voices, but almost one quarter of the Year 6 ten- to eleven-year-olds) showed possible signs of having reached pubertal onset. A year later, the eleven- to twelve-year-olds were almost evenly split between those that had still not reached pubertal onset and those that had, though the former were still a little greater in number. What cannot be discerned from this graph is the fact that the Year 6 and Year 7 boys were, at least on the basis of their individual performances in the test room, the ones that were really carrying the treble sections of their choirs. This was the case regardless of whether or not pubertal onset had occurred. The Year 5 boys, though possessing pure treble voices were on the whole less accurate singers than their older peers. When we go up to Year 8 (twelve- to thirteen-year-olds) we see clearly that this is a time of big change. Only 15 per cent of this age group had not begun puberty. The largest group (44 per cent) were 'in-puberty', but almost as many (42 per cent) had reached the 'completing puberty' stage.

The way in which the 'completing puberty' boys were handled varied from choir to choir. In one of the choirs, I met three Year 8 boys who had actually ceased to sing. In another, I found two boys who could complete the test bank only in the tenor register, but who remained in the choir, claiming that they mimed or sang only in falsetto. I also found three instances in which the boys, though possessing tessitura in the tenor octave, attempted to perform the test bank an octave higher in falsetto. These boys did not seem aware that they were singing in falsetto and one was shocked and surprised to discover that he had a tenor voice he did not appear to know about.

These results are quite perplexing and difficult to interpret. Clearly, there were some boys remaining in choirs as trebles who really ought to have been 'retired'. It is difficult to imagine in such cases that either the boy's vocal health and technique, or the choir's tone, would be well served by those remaining. The larger number of boys who were not 'completing puberty' but 'in-puberty' is the more intriguing. Were these boys under a strict 'Cooksey regime', they too might have been relieved of a high treble line. Yet there seems to be some kind of bonus whereby a regular and reasonably demanding choral singing regime allows such boys to flout Cooksey's predictions and remain not only as trebles, but as trebles with powerful, reliable voices who are often the backbone of the choir. This phenomenon has been noted by other researchers.

Jenevora Williams (2010), in her extensive study of London choristers, noted that falsetto phonation did not emerge as predicted by Cooksey as the majority of boys entered the third stage of change (we shall look at the vexed question of what is and is not falsetto in some detail very shortly). The boys in Williams' study were reported as continuing to sing with efficient fold closure in the upper ranges and with a laryngeal waveform having more similarities with an adult female or a trained adult counter-tenor. Williams suggests that the intensive training of these boys permits a hybrid phonation that seamlessly bridges the gap between child and adult. Colin Baldy also has substantial experience of teaching English professional choristers. He has similarly noted the phenomenon, though he calls it a 'supercharged falsetto'. He sees no harm and regards the 'enormous amount of noise' they are able to produce as 'rather a nice final flourish for them'. Williams asks the crucial question, how high should boys sing?: 'When they are actually capable of singing both parts, should they sing soprano or baritone?'

There is little doubt in my mind that if the boys are happy to do so and no damage is being done to them, their musical experience and maturity is of considerable value to the choir. They should sing soprano in choir, though perhaps baritone at school where a high soprano voice in a boy of that age might be though inappropriate by critical non-choir peers. This is indeed what often happens. My own research has revealed time and time again that boys are quite articulate about this situation and fully capable of managing it.

I have, though, experienced on several occasions a split of the choral world into camps of 'fundamentalists' and 'liberals'. The fundamentalist view is that as soon as there is any evidence of pubertal onset, the boy must stop singing treble. The liberal view is that a boy may continue to sing treble for as long as he is able to do so with ease and reports no discomfort. My own position over the years has shifted from the fundamentalist to the liberal. However, I say this with one important caveat: once boys attain the age of twelve years, they should be observed carefully and heard on an individual basis regularly. Each boy's progression through puberty is unique and every case needs to be considered on merit.

I have in my own 1000 voices archive a good number of boy treble voices where the boys are very clearly 'in-puberty', yet sing easily with useful treble voices. In some cases, the speaking voices are well down in the 'green shirt' range, yet almost every listener declares the sound to be a good treble up to G5. The boys themselves report no difficulty with their singing and are able to sing across the whole treble range with little in the way of difficult register breaks. However, this is not invariably the case. As my own cross-sectional study of seven cathedral choirs demonstrated, not all boys achieve a comfortable hybrid phonation. We do not yet understand why some boys do and others do not. In one choir I found two thirteen-year-olds clearly 'in-puberty'. Both were leading trebles, but under test the one with the lower speaking voice sang an easy, free treble with barely perceptible register breaks, whereas the one with the slightly higher speaking voice audibly crossed a lift point between B4 and C5. I have heard the sound of the first boy described as 'unchanged' by audiences of conductors but 'falsetto' by a voice coach. There is no clear explanation that I have been able to find for the fact that two boys of near equal stature, pubertal status and singing experience might end up with quite different adaptations to voice change. At the extremes of what is experienced, one boy may sing in a painful falsetto, another of apparently similar physical development in a treble that sounds pure and clear to the majority of listeners.

The majority of voices coaches I have consulted for this book take the view that provided there is no discomfort or tension that would result in the ingraining of bad habits requiring future remediation, the boy can continue. Quite how the final decision is made and who is to make it requires some thought. I believe that the days of the choir director's 'secret garden' are, or should be, over. The guiding principle has to be the familiar one of best interests of the child. This is better made in my view by at least two professionals, and the views of the boy himself and his parents need also to be considered. The view of the boy is important. His voice belongs to him and present-day ethical standards are grounded in the recognition that a child has sovereignty over his or her body.

On the other hand, a boy may not always make decisions that a wiser person might regard as in his own best interests. It is not uncommon, in my experience, for boys to wish to extend their time as trebles in order to reach a coveted position of seniority in the choir or to be able to participate in a forthcoming tour. Parents may also be reluctant to admit that the biddable son who has charmed the family for several years with his angelic voice is turning into a potentially rebellious teenager. Hearing boys regularly from the age of twelve is probably the best way to prepare everybody for the inevitable and reach a reasonable compromise. Sometimes it may be necessary to tolerate a changed voice treble because to deny the boy the opportunity of participating as a senior leader in a major concert he had been looking forwards to for months would the greater of the two evils. If this is done with understanding on both sides and the boy is counseled not to push his voice and to mime

70

for rest periods, I can see little harm resulting. The choir should not, however, rely on the boy's voice for its own survival in the concert.

My key point in concluding this section, however, is that it is probable that the timing of puberty has in the past been wrongly estimated because people have operated in a culture of ignorance that believes that 'puberty begins when the voice breaks'. A better understanding that puberty begins on average two or more years before any such event and that boys sing treble for some time during and even after puberty ought to result in improved public understanding of the timing of puberty. As I pointed out in the Chapter 3, if public visibility is the marker, the change of voice is the boy equivalent of menarche in girls. Although Tanner did not hold much store by voice assessment, the more we understand about voice change, the more we are inclined to trust vocal status as a reliable indicator, to the extent that it is now recognized in the national standards for adolescent growth. For much of adolescence, however, the singing voice is able to buck the trend of the speaking voice. That is where so much of the confusion comes from. We look in detail at what is going on in section 4.3 .

4.3   Head voice and falsetto

In Chapter 3 I warned that puberty plays complete havoc with registration. Boys who transitioned from cricothyroid to thyroarytenoid production with relative ease as trebles are going to have to handle a much more pronounced register break. The different parts of the voice are going to become much more apparent. We shall have to think much more about what boys might be doing when they sing treble during puberty. This means that we shall have to tackle the question of how 'head voice' and falsetto might be defined and understood. There are plenty of texts that make confident assertions about what such qualities are in boys' voices. Some make no distinction between falsetto and head voice at all. Others argue with conviction that the two phenomena are quite different. I have come to a healthy scepticism about this and regard any author who writes as though there are no unknowns as probably untrustworthy. There is simply no reliable scientific definition of 'head voice' and falsetto in a boy's voice that all are agreed upon.

I am fairly confident that Kenneth Phillips' (1996) belief that English choirboys sing only in the 'head voice' derives at least in part from the old belief of the nineteenth-century writers that the 'chest voice' should not be used. This belief has long since disappeared from the mainstream of choral work in the UK, though treble choristers continue to employ more 'head' than 'chest' in their singing simply because that is where their repertoire takes them. This is where a great split has come about over the question of how high boys should sing, and how big their range ought to be. A recent doctoral thesis summarised the position at the end of the twentieth century in terms of three distinct schools of thought:

- School A believes that the boy's voice changes in a predictable manner, lowering in pitch gradually and that voices are limited to a mid-voice tessitura of an octave or less.
- School B states that the boy's voice may change slowly or quickly and is not limited to a mid-voice comfort range of an octave or less.
- School C advises a period of rest once the voice begins to change.

School A has been highly influential. Cooksey's work might be included within it as well as whole singing movements such as the Cambiata principle of Irvin Cooper (see Chapter 5). Far from a boy remaining in ignorance of his new voice, School A believes that the boy should know about it and work to develop it. Its advocates are of the view that the safest and healthiest means of guiding the voice through change is through work on the lower register whilst the upper register rests. The new voice should be built on from a secure lower register in the initial stages. It is School C, on the other hand, that has tended to keep the boy in ignorance of the new lower register until there is a sudden, traumatic 'break' and whatever technique he has been using to maintain a high treble range just ceases to be possible.

I do not subscribe in a doctrinaire way to any of these schools. As with developmental stage theories, they can perhaps mislead the observer into seeing what the theory sees rather than what is actually there. It is School B, sometimes associated with the pioneering work of Frederick Swanson, that is perhaps the most likely to alert the well-informed observer to what is actually there. Although Swanson's work has fallen out of favour relative to Cooksey's, the most recent work on adolescent growth has reiterated the idiosyncratic nature of the process and the unpredictability of growth spurts. Cooksey did acknowledge this, but a tendency to generalize through a focus on mean trends has perhaps obscured the extent to which individuals vary.

Nearly every choir director I have interviewed for this book has told me that some voices change quickly and others slowly. This is observation of what happens when the voice is allowed to do its work in the real world of the choir rather than conform to what ought to happen according to a theory. We also know quite clearly that mid-pubertal choristers are not limited to a comfort range of less than an octave. Equally, there is ample evidence that if the modal voice alone is employed, as in the singing of pubertal boys lacking chorister training, the comfort range probably is less than an octave. So there may not be a definitive 'one size fits all' solution. I have come to believe that we need a flexible system based on sound professional judgement. Such judgements, to be professional, do need to be based on some systematic understanding of what may happen. There are certain things to look for.

The unchanged voice, according to at least one study, is capable of reaching C_5 without drawing on the resource of the 'head voice' or cricothyroid action. Boys who have learned to sing in head voice can almost certainly produce better tone and more accurate intonation in the C_4–C_5 octave, but will need to cope with big registration shifts once puberty begins. Boys who have never sung in 'head voice' on the other hand simply shift downwards. The possible range, however, does contract to as little as about a sixth as School A describes. To go beyond this without a result that is strained and unpleasant may require the crossing of a passagio. Boys who previously sang successfully in their whole voice as trebles may well need coaching as their passagio becomes much more pronounced with the emergence of the new voice. For boys with little or no such experience, this is not the time to start! The advice of School A is probably the most appropriate in such circumstances.

Most writers agree that there are two lift points or passagio regions that are easy to detect in pubertal boys but often much harder to perceive in pre-pubertal voices. I have certainly found evidence of this, but the extent to which it is clearly perceptual is variable. I have even experienced variation in the same boy from one week to another. Also variable is the degree to which a boy manages his passagio, an indicator of general vocal health and learned skill. The two passagio regions of the boy voice may well correspond to the primo and secondo passagio of the adult voice, though I am not aware of any study that has specifically addressed this question, so it would be unwise to regard it as a certainty.

The first lift point is the more obvious and is generally regarded as the result of a shift from thyroarytenoid to crycoarytenoid production. The point at which it occurs is not fixed and boys can be taught some control over its placement as well as techniques for covering sudden breaks. In upward vocalization it occurs around A or B_4 to C or D_5 and is certainly described by Cooksey. It is heard most typically in light green shirt boys, i.e. boys who are without doubt at the 'in-puberty' phase. These boys simply cannot push their modal voice beyond this point without breaking into a clearly different tone that is lighter and flutier and, for the sake of argument, 'falsetto'. A plausible though not proven beyond doubt explanation for this is that maturation of the ligament plays some part in restraining the pre-pubertal ability to push the modal voice higher. Loud or forced singing will also raise the pitch of the transition, creating a more obvious break when the aim should be to minimize the perception of register shift.

In downward vocalization, this same lift point can be depressed to somewhere between middle C to E and can be the most troublesome point for 'in-puberty' boys. It can lead to a complete phonational gap where the voice literally 'breaks' into two halves and no notes at all can be sounded in the space between. Above the gap is the old 'choirboy voice' and below it, the newly emerging young adult voice. The join between the two is what many people refer to as the 'clunk'. If boys are not taught in a way that allows them to manage this transition, they may be unable to sing at all in precisely the range that a lot of school singing is thoughtlessly pitched. Unsurprisingly, many give up in frustration and embarrassment that they cannot do what seems to come easily to girls.

One recent study has drawn on the work of Swanson (1977) to revive the notion of a phonational gap as though it were an inevitable feature of voice change. This is not so in my experience and there is little doubt that most boys can be taught to cover the gap if they have not already discovered for themselves how to do it. As Leck (2009) suggests, this is most readily done by vocalizing downwards from the old 'head voice' but, unlike School C, also exercising the new 'chest voice'. During individual lessons boys who are aware of a clearly developing register shift may sing scales as '4×4s'—four notes in one register and four in the other. Practising this over a range of keys will give boys the facility to diminish the 'clunk'. I am not aware of any well-developed practice that attempts such an exercise en masse with the boys of a choir. It is probably over-fussy and not necessary because of the extent to which individual differences are over-ridden by the chorus effect (see Chapter 10).

As we have seen, if the Cooksey scheme is followed to the letter, a boy's treble career is largely over once puberty begins and this is patently not what I have observed to be the case in my own studies of choral work in the UK. We saw in section 4.3 that boys continue to sing treble for some time after pubertal onset. I have also raised previously the possibility that a boy's voice actually expands in range during puberty. The principal advocate of the expanding voice in recent times has been Henry Leck. Whilst a member of an academic faculty, Leck's contribution has been primarily as a leading practitioner and his work with the Indianapolis Children's Choir has received growing attention. Leck describes how he came to his position, less through academic research than through a sudden insight in the course of his choral directing practice. This, then, is theorization from practice:

> I came to this whole process somewhat by accident, through ignorance. I knew that the classifications did not fit. I didn't know what to do with the boys in my first treble chorus of eighty-six singers because there were not enough to do SATB. Since the vocal classifications that I had studied were of no help, I told them just to sing high. I knew that it meant their voices would tire more quickly, they wouldn't be able to sing some notes, and their voices might crack . . . But I wasn't smart enough to know

what to do with them. I continued to vocalize them down across their break from their old voice to the new. Lo and behold, A MIRACLE HAPPENED and I discovered that if a boy sings from his high voice to his low range consistently and continues to sing in the old voice while developing the new, the break eventually disappears. What emerges is a voice that we do not recognize in our culture—a three-octave voice without a break.

I place some credibility in Leck's work because I regularly come across boys, typically aged thirteen or fourteen, who do have three-octave ranges. Indeed, I have one in my database with a five-octave range, which always amuses when played at conferences. There is, however, one very big question. Exactly of what use is a three-octave range? There is very little repertoire for singers with a three-octave range. As Leck himself states, this is a voice that we do not recognize in our culture. Boys who perform the classical choral repertoire as trebles are not going to need a three-octave range. Either they can sing in the crucial D_4–G_5 range or they are of little use to the choir director.

What I have seen time and time again is pubertal boys singing in this range who have not discovered that they have another voice in the range of E_3–D_4. Unless a voice coach takes the boy aside and explores with him his voice after pubertal onset, he may well not understand what is happening and will continue to self-identify as an unchanged treble. Though of somewhat lesser consequence, it is a form of ignorance almost on a par with teenage girls who did not know they were pregnant because nobody had ever told them the facts of life.

The upper passagio point is less well understood. It can occur in children's voices at around D_5–E_5 and may conceivably be confused with a lower passagio forced upwards. If there is a second lift point, the voice will already be in crycoarytenoid production, but the singer will feel that another change has occurred and this is often detectable by ear. This is probably not a transition from 'head' to 'whistle' register, simply a shift in resonance pattern. A further change into true 'whistle' register is not at all uncommon in boys under test, but would not normally be used in choral singing.

For how long into a boy's career 'choiry tone' can and should be brought down from upper regions of the voice is the final point to be considered in this chapter. A substantial amount of evidence points to the possibility than in some boys, though not all, it can be brought down for some time after the boy enters the completing-puberty phase. To all intents and purposes, the young man will present as a normal mid-adolescent. He will speak in a baritone range and he will be of stature and musculature that sets him apart from the lighter frames of the in-puberty boys. He will sing, however, with a soprano voice. The word 'soprano' is used advisedly. The tone will be more like that of a female adult than the pure, naive treble we have come to expect from younger boys or even to some extent by pre- to early puberty girls trained as trebles. The 'boy soprano' is an acquired taste and few people today have acquired it or wish to when they hear it.

I am as near to wholly convinced as I feel it safe to be to give this as the reason why it is erroneously imagined that puberty was so much later during the pre-World War II years when artists such as Ernest Lough made headlines. Whilst a secular trend might account for perhaps as much as a year's difference, training methods that resulted in the extension of upper register life throughout puberty probably counted for as much as two further year's difference relative to the practice of ending the treble career in early to mid-puberty. I believe this question opens up whole new unknowns for research into boys' choral voices. There is an urgent need to understand why some boys can produce a beautiful treble in what a majority of singing teachers would call 'falsetto' whilst the falsetto of other boys of similar age, development and SF_0 sounds clearly forced and like an adult's untrained falsetto.

Some texts seem to regard almost any use of falsetto by boys as a fault. I believe they are mistaken to do so and my evidence is the number of older boy trebles who sing quite beautifully and without any strain or tension, even though well-qualified voice coaches judge them to be employing falsetto. Not all boys succeed in doing this, however. Some lose any ease of production or purity of tone very quickly as the end of puberty approaches. Their falsetto sounds strained and unpleasant. Others keep going for a surprisingly long time. Their voice in the upper register becomes very powerful and it is a temptation for choir directors hard-pressed with recruitment difficulties to retain their services into Year 10 or even Year 11 of the English National Curriculum as they can equal two or three smaller boys in pure power output. This is a step beyond the super-charged falsetto Colin Baldy describes and I know of no experienced voice coach or well-run professional choir that adopts such a practice. The consensus is that it is harmful to the boy and does little to improve the tone of the choir.

Jenevora Williams currently differentiates 'head voice' from 'falsetto' by defining both 'chest' and 'head' as 'modal'. Thyroarytenoid action therefore is involved in the 'head voice'. Although the cricothyroids are dominant, some tension in the thyroarytenoids prevents the voice from flipping over into falsetto. This is likely to be a learned skill. True falsetto, in this understanding, occurs when the thyroarytenoid becomes passive and flaccid whilst the voice is controlled only through the cricothyroid muscles. For most in-puberty boys, transition into this mode is what happens abruptly and involuntarily at the B_4–D_5 lift point. This event, which I have witnessed on innumerable occasions, accords beautifully with the work of Cooksey. On this point Cooksey is quite clear that this falsetto voice does not, indeed cannot, exist in boys until they reach this mid-pubertal stage with its maturing ligament.

Cooksey did recognise that there may be a transitional voice between 'chest' and falsetto, but he never investigated the practice of training boys so that they are able to preserve enough thyroarytenoid tension to avoid a complete break into falsetto. As with all things, boys are most likely to learn this skill by imitation. Perhaps Cooksey did not do this because nobody would want boys to sing in such a way and the practice was less familiar in boys' choral work in the United States. The sound of a boy 'soprano' warbling and wobbling in a prolonged head voice is indeed regarded by most present-day listeners as demeaning for the boy. I address this in Chapter 5.

References

Ashley, M. & Mecke, A-C. (2013). 'Boyes are apt to change their voices at about fourteen yeares of age': an historical background to the debate about longevity in boy treble singers.' *Reviews of Research in Human Learning and Music*, 1. Available at: <http://rrhlm.org/index.php/RRHLM/article/view/13>.

Baldy, C. (2010). *The Student Voice: An Introduction to Developing the Singing Voice.* Edinburgh: Dunedin.

Cooksey, J. (1977) The development of a contemporary eclectic theory for the training and cultivation of the junior high school male changing voice: Part III: Developing an integrated approach to the care and training of the junior high school male changing voice. *The Choral Journal*, 18(4):5–15.

Leck, H. (2009). The boy's changing voice expanding: take the high road. *Choral Journal*, (May):49–60.

Phillips, K. (1996). *Teaching Kids to Sing.* New York, NY: Schirmer Books.

Swanson, F. (1977). *The Male Singing Voice Ages Eight to Eighteen.* Cedar Rapids, LA: Laurance Press.

Williams, J. (2010). The implications of intensive singing training on the vocal health and development of boy choristers in an English cathedral choir. Ph.D. thesis, Institute of Education, London.

Further reading

Ashley, M. & Mecke, A-C. (2013). 'Boyes are apt to change their voices at about fourteen yeares of age': an historical background to the debate about longevity in boy treble singers. *Reviews of Research in Human Learning and Music*, 1. Available at: <http://rrhlm.org/index.php/RRHLM/article/view/13>.

Baldy, C. (2010). *The Student Voice: An Introduction to Developing the Singing Voice.* Edinburgh: Dunedin.

Cooksey, J. (1999) *Working With Adolescent Voices.* St Louis, MO: Concordia.

Interlude 2: William

At the time of writing, William, aged fourteen years and two months, is in what may be his final term as head chorister of Blackburn Cathedral (see Chapter 10). 'What may be' are words that describe a common situation with such boys. How long is the treble voice going to last? Will it last until Christmas? William is in no hurry to lose it, though he is very well aware of how far he has progressed through voice change on account of my regular termly visits to his home to conduct detailed longitudinal assessments. Born in August, William is one of the youngest in his school year. That year, nevertheless, is UK National Curriculum Year 10 (US Grade 9) and it is not that common to find treble choristers in Year 10. Blackburn had had no choir school (though this is changing, see Chapter 10) and William attends the Queen Elizabeth Grammar School where he is something of a musical star. He plays the organ in the school hall, he has sung the part of Oliver in a school production, and large pictures of a younger William in evening dress playing the cello adorn the stairway in the school's music building.

Had he attended a conventional 7–13 choir school, William's career as a chorister would have been over at least a year and a term sooner. In William's case, that would undoubtedly have been a grave loss, both to the boy and to the cathedral. Statistically, there is an almost 50:50 chance that a boy of that age would no longer have a good, clear treble (see Chapter 4). On the one hand, this means that approximately fifty per cent of boys quite correctly leave the choir during their last year at choir school, but the other fifty per cent are good trebles the choir could have retained for longer. William did some very good work as a senior treble throughout his time as a young member of Year 9. He was certainly able to continue beyond the age of thirteen-and-a-half and the case illustrates well the unsuitability of the school year system, probably for many aspects of education, certainly for choir. When a boy's life as an experienced, mature treble may be only two or three years, the eleven months leeway of an August/September birthday makes a something of a nonsense of the system.

One of the first recordings William made for me when he was twelve was of the Welsh lullaby Suo Gan. Throughout that year, William's SF_0 hovered around a mean of 213 Hz, making him a 'light blue shirt' or pre-pubertal treble. The voice was pure, clear and well-developed with unmistakable evidence of 'ring' (harmonic enhancement in the regions of an adult's singer's formant but about 1 kHz higher in a child). I was anxious for William to record more because the voice was a good one and I had so often experienced boys with beautiful treble voices who did not record them until past their peak as unchanged trebles. Many such recordings are available commercially. In the event, we did not get around to a proper recording session until William was thirteen. The same organisational difficulties got in the way!

For the recordings made at the age of thirteen, William sang such pieces as 'Hear My Prayer' and Britten's 'Corpus Christi Carol' with the consummate ease of an unchanged voice and the professionalism of an experienced, senior cathedral chorister. The recording session was a real pleasure! His SF_0 at the time was just under 200 Hz, which is the cut-off point in the app for 'in-puberty', a 'slightly deepened' voice. Taken as a single measurement, an SF_0 of 196 Hz does not necessarily mean puberty has begun: the voice could be naturally low. However, Table 4 shows William's progression since the age of 11 years and 10 months. Between the ages of 11:10 and 12:11, the SF_0 has hovered around a mean of 213 Hz. By the time William was thirteen, however, there was a clear falling trend below 200 Hz, indicating 'in-puberty'. For the zealous 'Cooksey fundamentalist' (see Chapter 4) this might be the time to leave the choir. William's potential singing range at the time, however, was expanding. At the age of 13:08 he had retained his ability to reach a $C\#_6$ (1157 Hz) in whistle but had extended his lower register just about to E_3 (164 Hz). A lift point was beginning to appear between E_4 and D_4 (320–295 Hz) on the downward glide where a change could be seen on the electroglottogram (EGG), though still very hard to detect by ear in pitched scales.

Age (years:months)	EGG
11:10	210
12:02	215
12:06	209
12:08	220
12:11	213
13:03	196
13:08	189
13:09	176
14:01	157

Table 4: Electroglottogram readings of William.

EGG recordings of William between the ages of 11:10 and 13:09 illustrated that he was making very little obvious use of his lower register as a cathedral chorister. This was an almost pure 'head voice', probably the result of a repertoire that seldom required the lower reaches of the voice. Glides from highest to lowest point in the voice as well as keyboard pitched scales and vocalises revealed no significant lift points when William was twelve. The spectral lines were continuous throughout the voice and no characteristic shifts in mucosal waveform appeared. This began to change almost imperceptibly from about the age of thirteen-and-a-half but then quite clearly around the time William became fourteen years old.

As Table 4 shows, the fall in William's SF_0 was beginning to accelerate, reaching 157 Hz by 14:01. This is indicative of well-advancing puberty, confirmed by a bigger than expected gain in height, but also on this occasion, muscular weight. I had with me (quite intentionally) a copy of Orlando Gibbons' 'This is the Record of John', which the reader may well appreciate is a verse anthem that features as a classic of the counter-tenor repertoire. I asked William to sing the opening counter-tenor verse. His first attempt was nothing special because he was using only his customary 'head voice'. The lower notes were weak, insecure and insipid. I pointed this out to him and with the matter-of-fact nonchalance that I had come to associate with him, he switched to a blended production. This was instantly visible on the EGG where the characteristic wave-form of the lower register appeared as if by magic. The result was, to my ears, a beautiful sounding boy alto.

Perhaps the most remarkable feature of this particular episode was William's ability to switch to blended production and manage the passagio region with little or no instruction beyond saying 'you need to use your lower register'. I have encountered the same kind of instinctive vocal intelligence in other musical boys, though in different contexts of singing (see Interlude 3: Ben and George). How long William's capability as a boy alto will last is difficult to say, but the alto would the last phase of William's vocal boyhood, not what he should aspire to as an older teenager. In the German choirs, boys seem to remain at this level for long enough to be useful. What is important is that he is employing no falsetto at all and singing completely at the opposite end of his range to an adult male falsetto alto. There is no doubt in my mind as to which is the preferable sound: I prefer the boy any day! This is not to say that I have no time for the true adult counter-tenor. Such a voice takes time and skill to perfect. It is rare in relation to the number of amateur basses singing a falsetto that to my ears is often the weakness in an all-male choir.

On the subject of falsetto, a couple of sessions before the Record of John recording when William's SF_0 was much closer to the $200\,Hz$ cut-off, I asked him to participate in the Denis Barthel experiment (see section 5.2 on the Temple Church). I was able to play William a recording both of Denis Barthel and a boy who was a near-contemporary of William's but at the completing-puberty stage singing in a Barthel like post-pubertal soprano.

William sang with Barthel's voice in a pair of headphones, following exactly the extensive rubato and other interpretative nuances. He was quite capable of following these with good understanding, which I think is of significance in itself. A boy does not have to be sixteen years old to give a 'mature interpretation' (see Chapter 4). He was not, however, at all impressed by Barthel's sound, which he regarded as improper for a boy chorister. What he had to say is worth repeating for what it tells us about vocal identity and authenticity. In this interview, William clearly identifies himself as a boy who has yet to develop into an adult. There is, in William's view, a 'proper' way for boys to sing. Sounding like a woman, or indeed any mature trained adult singer, is 'false' for a boy. Boys are children and should have childlike qualities in their voices.

> INTERVIEWER: OK William, you were shaking your head while you were listening to that. What did you just say?
>
> WILLIAM: I could have mistaken it for a woman.
>
> INTERVIEWER: You could have mistaken it for a woman? Why?
>
> WILLIAM: The tone and the vibrato.
>
> INTERVIEWER: What was woman-like about the tone?
>
> WILLIAM: It was too rounded, that sort of thick and heavy tone that projects a long way, like the women singers try to project to the back of the hall. They make a big sound, a sort of round and large sound.
>
> INTERVIEWER: So should choristers not project their voices?
>
> WILLIAM: Yes, but not in the same way that adult singers do because they make the tone really thick and heavy. Choristers should do it with different tone, a chorister like tone.
>
> INTERVIEWER: Hmmm . . . well, that wasn't a woman. It was a boy. What kind of boy do you think it was?
>
> WILLIAM: Well it wasn't a chorister, not a cathedral chorister. Somehow it sounded like he'd been forced to use the vibrato he did...At that age, if you can sing bass you should. You shouldn't be still trying to sing treble because it's not meant to be really.
>
> INTERVIEWER: Do you think we should have choirs with boys like that in them?
>
> WILLIAM: No.
>
> INTERVIEWER: Why not?
>
> WILLIAM: Because I think it spoils boys' reputation. Obviously they've had boys that are that old in choirs before, but I think they should keep, 'cos it's a boys' choir, not a man's choir or a falsetto choir or something. It's supposed to be boys with a boy tone, not a false boy tone.

Chapter 5: Achieving authenticity

How many of us have dreamed of time travel? What would it be like to set the coordinates of a time machine for Lincoln Cathedral in the 1500s? What would a choir actually directed by William Byrd have sounded like? What would the boys have been like? How would they have compared in sound, physical size, intellect, appearance, cleanliness and character to the Lincoln choristers I knew so well during the 1980s? Would the men, indeed, have sounded anything like present day choir men? One meaning of the word 'authenticity' is related closely to this question. Much scholarship and creative energy has been expended by the early music movement on the development of authenticity in performance. There is almost an expectation now that the music of Bach will be played on reproduction period instruments. The same question can arise about the singers as arises about the instruments and I address it in this chapter.

There is another, equally important understanding of authenticity that we can have. This concerns the legitimacy of the expectations we place on our boys for the way they will use their voices. Chapter 2 was entitled 'understanding the instrument', the instrument being the boy chorister. Boys are not like period instruments. They cannot be constructed according to a series of dimensions and specifications arrived at by historical musical scholarship. They are living beings with identities fashioned out of social interactions within a given culture. Moreover, their bio-physical properties too are outside our control, as we have seen in earlier chapters on the secular trends in stature and puberty. Authenticity here means requiring of our boys a choral sound that will respect their identity and personhood.

One of the most fundamental questions that this requirement raises is one I have previously attempted to answer in my book *How High Should Boys Sing?* (Ashley, 2009). In this chapter, which concludes part one of the present book (the sections are punctuated by the three Interludes) , I want to re-open this question in the light of the preceding four chapters. The discussion will be relevant also to what is to come in the next section where we analyse the work of some actual choirs. I have already made an important statement about authenticity through drawing a particular distinction between 'boys', defined as younger adolescents who sing treble, and 'young men', defined as older adolescents who attempt the voice parts of adult men. As with the lift point within the passagio region, the break between 'boy' and 'young man' is moveable and no respecter of chronological age.

In this chapter I want to look at three scenarios related to the authenticity question. The first concerns what I regard as the folly of applying similar standards to voices as to musical instruments. The second concerns the change from boy soprano to boy treble. The third concerns what happens if we relax the 'rules' about the acoustic definition of 'boy'.

5.1   Bach's boy sopranos

The interest in Bach's boy sopranos is largely driven by musicologists' quest for authenticity in performance. David Wulstan is one such to have been much attracted by the chimera of boys with high lung power and emotional maturity but still soprano voices. This interest, which might be likened to a quest for the Holy Grail, I suspect drives an almost certainly erroneous belief that boys' puberty in Bach's time was later by several years than it is now. An important study by Bowers (1987) points out that Wulstan's belief in the existence of such boys is 'misconceived on a number of grounds'. Wulstan's attempts to estimate the timing of puberty from biographical accounts do indeed seem rather naive from a medical point of view. He concludes somewhat implausibly that mutation occurred at age eighteen in 1475, at sixteen in 1550, at fifteen in 1600, and again at eighteen in 1850. Such figures, even if based on accurate medical information (which they are not), might at best represent localised variations and not a secular trend.

Whilst some variations in the mean timing of pubertal onset and climax are to be expected, we saw in Chapter 4 that this is unlikely to deviate more than a year or two from mutational climax at around age fourteen. That it was as late as age eighteen in Bach's day, as is often suggested, is highly improbable. The more sober appraisal by Bowers rightly takes Wulstan to task for his fanciful speculation. Bowers states that 'it is entirely clear that in the fifteenth and early sixteenth century the trained singing-boy's voice broke [sic] not at 18 but at about 14 or 15' (p. 48). He cites a recognised medical authority (J.M. Tanner) and an analysis of the careers of almost 100 boys who sung at St George's Chapel, Windsor between 1461 and 1499. Chapel records indicate that none of these boys exceeded the age of fifteen, though a number were retained to sing with 'broken' voices in order that they could qualify for an ex gratia payment as compensation for loss of employment.

Let us look at what may really have happened and deconstruct the myth of the mature adolescent with the lung power and voice of a castrato. As is probably quite well known, J.S. Bach occupied the position of Thomaskantor in Lepzig from 1723 until his death in 1750. This was his final position and the period that saw such momentous events as the first performance of the *St Matthew Passion*. It was a strange relocation in many ways. The move from Köthen entailed a reduction in salary for Bach himself and the loss of Anna Magdalena's income as a singer. Most biographers see it as representing a decrease in social status from the position of Kapellmeister and Hofkomponist to mere cantor and teacher in the Thomanerschule. Of interest to us is the fact that the resources available to Bach for the performance of his music also represented a retrograde career move. Bach is known to have complained frequently about the quality of his singers and he hardly had the kind of inspirational working relationship with the boys that we would expect in one of our better choir schools today.

One in-depth study of Bach's performance conditions in Leipzig seems to have revealed that Bach was also irritated by pedagogical obligations that got in the way of perfect performance. Bach used singers from the local university whenever he could in order to create the sound he aspired to. This was not easy for him. In a historically important memorandum of 1730 to the city council, he complained that 'the state of music is quite different from what it was', and warned that the forces of the Thomanerschule and the civic musicians were not adequate to perform his music. Intriguingly, there are suggestions that Bach was forced to compromise. Had he had access to better sopranos, the soprano parts of his great Leipzig works might have been significantly more elaborate and demanding than those that have come down to us. The more demanding arias, it seems, may in any case have been sung by adult male sopranists, there being no boys capable. One such singer appears to have been Christian Friedrich Schemelli, who had attended the Thomanerschule between ages eighteen and twenty-one, by which time his 'voice had almost certainly broken'.

It is an intriguing situation that whilst Bach has handed down to us some the greatest choral compositions the world has ever known, Bach himself may never have heard them performed to anything like the standard we are accustomed to today. The same may also be true of William Byrd. How I long for that time machine! The desire for authenticity is thus entirely understandable. However, it may be taking things just a step too far when it comes to the singers. My own take on this is relatively simple. We need to remember that Bach was not the international celebrity at Leipzig that he has subsequently become. He inherited the indifferent resources of a provincial school and a motley band of civic musicians. He would surely have wished he could have had some of his singers from Köthen. I can really see no reason, other than a purely scientific interest in the exercise of recreating a lost sound, for a truly authentic performance to be created. We should perhaps be careful about what we ask for!

My reasons for supposing that the choir lacked any real merit in choral tone are based upon my understanding of puberty and the secular trend. Here, my scientific curiosity is aroused. I would like to recreate Bach's Leipzig choir for scientific rather than artistic reasons. How would one go about this? I believe that one would need to assemble a choir consisting of a number of boys whose voices, to all intents and purposes, had 'broken' but who were still contriving by some means to sing soprano. The idea that Bach's boys would have been older than a choir of present-day boy trebles does have some evidential basis. There is sufficient documentary source material available to support the contention that many of Bach's boys were of (for a boy) advanced years. Adult male sopranists were also employed to bolster the boys' sound. The following is typical of what tends to be written in generalist biographies of Bach:

> Here Bach had to rely upon the hoarse and oversung voices of the boys plus an occasional singer from the community or the University. In those days a boy's voice would change at around 17 or 18, so Bach would normally have his sopranos and altos for about five years. Although they were not the best of musicians, because their voices changed late, the treble voices of Bach's choir would have been more accomplished than today's boys.

<http://www2.nau.edu/tas3/leipzig.html>

I do not, however, think that this is a very thoroughly thought-through position. We know that Bach was not satisfied with the quality of the voices, but this does not necessarily mean that they were 'hoarse' as we now understand the term. If there was some kind of rough quality to the voices and a good number of the boys were in their mid- to late teens, the 'hoarseness' is almost certainly due to pubertal mutation. 'Oversung' would suggest some kind of misuse, but oversung in what way? We know that intensive daily use of treble voices can strengthen them. 'Oversinging' might therefore refer less to the intensity of use than to forcing a soprano register out of voices that were well beyond the point of mutation. We cannot know this for certain, but it seems more plausible than the belief that puberty was long delayed.

The statements 'although they were not the best of musicians' and 'would have been more accomplished than today's boys' are similarly speculative, perhaps driven by the desire to 'prove' the myth of physically and mentally mature boys with soprano voices. There is plenty of evidence in high-quality CD recordings that a good number of today's boys are quite highly accomplished young musicians by the age of thirteen. Unlike Bach's boys, such boys of today would also have voices that sound beautiful rather than 'hoarse', albeit in the way of a boy rather than a mature soprano. Similarly, there is no point of scientific comparison between the mental, emotional and cultural development of boys over 250 years apart. The uncritical assumption that they would have been on the same trajectory of mental development is not necessarily warranted.

The belief in improbably late puberty in Leipzig, however, probably owes most to another scholar, Stephen Daw (1970). Daw attempts to demonstrate a secular trend by drawing on a list, published in 1904, of the ages and voice parts of Bach's singers in the year 1744. This appears to be the only extant primary source. Unfortunately, in his paper, Daw seems to confuse altos with sopranos, which seems a rather elementary mistake to make. He suggests that altos are partially changed voices and then produces a graph that shows the probable age extremes of Bach's altos between 1723 and 1750. Quite how this is done, given that by his own admission 'we do not know for certain the voices of individual scholars except for the year 1744', is something of a mystery. This graph shows the youngest alto age as about fifteen-and-a-half and the oldest as just under nineteen. We are left conjecturing the extent to which boys who were altos were forced to sing soprano parts and whether there might also have been younger soprano boys.

Daw's graph also shows a rising trend that he attempts to explain as a consequence of the War of Austrian Succession (1740–1748). Leipzig was occupied by a Prussian army and its citizens suffered considerable privations. Death rates at the Thomanerschule rose during this time. Daw's explanation here can be considered in the light of the recent medical studies of the conflict in Croatia and Bosnia which did show a small delay in the timing of boys' puberty attributable to stress. Elsewhere, Daw writes of a 'blanket virus epidemic which swept Germany in particular, and much of Europe in general, around 1700' as being the cause of unusually late puberty. This again strays too far into speculation, but it is possible that Bach did live in a time and place where boys may not have attained the physical maturity of today's fourteen-year-olds until a year or so later. Daw's concluding blanket claim that the 'secular trend from 1740 to 1959 is about four years', however, goes too far beyond the evidence he was able to produce. Mecke (2007) has examined the German-speaking literature on the topic and concludes that Daw overestimates the timing of puberty in the eighteenth century by about two years. Thus if Daw gives an age of seventeen or eighteen, actual ages of fifteen or sixteen may be more likely.

This makes the scientific question of what these boys were like all the more interesting. No data are available on their stature or general health. If puberty were later as a result of stressful living conditions and poor nutrition, then stature would very probably also have been less. Thus what boys 'gained' through delayed puberty, they also 'lost' through diminished stature. How tall and heavy would one of Bach's seventeen-year-olds have been? Quite possibly a seventeen-year-old in Bach's time may have weighed no more than a healthy present-day fourteen-year-old. What would have been their vital capacity or muscular development? These questions are important because the belief that boys capable of adult power and insight without castration once existed is so persistent.

I think it more likely that boys of any age have never been capable of matching the performance of mature female sopranos, nor ever will be. The authenticity enterprise itself is fundamentally flawed on this issue. As Edward Higginbottom (1997) was once forced to observe in a public spat with Peter Phillips, 'We are forced to accord to young musicians (and to children's choirs) a value springing from their very 'childishness', and we have to recognise the part it plays in the aesthetic experience' (*Musical Times*, December 1977). In my view, if you desire perfect performances, recruit—as does Phillips—mature females with pure, vibrato-free voices of the power ascribed to these fictional boys reaching puberty at age eighteen. Are some of us forgetting here the crucial difference between pedagogic choirs and performance choirs? I enjoy working with boys' choirs because I value the very childish flaws that make them attractive. The satisfaction comes from fashioning these young people into highly capable future musicians and confronting the boisterous antics that musicians such as Phillips would presumably find an irritating distraction.

5.2   The Temple Church and the pre-war boy soprano

A contemporary choir director recently observed in the national press that 'the emotional depth and finesse of a youth of fifteen or sixteen cannot be replicated by an eleven- or twelve-year-old'. Whilst this statement alone is defensible and coherent, in the context of the secular trend in puberty, it loses any real sense. 'Youths' of fifteen or sixteen have never sounded like eleven- or twelve-year-old trebles, as I shall attempt to demonstrate in this section. Bach was not the only historical musical figure to have struggled with poor-quality singers and indifferent civic and church authorities. 1750, the year of Bach's death roughly coincided with a 100-year nadir of English cathedral music. Alan Mould's definitive history of the English chorister (2007) paints a gloomy picture of abuse, neglect, and poor musical standards during this period. Records of how boys were educated and cared for during this time are extremely rare. Evidence of how they were trained to sing and how their voices were treated at puberty is to all intents and purposes non-existent. This changed from 1850 onwards as zealous Victorian reformers rebuilt the entire edifice.

A number of choirs led the field of revival. The story of Maria Hackett's campaign at St Paul's Cathedral and its eventual blossoming through the work of John Stainer is well known. King's College Cambridge was another early pioneer of improved conditions for choristers. The commitment of the College was rewarded in 1928 with the first broadcast of what has become the internationally renowned Christmas Eve service of lessons and carols. This broadcast presaged an era where 'King's' came to define a particular type of boy chorister sound, sometimes disparagingly referred to now as the 'Wilcox coo'. There are grounds to argue, however, that as a documentary source for the history of boys' singing, King's College Cambridge might be eclipsed by London's Temple Church. There are three reasons for this. First, the remarkable fifty-nine-year reign of Sir George Thalben-Ball, director of the choir from 1923 until 1982. Second, the game-changing recording of 'Hear My Prayer' by Ernest Lough in 1927, repeated in 1928. Third, some notable oral histories and re-masterings of a wide range of early recordings compiled by Stephen Beet (2005) which deserve to be better known. These three things add up to a rare window into the secular trend in puberty and its impact on boys' choral singing.

In Chapter 2 we saw that the late nineteenth century was also a highly productive period in terms of texts on singing. There are reasonable grounds to suppose from these texts that most English choirboys, in the decades following their publication, were trained to sing in 'head voice' only. In Chapter 2, we considered the likely effect of this. Downward vocalisations and a repertoire that seldom required regular phonation much below E_4 ensured that boys seldom, if ever, crossed the passagio point that would have required clear thyroarytenoid production. These muscles were probably, to all intents and purposes, fairly easily 'switched off' during much of the boys' singing. A result was that singing in the soprano range was possible right up to the completion of puberty and possibly for a year or more beyond that time in some cases.

For the first time, we have primary sources that describe the technicalities of how boys were taught to sing and how this related to puberty and the changing voice. Of at least equal importance was the rise of sound recording. The evidence base we have to draw on is one that allows us for the first time in history to listen to the sounds that were actually created. Whilst unfortunately we do not have measurements such as the boys' heights and weights, there is quite a good photographic record. From extant photographs of Thalben-Ball's Temple choristers, we can see that a good many of the boys are at the completing-puberty phase. They appear in the photographs equal in height to the adult men in the choir and their faces have lost the softness of childhood and assumed the angularity of the maturing teenager. There is also a small but precious number of recordings of some of the boys' speaking voices. Recordings of speaking voices in a baritone register confirm what the photographic evidence suggests.

Most important of all, we know what these boys' singing voices sounded like. The tone was quite different to that of most present-day boy trebles. Without exception, everyone to whom I have played the recordings states that the sound had something in common with an adult female soprano. For the majority of listeners, this is not intended as a compliment. The most strident critics are almost invariably same-age peers who express shock, dismay and incredulity that any boy could sound so (see Interlude 1: William, for example). In a chapter on authenticity, we should take particular note of this: a number of texts report how often boys are reluctant to sing at all 'in case they sound like girls'. Provided this is not interpreted as a put-down of the female sex, boys are surely entitled to create sound that they can recognise as uniquely theirs. Only one thing, probably, is worse for boys than sounding like girls, and that is sounding like old women with wobbly voices. This was the point might by George Malcolm when he introduced a new way of singing at Westminster Cathedral (see Chapter 2) that received the endorsement of Benjamin Britten.

The context needs to be understood. There is evidence that in the early twentieth century, it was not considered such an issue for males to imitate female sound. John Curwen (1891) describes the means for teaching boys to find their 'head voice' thus:

> Shew him first that he has two voices, and that he must use the one that is most like a woman's.

No sane practitioner of contemporary choral work with boys who had swum to exhaustion against a heavy current to convince his singers that a boy's upper register is appropriate to use would then send them running with such advice! The meaning, however, would have been different in an age where it was not expected that girls or women would invade male-only domains and it was even reported that boys could sing better than trained women sopranos.

Nevertheless, the Temple Church under Thalben-Ball differs from what we might attempt to piece together from fragments of evidence relating to J.S. Bach. No one who has heard the Temple recordings and others similar could possibly describe the voices as 'hoarse and oversung'. Jenevora Williams (2013) describes them in these terms:

> Many of these young male singers have a sound that is not dissimilar to a mature female voice. There is more power, flexibility and control than in an unchanged male voice and yet a lightness which is not possible in an adult male alto singer.
>
> (Williams, 2013, p.70)

I have been interested in this type of voice and its possibilities for some time and have conducted various experiments over the years to compare it with the now more familiar boy treble voice. Most of my experiments have used the voice of Denis Barthel, which I think is a particularly fine example. Barthel was a probationer in the Temple Choir in the year 1927, when the first Lough recording was made. He became head chorister himself in 1932 and enjoyed a career almost on a par with Lough. Indeed, his own recording of Jerusalem sold half a million copies. I was privileged to correspond with Barthel shortly before he died. Here is what he said:

> [T]he fact that the Temple chorister's voices often did not break early was due to the 'Temple tone' and the manner in which Dr Sir George Thalben-Ball (whom we all loved very much) taught us to project our voices. For example, my voice and that of Ernest Lough did not break until we were both seventeen.

Here, then, is an example of the boy soprano voice sustained until the very end of puberty, perhaps into the third and final phase of adolescence. Would this have been the kind of sound made by Bach's boys? There is little doubt that the Temple boys were very well taught and, unlike Bach's boys, enjoyed a devoted relationship with their director. Some people argue that the Temple boys sang only in falsetto, but I am fairly sure this is not the case. It is more likely to be the hybrid phonation observed by Williams, carried perhaps a stage further. Barthel's voice is remarkable in that he is able to carry good tone with little perceptible register shift as low as B3, which he demonstrates in his astonishing recording of 'He Was Despised' from *Messiah*. For this reason, I doubt that the Temple boys sang only in pure 'head voice' as advocated by the nineteenth-century writers. A more sophisticated and skilful blending of registers in which some tensioning was provided by the thyroarytenoid must have been used.

For my first experiment I recruited two present-day choristers, aged twelve and thirteen, who were keen to participate. We used a recording made by Denis Barthel at the age of sixteen. The recording was of Walford Davies' setting of 'O Little Town of Bethlehem'. A contemporary review of this recording in the December 1932 issue of Gramophone magazine described it as a 'notably good record for anyone who cares for emotional singing from a boy'. The twelve- and thirteen-year-old rehearsed the piece, which we then recorded. I edited the 1932 and 2006 recordings together and played them to an international conference of leading voice specialists and singing teachers.

The twelve- and thirteen-year-old were called 'nice ordinary boys' but Barthel's voice was recognized as something quite different. Comments included 'beautifully produced' and 'amazingly rich and powerful'. Most tellingly of all, perhaps: 'imagine a choir of sixteen of them'. Well, were we able to travel back in time to the Temple Church of the 1930s, we could have heard more or less exactly that sound. These experts confined their remarks to the quality of the vocal production, which clearly impressed them. None suggested that the sound was inauthentic for a boy (or should I say young man). However, I have heard such suggestions quite frequently from those who expect only the more naive 'treble' sound from boys.

The matter might rest there were it not for a most fortuitous opportunity to come as close to time travel as will probably ever be possible. I received, quite out of the blue, a video audition tape of a boy one month short of fourteen. The audition was for a prestigious choir and the director of the organization was intrigued by the fact that the boy spoke in a remarkably deep baritone voice for one so young, yet performed his audition piece (Handel's 'Where E'r You Walk') in what sounded very much like a pre-war boy soprano. I suspected from the audition tape that this might be close to the way the old pre-war boy sopranos sang.

I was on a train to meet this young man, armed with recording gear, electroglottogram, video camera and miscellaneous measuring paraphernalia a month later. We recorded 'O Little Town of Bethlehem' as well as 'Where E'r You Walk' and a whole range of speaking and singing tests. The analysis of the vocal exercises shows a voice split into three regions. There was a strong soprano register that faded to nothing at around E_4. There was then a gap from about E_4 to B_3 where the boy really struggled. From about A_3 right down to E_2 the voice resumed as a rich baritone of surprising maturity. The baritone, indeed, was of a quality that might make a musical seventeen-year-old envious. There were thus similarities and differences between this boy and the old Temple boys. The upper register in both cases, to use Jenevora Williams' words, had 'power and flexibility but a lightness not possible from an adult male alto'. Unlike Barthel, however, this boy could not carry this production comfortably into his passagio region, very probably because nobody had taught him how to support cricothyroid production with a little thyroarytenoid tension.

For this to happen to a fourteen-year-old rather than the more customary fifteen- to seventeen-year age range of Thalben-Ball's day might be a manifestation of the secular trend. For such a deep baritone voice to have developed, pubertal onset must almost certainly have been no later than age twelve, possibly as early as eleven. Interestingly, when I asked him why he chose to sing soprano for his audition, we got into a fascinating conversation about how he was one of the more physically mature boys in his year. His reasons for preferring soprano were that it made him less different to the other boys in his year (Year 9 of the English National Curriculum or US Grade 8). In other words, he felt safer and less different with a high voice than a deep one that marked him out from peers who actually sang higher. He eventually decided he would join the bass section of the choir he had auditioned for and seemed very happy and well-integrated into that on the next occasion I saw him.

I rounded off the opportunity by asking William (see Interlude 1 above) to repeat the Barthel experiment. William followed Barthel's interpretation, with its incredibly long drawnout rubato, to the letter. He proved himself quite capable of the 'mature interpretation' though in the voice of a treble in early change rather than a boy who had completed puberty. William's clearly expressed view was that this was only for the experiment and not at all the way he wished to be remembered as a treble. This is indicative of the way taste has changed, perhaps irrevocably, since Barthel's day.

Boys, nevertheless, will only judge by what is familiar to them. Part of the role of the educator is to challenge with the unfamiliar, so I would be reluctant to write something off just because it is different. There has to be a difference between cultural taste and necessity. Bach used ageing boys, probably in bad grace, out of necessity. The voices were described as 'hoarse and oversung'. Thalben Ball, on the other hand, was clearly greatly loved by the boys he worked with and possessed of a unique gift to create 'beautifully produced' sounds. It is not inconceivable that the old technique of training 'head tone' might enjoy something of a revival if the proportion of boys beginning puberty earlier increases and our understanding of the management of a boy's falsetto improves. The technique used by Thalben-Ball, however, is almost completely lost and may need to be rediscovered by experimentation should anyone want to revive that sound.

5.3   Authenticity through unique parts for boys

We have also to consider that many boys of the Lough/Barthel era would have left school at the age of fourteen. The notion of a complete rest after voice 'break' would not have the same impact in schools as it would today. Neither had the hedonistic teenager of the 1950s onwards been invented. There were no role models of loud 'chest voice' singing by older adolescents to call into question the authenticity of 'young men' singing soprano. One of my favourite quotations is from the 1930s and by the mid-twentieth century English composer and choir director Edward Bairstow. It bears endless repetition in order to make the point that there was little motivation in those days to discover whether pubertal boys had voices that were distinct from either pre-pubertal trebles or young tenors and basses.

> My experience is that if a boy uses his voice naturally and without forcing it, he never goes through a period when he cannot sing at all but, while in such cases it does very little harm for him to sing, it is no use him trying, as his voice is gradually changing in compass and in timbre.
>
> (Bairstow, 1930, pp.11–12)

Bairstow does not appear in this extract to have considered that harm might be done by the boy's not singing. Bairstow, of course, wrote from the privileged position of director of an elite performance choir. Those whose concern lies more with the general population than the privileged minority have tended to see things differently. Herbert Wiseman stressed to the contrary the importance of boys continuing to sing precisely at the time the voice is gradually changing in compass and timbre. The harm that would be done by boys not trying was that many of them would be lost to singing, possibly for the rest of their lives. His book *The Singing Class* (1967) described how this might be done, but has had little lasting impact on choral practice in the UK.

Irvin Cooper in the United States was particularly concerned with this agenda during the 1960s. One story that is told is of how Cooper, as a young music supervisor in Montreal, was inspired by the singing of young adolescent Boy Scouts around their campfire. Why, he wondered, could these boys sing so lustily at camp whilst remaining silent in the school music class? This is a question that should challenge us in choral work, because campfire singing is not choral singing. The boys pick their own pitch and do not have to fit their voices to SATB parts where they do not necessarily belong. Moreover, the tradition is largely oral, so perhaps some way distant from the choral conventions of formally notated compositions. The same, of course, is true of the more contemporary context where solo and small band singing has overtaken any form of choral singing in popularity for the majority of boys. Boys in a band can readily pitch the music to fit their voices. Most do so without having to think how they are going to fit voices to parts and attempts to notate genres such as rock for choral singing have often seemed somewhat contrived to me.

Whether or not parts other than SATB are provided for adolescent voices is perhaps one of the most challenging of all issues in contemporary choral work with boys. It may be helpful at this stage to review what the difficulties and possibilities are. Boys who keep singing during adolescence might be accommodated in any of soprano, alto, 'alto-tenors', Cambiati, new or emerging baritones, tenors, or basses.

Soprano. As we have seen, boys as old as fifteen or so can be still capable of singing in the soprano range. If the old 'head tone' technique is taught, the boy soprano voice can last right up to the end of puberty and into the years of later adolescence, though it sounds literally more like a soprano than the younger 'treble' sound. This is perhaps controversial, but it is a possibility. A boy who has endured 'ooh girl' taunts at the age of twelve or thirteen may as well continue to put up with this for another couple of years or so and some do quite happily out of their own agency.

Alto. A seemingly obvious first port of call for ex-trebles is the alto part. As we have seen in Chapters 1–4, boys in some cultures always sang alto, never treble. Boy altos are relatively common in Germany, but a clear distinction needs to be made as to whether these are naturally low unchanged voices or former high voices that are descending in pitch. Both are possible at the earlier in-puberty stage (light green shirt). Singing alto later into puberty is not recommended by a number of respected authorities that advocate that an ex-treble should use the lowest voice available until this is properly developed. This is seldom likely to be alto and may well be 'emerging baritone' (see 'New or emerging and settling baritone' below). We can fairly safely say that an average boy treble who admires the counter-tenor voice and imagines he can attain one simply by switching to alto during adolescence is making a fairly serious mistake. Church choirs sometimes have men singing an insipid falsetto alto. This is usually produced by a flaccid thyroarytenoid and is not at all the same technique as a trained counter-tenor.

Alto-tenors. The term 'alto-tenor' is generally credited to Duncan McKenzie (1956), one of the early pioneers in changing voice research. McKenzie had discovered, as will anyone else who attends carefully to the voices of adolescent boys, that there is a period during which a boy is neither alto nor tenor, but somewhere in between. So the term means effectively 'what it says on the tin'. The 'somewhere in between', according to McKenzie, was an approximate octave between about G below middle C to the G above. McKenzie admitted that such a range was not well-suited to the conventional choral ensemble, but as near perfect as possible for what in this book would be recognised as pedagogical choral singing. Significantly, McKenzie was keen to incorporate 'head' and 'chest' registers and to develop a smooth transition between the two. In this way, his alto-tenor plan differed from the now more popular cambiata system.

Cambiata. The cambiata voice has caught on to a degree that the alto-tenor never did, partly due to its systematic classification and promotion by the Cambiata Vocal Institute of America (CVIA) under the direction of Cooper's energetic successor, Don Collins. A Cambiata I part will be similar to a treble part with A below middle C at the bottom, but will not go above the point where 'light green shirts' are in danger of crossing into falsetto. A Cambiata II part will range from E in the tenor octave (E3) to roughly the E above middle C (E4). The E above middle C is another danger area for adolescent boys' voices. For many it will be the upper region of the passagio where the pronounced register shift into crycoarytenoid occurs. Avoidance of this difficult passagio is what marks out the cambiata scheme as clearly belonging to School A, the belief that voices descend in gradual, predictable steps and that the new lower voice should be developed before attention is given to the whole voice. Whilst this undoubtedly works well in school singing, it is a less certain proposition for experienced choral singers or ambitious choir directors. The cambiata voice, with its similarities to and differences from the alto-tenor, is the most crucial phase around which much else revolves. I shall return to it shortly.

New or emerging and settling baritone. This is another singing range unique to adolescence and is used in the cambiata system. The A below tenor C (A2) can be thought of as the bottom of the range, although new baritones may be a little higher (B2 is sometimes given). Settling baritones may get the bass G (G2). This is not at all uncommon in my experience and such boys may call themselves, or be called, 'basses'. The new baritone phase is obviously for boys who have newly passed the high mutation point and would be recognised straightaway by lay people as the 'broken voice'. The upper limit of emerging baritone will vary according to the way register change (if any) is managed. Although voices at this stage share much of the range of adult male voices, they are still immature and unformed. Cooksey (2000) insists that there is no such thing as a mature bass or tenor amongst adolescent boys. His extensive sonographic analyses reveal that upper partials present in younger boys' voices disappear during the emerging baritone phase and take some years to fully reform. Hence the paradox that a young boy's treble voice may sound acoustically rich, perhaps crowned by 'ring' harmonics, whilst the voice of an older boy who may be physically a lot bigger than the treble will simply sound 'weedy'. There is also the question of larynx descent. The fifteen- or sixteen-year-old will be unlikely to have a fully descended larynx. He will thus have a shorter and smaller vocal tract, even though his vocal folds may be approaching adult length.

Tenor or bass. In spite of the above, boys at the emerging and settling baritone stage are often found singing either tenor or bass parts. The question might well be asked, why bother with a baritone stage if young men can simply be placed with older men to learn to be tenors or basses on an apprenticeship scheme? Cooksey provides an answer to this. He states that if boys are asked to produce vocal sounds that imitate adult-like qualities, they must use their laryngeal and vocal tract muscles with excess effort to do so. Any number of bad singing habits may thus emerge. This, in fact, is an extremely important consideration, given the extent to which young singers learn choral tone production predominantly by imitation, in spite of considerable sums that might be spent on singing lessons. There is an obvious difference between a school choir where few of the lower voices have mature adult-like qualities and a community choir where sixteen- or seventeen-year-olds may sing next to mature men. I address this question in the Chapter 10. Cooksey advises that emerging adult voices 'can sing most bass parts'. Their optimum pitch area is B2–A3. Tenor, then, would seem to be the least appropriate part for boys at this stage.

The management of young men's baritone voices has perhaps received less attention than younger boys' treble and alto voices. This can hardly be right, given that many older boys set their sights on becoming a tenor, bass or perhaps counter-tenor because of adult voices they admire and aspire to. Boys may well ask whether you can tell them whether they will be tenor or bass when adult. The answer is, no you can't! They must just be patient and prepared to enjoy the process of experimentation. If singing in an SATB choir, they might try a time in different sections. Tenor is usually the most problematic range and a fifteen-year-old should not be thinking 'I'm now a tenor'. Those authoritative texts that do tackle the issue suggest sing the lowest available part, move around, omit uncomfortable notes or passages but above all, do not attempt to compete with more mature voices in volume or tone. Colin Baldy (2010) describes how ignoring this advice has been a particular problem in schools where adolescents are required to take leading tenor roles. In one particular case:

> Not having yet worked out the relationship between his falsetto and full voice, and having no concept of tilting the thyroid cartilage, he resorted to dragging the larynx up to an uncomfortable position. Indeed, so reliant had he become on this particular method, and so pronounced was the tension involved, that his chin was thrust upwards an out. The result was uncomfortable both for him and the audience. It took several years before he was able to remedy these habits.

This is the situation we are faced with in contemporary choral work with boys. Older adolescents are not men, yet surprisingly few texts tackle the practical implications of research into emerging baritone voices and how they are to be fitted into conventional SATB choral music. Many are simply content to parrot Cooksey's scheme as though that were all that is necessary.

5.4   Are unique vocal parts really necessary?

Cooksey's scheme, as I have already pointed out, is not a 'system' that prescribes repertoire. The basic tenet which Irvine Cooper (Cooper and Wikstrom, 1962) is said to have derived from the boys around the camp-fire and on which the cambiata principle is founded comes much closer to this. Cooper formulated it thus:

> Music should be written to fit the voice instead of attempting to make
> the voice fit the music.

This is a far-reaching statement of profound importance and it means what it says. It means that most of the standard choral repertoire is unsuitable for adolescent boys' voices. It also means that music has to be specially composed or arranged for adolescent boys' choirs, changing voice choirs, cambiata choirs, call them what you will. Understandably, this has led to short shrift from music publishers. The potential market, certainly in the UK, is small and uncertain. The risk of large print runs that may not sell is an understandably high one. This could change with new means of music distribution where the purchaser downloads an e-copy and bears the cost of printing. However, there is then the question of interesting composers and arrangers where I have found the same problem. Most of our best composers have plenty of work and are seldom motivated to prioritize unconventional part-writing for adolescent boys. When it comes to 'lesser composers' having a go, I am minded to quote Kodály:

> Let us take our children seriously! Everything else follows from this . . .
> only the best is good enough for a child.

(Kodály, 1941)

The Cambiata Press publishes music arranged according to Cooper's principles and it certainly does take the needs of adolescent boys seriously. Unfortunately for contemporary choral directors outside the US the catalogue is quite strongly biased to US culture and some, I'm sure, would call it rather conservative. Technically, there is little doubt that it works. I have used some of their arrangements and have been struck by the goodness of fit between parts and voices. More particularly I have been impressed by comments made by lay listeners who have spontaneously remarked on the authenticity of the sound for boys of that age (roughly 12–16). For example the arrangement of Scarborough Fair by Harry Swenson is in three parts, Cambiata I, Cambiata II and Baritone. The Cambiata I part ranges from A_3–A_4, the Cambiata II from F_3–E_4 and the Baritone from D_3–C_4. When the voice parts are correctly matched to pubertal stage the sound is, as predicted by Cooper, 'rich, undeniably masculine almost to the point of belligerency'. Cooper also describes it as 'truly beautiful if the sound is controlled in volume and not permitted to become strident from sheer vocal exuberance'. The admonition to control the volume is perhaps a clue that choral quality is expected.

Successful and authentic though this arrangement and ones like it are, the question inevitably arises as to whether the approach is too limiting for choral work. Embedded within the conundrum are two wider questions about authenticity:

- Is it always authentic to disengage adolescent boys from the choral mainstream?
- If young people describe the choral mainstream with words such as 'posh' and 'elderly', under what circumstances is their participation in it authentic?

I shall discuss these questions in company with the directors of some real choirs in Chapters 7–10.

References

Baldy, C. (2010). *The Student Voice: An Introduction to Developing the Singing Voice.* Edinburgh: Dunedin.

Bairstow, E. (1930). Should breaking voices be rested? *The Music Teacher*, (April):11–12.

Beet, S. (2005). *The Better Land: In Search of the Lost Boy Sopranos.* Waterford: Rectory Press.

Bowers, R. (1987). The vocal scoring, choral balance and performing pitch of Latin Church Polyphony in England, c. 1500–58. *Journal of the Royal Musical Association*, 112(1):38–76. doi:10.1093/jrma/112.1.38

Cooksey, J. (2000). Voice transformation in male adolescents. In L. Thurman and G. Welch (eds.), *Bodymind and Voice: Foundations of Voice Education* (pp. 718–38). Iowa City, IA: The VoiceCare Network.

Cooper, I. & Wikstrom, T. (1962). Changing Voices. *Music Educators Journal*, 48(4): 148–51. doi:10.2307/3389562

Curwen, J. (1891). *The Boy's Voice: A book of practical information on the training of boys' voices for church choirs &c.* London: Curwen.

Daw, S. (1970). Age of boys' puberty in Leipzig, 1727–49, as indicated by voice breaking in J. S. Bach's choir members. *Human Biology*, 42(1):87–89. Available at <http://www.jstor.org/stable/41449007>

Higginbottom, E. (1997). Laudate Pueri. *The Musical Times*, 138(1858): 3–4.

Kodály, Z. (1976). *The Selected Writings of Zoltán Kodály.* New York, NY: Boosey & Hawkes.

McKenzie, D. (1956). *Training the Boy's Changing Voice.* New Brunswick: Rutgers University Press.

Mould, A. (2007). *The English Chorister.* London: Hambledon/Continuum.

Mecke, A.-C. (2007). *Mutantenstadt. Der Stimmwechsel und die deutsche Chorpraxis im 18. und 19. Jahrhundert* [*Mutants' House: Voice change and German choir practice in 18th and 19th century*]. Berlin: Wissenschaftlicher Verlag Berlin.

Williams, J. (2013). *Teaching Singing to Children and Young Adults.* Abingdon, UK: Compton.

Wiseman, H. (1967). *The Singing Class.* Oxford: Pergamon.

Wulstan, D. (1986). *Tudor Music.* Iowa City, IA: University of Iowa Press.

Further reading

Beet, S. (2005). *The Better Land: In Search of the Lost Boy Sopranos.* Waterford: Rectory Press.

Mould, A. (2007). *The English Chorister: A History.* London: Continuum.

Chapter 6: The power and the passion

In this chapter, we take a break from examining boys and their voices and turn our attentions instead to the choir director him or herself. I attempt to set out what I have learned about the nature, personality and skill set needed to be the successful director of a boys' choir. I am not referring here to the skill set that any conductor must have. I am assuming that you either already have that or are well on the way to acquiring it. I am referring to those additional qualities needed to make it work with boys. Good boys' choirs are relatively uncommon, as is the participation of boys in choral work more generally. The most frequently given explanation for this is that boys think singing is 'uncool' or 'unmanly'. These explanations are misleading. Boys judge singing according to the social climate set by the adults that are important to them: a thought such as that should sober up the most hardened alcoholic choral director.

I have titled this chapter 'The power and the passion' because both are involved in large measure in the running of boys' choirs. Power and passion are necessary but dangerous ingredients of choral work with boys. This chapter will not be entirely comfortable reading. It is being written at a time shortly after the youth singing world was rocked to its foundations by a major scandal involving one of its best known and admired leaders. The events that culminated in the suicide of an abused former pupil of a specialist music school were widely reported in the global media and will remain in cyberspace for decades to come. Nothing is to be gained through a naming and shaming of the organisation concerned, so I will leave it to the reader if they wish to go searching on the web for the details.

What I am able to say, though, is that a tragic feature of this case is that, far from 'shame', the organisation involved had had in place for some time comprehensive and efficient procedures for all aspects of the welfare and safeguarding of its young people. The events were historic and had occurred at some time in the past elsewhere. The organisation, in that sense, was itself a victim. The legacy of an era when young people were not afforded such protection will take some time to run its course. The event, moreover, occurred at a similar time to an even bigger scandal involving the former TV personality, Jimmy Savile. Two features of that case were particularly shocking. The first was the extent to which Savile gained access to his particularly vulnerable victims under the cover of philanthropy. The second was the level of institutional complicity by the BBC and perhaps even in a sense the State, which awarded Savile an MBE.

This is all very sadly relevant to choral work with boys because these, and too many other similar incidents that have involved boys in choirs, boil down to the abuse of power and the mismanagement of passion. Whilst it easy to express disgust and blame individuals, this negates the fact that problems of power abuse have long roots in the organisation of society. The society that allows these things to happen has been and largely still is organised along patriarchal lines that privilege men and structures of male power such as the Catholic Church as well as most national governments. These patriarchal structures are no more helpful to men than they are to society as a whole. Choral work with boys has to happen in environments where men (and much more rarely, women) who might be tempted to abuse their positions of power simply cannot do so. Thankfully we have made huge progress in this field in recent decades. Reports in the press are increasingly of historic rather than contemporary abuse.

The matter cannot rest there though because, after a lifetime studying the phenomenon, I have become convinced that choral singing with boys is highly unlikely to happen in any significant way unless driven by the right kind of passion. One cannot simply legislate to neuter all forms of passion, and the line between the right and wrong sorts of passion can be blurred in heady and intense situations of creativity involving persons of unequal power. This chapter, therefore, is about the proper place of passion and its management. It is necessarily also about the proper and benign use of power, for the two are closely linked. Both can be exercised benignly with life-affirming artistic results, or malevolently with tragic results. The practical link I make in the middle of the chapter between passion and power is relationships. The ability to form genuine, warm, respectful relationships with all involved is the key to getting passion and power under control. It is the key to successful choral work with boys.

6.1   The centrality of passion

As I stated in the Chapter 1, without a conductor fired and driven by passion, any boys' choir will slowly die. What exactly do I mean and what is the authority for my claim? It comes largely from the boys themselves. I have asked many boys what they think of the conductors of their choirs. I have been struck by the number of times they have used the word 'passion' for conductors they like and are loyal to. What do they mean? I think at one level it is probably a combination of obvious dedication, great knowledge of the subject, hard work and infectious enthusiasm. At another deeper level, I suspect it is the ability to communicate all this to boys through an affective disposition toward them. You can have great knowledge of choral music and work very hard at it, but if you don't like boys and enjoy their company, you won't communicate this to them. I shall return to this singularly important theme shortly.

My other reason for stressing the importance of passion is something of a confession. I managed to spend a quarter of a million pounds of public money on a research programme to increase boys' participation in choral singing. Well before beginning it, I had known that there is a postcode lottery with regard not only to boys' singing, but towards much of music education. In other words, depending on where a boy lives, he may have access to an inspirational music teacher and a thriving, dynamically run choir. More likely, he will endure music teaching of indifferent quality and have access, not to a choir that is an activity of choice for boys, but one which is nearly all girls. Rather than tackle the difficult question of why some teachers have a magic ingredient but many do not, I chose instead to focus on the easier topic of teachers' subject knowledge. There were good reasons for this. I had conducted research which revealed great ignorance amongst English schoolteachers of boys' voices and what they were capable of. Many conductors knew little more.

It is a lesson learned, however, that subject knowledge is not the most important dimension of teaching. It is, of course, important, but an infectious enthusiasm for the subject is invariably reported by young people as a quality of teachers they will work hard for and whose subject they enjoy. This is true for any subject, but especially true for subjects seen as less essential. Here, learners may need to be won over. I once worked on a project for the Institute of Physics to address the shortage of girls opting for advanced study of physics. One of the findings was that girls would study physics if the teacher communicated an infectious enthusiasm for it. Teachers with high academic qualifications, if dull and boring in their presentation, would attract only boys for whom physics was seen as a 'boy's subject'.

I am confident that a similar principle operates in reverse for choir singing. Girls are on average more likely than boys to tolerate routine and unexceptional choral teaching. The majority of boys have to be won over and the empirical evidence that what wins them over is an infectious enthusiasm turbo-charged by passion is all but unanswerable. Is this something that can be taught? My answer to this question, after many years' work in the training and development of teachers, is probably not. It is a quality that one needs to look for at the selection stage. After many informal conversations and formal interviews with boys, together with a lifetime's observation of choral work, I am inclined to believe in the existence of small boys with a latent love of music whose lifetime passion will be kindled by an inspirational choir director they may secretly adore.

In other words, there is an ancient apostolic tradition. Our ability to select candidates who will become passionate and successful directors of boys' choirs at the present time depends more upon the continuance of this tradition than any amount of clever psychology in the training of teachers and conductors. Perhaps you have bought this book because you were once the small boy I describe above. On the other hand, you may never have been a small boy! After the 'puberty begins when the voice breaks' misconception, the misconception I have most frequently to deal with is that you have to be a man to be a successful boys' choir director. Nothing could be further from the truth. The idea probably arises from a misguided belief in the old sex role-modelling theory. This is not how things work at all.

Much can be learned about the nature of passion from the fact that many women have been and are successful directors of boys' choirs. The ability of women to motivate reluctant boy singers (as opposed to the much easier task of motivating elite, selected boys) in fact often exceeds that of men. There are things to learn here so let us delve more deeply.

At one level, a comparison can be drawn with passion in other fields that do not involve boys in choirs. A man can be passionate about aircraft. This could mean that he has an encyclopaedic knowledge of aircraft types and their history. He will spend many hours reading up the subject and visiting airport observation galleries. He might be a highly talented craftsman who creates magnificent radio-controlled flying models of award-winning quality. He is just 'passionate' about aircraft. This is a very male kind of passion and it is seldom, in my experience, much understood by the majority of women.

It is not hard to transpose this kind of passion in one sense to choir work. The passionate choir director will have great knowledge of the music and will have worked hard to perfect his or her conducting skills. He or she, no matter how busy, will have found the time to create an arrangement for the choir, perhaps staying up until the early hours for several nights to do so. These qualities and efforts will be recognised by boys who may well respond positively, provided they are not negated by incompetence or ineptitude at human relationships. Therein lies the difference. There is no shortage of research that suggests that, on average, women are better at relationships than men.

Here are three actual quotes from three different conductors, each passionate about their successful boys' choir:

'I love them to bits.'
'They are so cute!'
'Oh [Quentin] is just so gorgeous.'

Now this might alarm you a little. Would it help if I revealed that all three were young and female? This is a passion not found in a man's enthusiasm for aircraft. It is also a reciprocated passion. The boys in these choirs were clearly attracted by the young female in front of them and not averse to the occasional mild flirtation in some cases. There is some complex 'chemistry' going on here and the difference between aircraft and boys is that boys are human beings and choir singing is an intensely human and emotional activity.

There are all sorts of complex reasons for why the expression and enactment of this kind of 'passion' is much easier between women and boys than men and boys. Much of it, of course, is social expectation and conditioning. Whatever private feelings may be harboured, no man is ever going to call a boy 'gorgeous' unless perhaps in the cloistered company of other men so inclined. Underpinning the social overlay, however, is a fundamental biological difference in the way men and women make relationships. Male relationships are more likely to be transitory and based upon power, hierarchy and conquest; female relationships upon cooperation, care and fidelity.

This, of course, is a huge generalisation. Between the two crude biological dimorphisms of the XX and XY chromosome lies a rainbow-panoply of gender performance. At one extreme of gender construction is what is commonly referred to in academia as 'hegemonic masculinity'—a much overrated concept in my view. The classic hegemonic male is loud, aggressive, boastful, single-minded about sport, emotionally illiterate, boorish in manner and unlikely to treat women with respect or as social equals. Fortunately, such an extreme caricature applies to only a minority of men.

The successful male director of a boys' choir is highly unlikely to be such a male. He will more likely be emotionally literate and to some degree wear his heart on his sleeve about the emotional power of the music and the choir's performance. At the extremes, such sympathetic, artistic qualities may be more likely in gay males than the hegemonic macho type, though plenty of heterosexual men can also be artistically sensitive and sexual orientation is really irrelevant and nobody's business. It is certainly irrelevant to any paedophile tendencies, though sadly an association in the public mind has been fuelled by some very unfortunate cases of abuse in boys' choirs. Men, therefore, have to exercise an additional layer of discretion above women.

At root, though, I simply cannot believe that anybody can successfully be in command of such an intensely human activity as a choir without at least some positive affect towards the singers. This positive affect has to be manifest in warm, open and trustworthy relationships that allow the choral art to flourish. If you feel the need to assert your alpha male status by yelling aggressively at boys, perhaps you should look at another outlook for your energy.

6.2   The importance of right relationships

The much-lamented Allan Wicks once said choir training is ninety-five per cent relationships. Dare I disagree with the hero, role model and mentor of my student days? Yes. With due deference to the late maestro I'd dare to say it's ninety-six per cent! You can have a PhD in your subject but if your relaɔnship skills are poor, the students will learn relatively little. If you have a music conservatoire diploma and musical doctorate but are a clanging gong at relationships with an amateur choir, the boys just won't come. You may think it's all to do with repertoire. A lot of people do. You'd be making a mistake. You have the wrong 'r'. It's not repertoire but relationships. If the relationships are right, boys will sing almost anything. Please don't make the mistake of thinking you make choir 'cool' by choosing the music you imagine they think is 'cool'. You make it cool through the kinds of relationships you create. Then your boys will sing anything from reggae to a Haydn mass.

Relationships are the social lubricant that permeate every interface associated with a choir. They exist at all sorts of levels in all sorts of combinations. Relationships with parents and families are of course important. If you work in a school, relationships with other teachers, particularly the sports teachers, are very important. Relationships between the boys themselves are vital. You need to set a climate in which these can be positive and productive and this is no easy task. There is perhaps a little truth in the adage that boys will thump each other and forget the incident whilst girls will bear complex and enduring networks of grudges. Don't be fooled, however, into thinking that boys won't bully each other or wind each other up to destructive levels if you don't set and maintain the climate of good relationships. At the top of the relationship tree, of course, is the very special relationship between you, the conductor, and the boys.

A positive affective disposition is necessary for the best choral work with boys. I think I have made that point sufficiently. If you only want to make music, why bother with boys? Adults or girls can be a much quicker route to a good musical result. An affective disposition does not mean you get all 'lovey dovey' or 'touchy feely'. Your boys may well think you 'weird' or 'creepy' and desert you if you do. Neither does it mean you come across as a 'soft touch' for you will never be able to control them if you communicate that you are that. Good relationships with boys are grounded in good discipline, firm, clear leadership and well-established, consistent and clear boundaries. Failure to set these is the quickest route to disintegrating relationships.

Gender is largely irrelevant to this. At least in theory, males or females are equally capable of setting clear, consistent boundaries. Provided that they do, boys will judge the gender of their conductor to be immaterial. Experience and no shortage of research has shown that the person who is most likely to fail is the loud, aggressive male who falsely imagines that his physical size and loud voice can make up for a lack of organisational skill and proper care. Caring is part and parcel of good relationship-building, but the concept of caring needs to be clarified.

In an earlier book , I drew on the work of James King to make an important distinction between caring about and caring for. Caring about implies a management function. If one cares about one's choir, then one is highly concerned to get everything right. One cares to choose a good programme of music the singers will enjoy, to organise one's rehearsals well and, of course, to deal effectively and quickly with any relationship issues such as bullying or parental misunderstanding of requirements. Caring for has a more intimate dimension, epitomised by the Florence Nightingale image of dressing wounds and soothing troubled spirits. When working with the youngest age groups, caring for can sometimes mean professional permission for intimate contact—potentially a difficulty for males working in nursery settings.

I have researched boys' views and understandings of this issue several times over the years, always with the same result. Boys' expectation is for caring about, carried out in a competent and professional manner. Boys have given me many times a consistent definition of the competent professional teacher who cares about them:

1. A good teacher is able to control them. They do not want someone who is their best mate. They want someone who can keep order.
2. A good teacher is knowledgeable, enthusiastic and perhaps passionate (there you are!) about the subject.
3. A good teacher is patient and can explain things well.
4. A good teacher is fair in their dealing, keeps confidences and does not pry into private lives or gossip about pupils.
5. A good teacher has a sense of humour. They can tell good jokes but restore order when the joke is over.

I have conducted similar research in a variety of locations specifically with boys in choirs and obtained a remarkably similar result. Here, for example, is what the members of the National Boys Choir of Scotland think:

1. Good discipline: can control boys
2. Passion or enthusiasm
3. Musical skill
4. Ability to explain things
5. Always fair, no favourites
6. Knowledge of voices
7. Fun and sense of humour
8. Patience.

All of this reduces to the fact that boys expect their choir director to be a professional, regardless of whether the choir itself is amateur or professional. When you are in charge of boys, only professionalism will do. A professional approach goes a long way to communicating to the boys that you do like them. Because of itself, the development of professionalism is something that requires care and dedication. A professional approach also means that you avoid such unprofessional behaviour as having favourites or being inconsistent in your moods and expectations.

How, then, do we add the final magic ingredient that really wins the undying loyalty of the boys and takes the choir to heights unattainable through mere competence? You are unlikely to achieve it if you suffer from empathy deficit. Statistically, as an actual neurological condition, this is more likely in men than women, but to some degree in all of us it is simply an attitude of mind. There are pedagogical and performance elements in the work of every boys' choir director. Part of caring about your boys in a professional manner is to expect and strive for the best you can get out of them in performance. Ultimately, though, you will have to decide where your heart really lies.

If you are a woman who is concerned about good relationships, you may well by virtue of your gender offer the boys a retreat from the constant demands of hegemonic male competition that they will appreciate. This is not 'mothering'. It is simply the provision of a feminine perspective on life that most boys crave right though to manhood. You will probably instinctively know how to do this. Assuming you are also a passionate choir conductor, you will also instinctively know how to get the balance between nurture of the music and nurture of the singers right.

Some men may need to work more consciously to develop this skill. I have interviewed boys who have described their male conductor as 'creepy'. It is very rare for this term to be applied to a woman. Here is a recent example:

INTERVIEWER: Now did you start singing low or did the teacher get you singing low?

BOY: No the teacher actually goes quite high, Mr [N]. I don't like him though.

INTERVIEWER: Why don't you like him?

BOY: He's very creepy. He's the creepiest person you'll ever meet. It's just his face. Like if he asks for choir and you want to quit he absolutely shouts at yer.

INTERVIEWER: He makes you sing high?

BOY: Well not high, just like aaah (demonstrates note) not (a.a) (coughs) wait, I've got a cough aaaaa (demonstrates high note) like uuu, aaah (demonstrates different notes).

'Creepy' might mean an uneasy feeling of discomfort in the presence of a particular adult. In this precise context, where the boy introduced the word 'creepy' quite out of the blue, I think the real problem may be lack of empathy.

The individual lacking empathy will be poor at reading the subtle signals sent out by boys and will fail to understand how they see things. Failure to understand how boys see things could be addressed to at least some extent by greater knowledge and a determination to improve. Time spent building relationships with parents will reveal much of value about the boys' perspectives. The 'creepy' teacher above could read Paul Freer's (2012) important chapter in Perspectives on Males and Singing:

> Boys report feeling a sense of pressure from their conductors to never withdraw from choral music, especially from school-based choirs. But, most boys would like to explore the many opportunities open to them, and this experimentation may lead to schedule conflicts requiring the withdrawal from choral music.
>
> (Freer, 2012, p.21)

The importance of synchronising singing and sport has already been discussed. It is equally important to appreciate though that whilst your mind may be focused singly on the technicalities of a choral performance, boys' minds may be elsewhere. If you cannot see that in an empathetic way, your 'passion' is more like that of the aircraft enthusiast and will not be reciprocated. If you prioritise relationships and have empathy, you will know how to take the boys with you. You will enjoy telling them jokes or even groaning at the awful ones they tell you. You will enjoy helping them when they find something difficult. You will take time and care to explain interesting points about the music or the composer to them. You may pause to enlighten them about a historic event or a philosophical belief.

Having gained their interest, you actually will gain satisfaction from bringing the boys up shortly if they overstep the mark or apply insufficient effort to what they are doing. This is not because you have sadistic tendencies. It is because you genuinely care for the boys and want them to succeed as individuals as well as a choir. Your firm admonitions will always be controlled and professional and balanced by genuine pleasure and approval when they get things right. The man who can build relationships with boys through all these means will be an inspiration to them and remembered by them for the rest of their lives. That is the difference between passion for aircraft and passion for conducting a boys' choir.

6.3   The abuse of power

I still remember an organ lesson in Canterbury Cathedral in the 1970s. This was shortly before being admitted to the hallowed ground of the morning practice room for observation of rehearsal technique. Though this was long before child protection had been legislated, the maestro clearly gave due thought to the welfare of his choristers, as well, perhaps as that of his organ students. He swung round on the organ bench and said, quite out of the blue, 'Now, about these choristers. If I came on you now, you'd be traumatised, so think how much worse it would be for them.' That was a succinct lesson about empathy and I like to think that I did not need it for I have always worried about how the boys are feeling and whether my actions make them feel better or worse. I think Allan Wicks also had the difference between the 'right' and 'wrong' sorts of passion nicely buttoned up.

If one takes genuine pleasure in the success of others, particularly when they are children, one is less likely to abuse one's power. The principle of the benign exercise of power is that one uses it to empower others. This is easy to do with boys if you use your skill to help them become good singers and rounded, socially competent people. Unfortunately, a large ego can sometimes be part of the psychological make-up of a conductor. This can make such a process harder. I do get a little irritated when I see presentations of 'my wonderful choir'. Of course, a conductor is entitled to feel proud of the choir they have led as well as to gain some personal reward from its success. When 'me, me' screams out constantly though, it is tiresome and indicative of dispositions that may not be entirely healthy. Facebook has a lot to answer for here and we need to be wary of conductors' vanity dressed up as praise and thanks for the choir. Boys seem to have a mysterious sixth sense for knowing when praise is genuine, but not always, as the Denchester Boys Choir case study (below) demonstrates.

Those responsible for the appointment (and dismissal) of conductors need to be wise enough to discriminate between the natural charisma that is necessary to inspire any choir, let alone a boys' one, and a power craze. They need also to have the necessary determination and strength to deal with a conductor whose behaviour is like the one I describe below. There are (unfortunately) many illustrative case studies available to choose from. I think the following illustrates well the points I am endeavouring to make. A recurring theme in the analysis of abuse cases is that boys (and their parents) can incorrectly perceive a conductor who turns out to have been grooming one of them for sex as the exact opposite of creepy. The names have been changed in this extract to protect the present-day reputation of the choir concerned.

Denchester Boys Choir

To understand the impact of the events on everyone connected with Denchester Boys Choir, it is necessary to know something about Brian Sopwith himself. This was a man whose life and passion was the choirs he had founded. He had a formidable reputation in the music world as a genius for getting the best musically out of boys, but is also described as a 'Jekyll and Hyde' by a former accompanist, for the rapidity with which he could switch from the epitome of charm to ferocious anger . . . His control was total. Parents signed a contract agreeing to rehearsals two nights a week, plus regular all-day sessions on Sundays, up to 20 concerts a year and overseas tours in the summer holidays lasting up to three weeks.

Nobody left the choir initially . . . One boy, overcome by the situation, burst into tears, others challenged their new director, saying: 'This is not the way we do it in Denchester Boys' Choir' . . . During a rehearsal break, one lad was found gathering signatures for a good luck card to send to Sopwith. On a bus journey back from a concert, a group of the older boys had to be reprimanded for displaying a window banner with the words 'Sopwith is innocent'.

The message here is all too clear. This is a conductor that boys today might describe as 'awesome' or 'legendary'. The classic ingredients are there. The word 'passion' is used by the reporter. The conductor had a 'genius for getting the best musically out of boys'. Readers with the time and the inclination to delve more deeply into such reports will find that this pattern of the male autocrat who is at first thought be a wonderful conductor and later found to be an abuser is a repeating one.

Is there anything that has been missed in the difficult task of discriminating between benign and malign passion? Some time after this particular offender was sentenced, a web forum was established for former members of the choir to come to terms with what had happened. It is very clear from an analysis of the posts that the recurring themes were those of the abuse of power and chilling self-centredness. The conductor was described as a total autocrat who got his way by fearsome fits of shouting and violent mood swings. Moreover, boys who had attended the school at which he taught music described an ingrained culture of bullying by a core of male staff. Some boys would take their cues from these 'role models' and bully other boys. The word 'passion' occurs yet again in this extract from one such a post. Here, the contributor appears to be discriminating between benign and malign passion, and it is the degree of complicity in the bullying culture that makes the difference:

I do feel, however, that he was part of a serious bullying culture within the school and that this reflected in the behaviour of both staff and pupils. Whereas I can identify many individual teachers who inspired me, taught me with passion and imagination and guided me towards a degree of academic success ([names] spring immediately to mind), many others were viscious [sic] and intolerant.

For me, a particularly tragic feature of this case is the obvious failure of the choir to tackle negative aspects of masculinity. In Chapter 1 I wrote these words:

It is from the population of men lacking emotional sensibility and empathetic capacity that the majority of the world's violent crimes from war to rape emanate. I am passionately against war, rape and all other crimes that arise from a lack of empathy. Boys should participate in activities that develop emotions and empathy.

Choral singing, then, should be an activity that develops emotions and empathy. I am not at all against boys participating in sport or in boyish horseplay if it is benign and subject to a watchful eye. A joyless approach to child protection that seeks to outlaw any form of exuberance or childish romping about goes too far in my view. During the serious business of the choir, however, boys should be in a time and space where respect for each other as co-creators of beauty is learned. Choir should be where boys learn emotional sensibility and develop empathetic capacity, not how to bully other boys. Bullying in any form, favouritism, unkind sarcasm, arrogance, inconsistent moods—these should not have any place in choir rehearsal. I suspect it unlikely that you would find them to be characteristics of a rehearsal where the female conductor 'loves her boys to bits'.

6.4   Safeguarding

Nobody should be engaged in contemporary choral work with boys unless they are working (paid or volunteer, it makes no difference) in an organisation that has proper and comprehensive policies and protocols covering what is now generally known as 'safeguarding'. Safeguarding should cover not only the territory of child protection, but also areas such as anti-bullying policies, health and safety, and risk assessment. Those policies should ensure that all who come into contact with boys through choir have enhanced Disclosure and Barring Service (DBS, previously Criminal Records Bureau or CRB) clearance or its equivalent in countries outside the UK. In my experience, there is now a well-established culture where these things are automatic. For example, if a singing teacher genuinely needs to touch a boy to correct a postural fault, he or she will first genuinely seek the boy's permission and do so only when a second adult is present or at the very least there is a glass door to the teaching room. I see this happening in practice regularly.

It is not the aim or purpose of this book to reiterate the contents of safeguarding training. In theory, cases such as Denchester could no longer happen in an age of safeguarding. However, there are reasons they still might that this chapter has touched on. A few brief words are therefore merited. First, there is a danger of complacency. It is all very well having a policy, but if there are no reasonably regular events to make sure that everyone in the organisation is aware of it and able to contribute concerns or suggestions for improvements, it can just become a dusty file with no practical impact. Second, there is still a big danger from naivety. The risk of this is perhaps highest in churches where there might exist attitudes such as 'because we're a church, we believe in trust' or 'because we're a church, there couldn't be bad people in our congregation'. These are exactly the conditions under which abuse thrives. Greater, not lesser, vigilance is required in voluntary organisations.

Most dangerous of all, however, is abuse that can happen through the conditions of 'power' and 'passion' that this chapter has addressed. A particularly chilling aspect in the reporting of the Jimmy Savile affair was the aura Savile was said to have cultivated that he was above the law. Nobody is above the law. It is an insidious abuse of power for an individual to suggest otherwise and an appalling dereliction of duty on the part of any organisation that allows an individual to do so. Inspirational musicians, however, can be powerful people. The very charisma that makes them successful in attracting large numbers of boys to choirs also makes them hard to challenge. As the Savile affair showed, an individual with a high-level national reputation is able to set themselves above the law through exercise of their charisma and the weakness or naivety of those whose duty it is to uphold the law.

6.5   A thorny question

In one of my earlier attempts to address this difficult issue, I chose an oblique approach based on the case study of Benjamin Britten. My idea was that intelligent readers might draw their own conclusions without my having to spell it out. I can see now that this was a mistake. Most commentators accepted passively what I had to say, even if only after drawing a deep breath. One campaigning organisation with a particularly narrow agenda bordering on the spiteful in its attacks on girl choristers, however, accused me of 'prurience'. Some eighteen months after this, a leading member of that organisation received a life sentence for historic offences during his time as a prep school teacher. Methinks the campaigning organisation did protest too much, so let us try again.

I do find Britten difficult. He is without doubt one of the greatest, if not the greatest, composer the UK has produced. His compositions for boys' voices are unsurpassed genius. Naturally I want to share them with boys I teach. What should one do? One can of course introduce them to the boys with little comment, as one often does with the works of other composers. The boys will innocently learn and sing them. Therein lies what I find difficult for I cannot feel I have been totally honest with the boys and may myself have been complicit in the exploitation of innocence. On the other hand, how does one begin to do justice to the complexities of the passions that beset Britten?

It is just not within the comprehension range of a twelve-year-old and simplistic and tarnished judgements will probably be made.

The positive interpretation of Britten's string of affairs with thirteen-year-old boys is perhaps, as David Hemmings is reported to have said, as a 'deeply considerate father figure'. Undoubtedly Britten (and his partner, Peter Pears, who did so much to keep Britten out of trouble) wrestled deeply with my question of the 'right kind of passion'. For the most part, perhaps, the writing of great music was a safe vent for a very deep passion that crossed over into the erotic. Without dwelling too much on this issue and straying into the 'prurient', amongst the many documented friendships with thirteen-year-old boys the only one known to have ended in an actual sexual encounter (strongly resisted by the boy) was the unfortunate case of Harry Morris.

At the time of the Harry Morris affair, Britten was only twenty-three-years-old (and thought of himself as a thirteen-year-old). This was not the act of a mature man who had struggled with his erotic passions, learning eventually to subdue them and sublimate them through great music. Today, though, we have become quite unforgiving of such lapses in young men. It is impossible really to justify the Harry Morris incident. It is not just the thirteen-year-old, though, that needs the protection. So also does the twenty-three-year old. History cannot be rewritten but one has to speculate on whether the world would ever have come to know great works such as the *War Requiem* had present-day attitudes and procedures caught up with Britten during his lifetime. I hope I have explained it better. It is not easy.

References
Freer, P. (2012). From Boys to Men: Male Choral Singing in the United States. In S.D. Harrison, G.F. Welch & A, Adler (eds.), *Perspectives on Males and Singing*. (Landscapes: the Arts, Aesthetics, and Education, Vol. 10). New York, NY: Springer.

Further reading
Bridcut, J. (2006). *Britten's Children*. London: Faber and Faber.

Durham, A. (2003). *Young Men Surviving Child Sexual Abuse: Research Stories and Lessons from Therapeutic Practice*. Chichester, UK: Wiley.

Hawes, M. (2004). *Never Take No for an Answer*. Lewes, UK: The Book Guild.

Chapter 7: Demographic management of boys' choral work

Phrases such as the demographic time bomb have become part and parcel of human resource management and economic planning. The workforce in developed Western countries is ageing and we all know what has happened to pensions. An ageing population spells bad news for the younger generation who are going to have to work harder and longer for proportionately smaller rewards in old age. Demographic time-bombs also tick under the feet of any boys' choir. There is a kind of inevitable entropy whereby if nothing is done, a boys' choir ages until it becomes top-heavy with 'pensioners'. You may once have had a treble line of bright, eager young faces. For your neglect of the never-ending process of recruitment, you will be rewarded by a choir of falsettists.

Demographic management applies not just to treble lines, of course. If your choir is made up of boys singing a range of parts, you will find that if you neglect demographic management the choir will inevitably gravitate towards a baritone ensemble. At the very least, the parts will become unbalanced. Demographic management is one of the most vital of all functions in choral work with boys. It begins with a clear view on where you stand in relation to the pedagogy/performance continuum. If your view of choir management is to audition occasionally in order to maintain a relatively static body of singers you know and trust, you are quite definitely in the wrong business. If, on the other hand, you think like a schoolteacher and see things in year cohorts that move on, you are more likely to enjoy success.

Boys' choirs are, by their nature, transitory phenomena in which young boys join, grow through the choir and leave. However good your performances may be, this unavoidable fact marks your work heavily as pedagogical. As with school cohorts, some years may be better than others and some degree of fluctuation in the choir's fortunes is part and parcel of the excitement of running a boys' choir. If you are fortunate enough to direct a professional choir supported by a choir school, your choir very probably will broadly correspond to the school years. Your main role (apart from directing the rehearsals and performances!) will be to ensure that a successful annual voice trial is held for eight- to nine-year-olds. You may be in the enviable position of directing a choir whose reputation alone is sufficient to ensure an adequate supply of applicants. Sadly it is increasingly likely that, even in some of the more prestigious choirs, you will have to engage in some form of outreach. I shall say more about that shortly.

I know of at least one professional choir that has invested heavily in a kindergarten section for the under-eights. The motives were twofold. First, the choir had noticed that it was losing older boys more frequently as a result of the secular trend to earlier puberty. Second, the choir authorities were concerned with the quality of applicants. The learning curve from entry to the choir to a position of usefulness was becoming too steep, largely as a result of the poor quality of musical education in the primary schools. A junior training or kindergarten choir, whatever it is called, seems to me an excellent idea. The need for one clearly underlines the pedagogic nature and function of boys' choirs. Aside from the obvious one of providing good musical training to small boys who would not otherwise receive it (see Chapter 8 for the importance of this), the advantages can be considerable. The choir is less vulnerable to unexpected losses whether these are due to early puberty or other family circumstances. There is an opportunity to induct parents and test out the likely level of commitment. This latter point has become of increasing importance in an age of unprecedented leisure choice and split families. Generally, the younger the age at which boys become loyal to choir, the less likely they are to choose other activities.

Table 5 shows an idealised demographic for a treble section of sixteen boys.

For the majority of choirs that function without the support of a dedicated choir school, I would strongly recommend that a chart like Table 5 be borne in mind. It is so easy to carry on from year to year without noticing how the demographic structure of the choir is changing, until the inevitable crisis point is reached. The choir either then folds or goes on an emergency recruiting campaign that floods it with an assortment of boys lacking the necessary musical experience and skill that is otherwise carefully built up by regular, planned recruitment and progression. I have seen this happen so many times! One possible means of focusing attention on demography is to maintain a choir register in year groups. Dangerous population bulges that result in a sudden haemorrhage at puberty show up more readily, as do under-representations of year groups. If the boys are seen individually for coaching on a regular basis and perhaps tested with the voice change app, a much more secure and demographically aware choir should result.

7.1   The 9–13 problem

Boys, as I have suggested several times, learn the most by imitation. Table 5 takes it almost for granted that the nine and ten-year-olds will be imbibing the skills of the twelve and thirteen-year-olds. Unfortunately, this is not how schooling is organised. Transfer from junior to senior school usually cuts ~~ s the natural demographic of a boys' choir. The most debilitating example ₃ is in England where transfer in the majority of state-funded schools at the unusually young age of eleven. The effect on boys' choirs is noth-

Year (age)	Number	Function
Year 4 (8–9)	0–2	The 'nursery'. May not yet join the choir, but the more advanced ones might become pro-bationers to replace losses.
Year 5 (9–10)	4	On a rapid learning curve. Finding their feet and becoming the next year's mainstay of the treble section.
Year 6 (10–11)	4	Key year in which the pinnacle of development may be approached. Vital part of the young sound of the choir.
Year 7 (11–12)	4	The second key year in which musical experience is added to voices at their peak. The 'golden year'. Some voices may become leading soloists, though a minority of others may begin to pass their best.
Year 8 (12–13)	3	At least one Year 8 pupil is likely to be lost to voice change. Others may assume useful leadership roles though their range and quality of their treble voices may diminish. Boys with later puberty may still peak as soloists or leading members during this year.
Year 9 (13–14)	0–2	One or two boys for whom puberty comes later may survive as useful members of the choir, possibly with very powerful top registers—a 'super nova of the dying treble voice'.

Table 5. An idealised demographic for a treble section of sixteen boys.

ing short of catastrophic and we need look no further than the age of transfer for a significant and often overlooked explanation for the dearth of boys' singing. Transfer at age eleven has three main results:

- Most primary schools lack skilled music teaching, let alone choral instruction. The consequence is that the majority of boys fail to develop adequate pitch-matching skills or find their upper registers, ever.
- Younger boys cannot learn by imitation of older boys. Good choral tone is very hard to develop and the expectations of what is possible are almost invariably too low.
- Boys approaching the age of eleven wrongly believe that singing is 'babyish' and something that must be discarded in order to show that they have 'grown up' on transfer to secondary school. Low expecta-

tions exacerbate this problem as singing in primary schools often is 'babyish'.

The situation can be less dire in those countries where transfer is at the age of twelve, though this may also exacerbate the problem of a lack of teaching skill and low expectation if all the teaching in the primary schools is generalist. In the majority of choir schools, transfer is a year later still at age thirteen. This is partly because a thirteen-plus transfer is the norm in the independent schools to which most choir schools are aligned, but also because of a tacit recognition that viable boys' choirs of quality simply cannot function with transfer at eleven. I have come over the years increasingly to believe that at least some of the belief in 'uncool' has developed largely as a result of this fundamental structural barricade.

Good boys' choirs with strong, capable treble sections have a much better prospect for functioning either in independent schools with a thirteen-plus transfer or outside the bounds of schooling altogether. Very occasionally an individual's exceptional genius overcomes the difficulties in other circumstances. 'Outside the bounds of schooling' may be something like a church choir or a county youth choir. Whatever it is, given all that has been said about pedagogy and demography, it occupies an uncomfortable and vulnerable position. Community choirs can easily lose boys at age eleven when new friends (and enemies) are made and new opportunities open up at secondary school. There really is only one infallible answer—step up the recruitment of younger boys to make good any possible losses! A strong influence of older boys (e.g. age fifteen or over) can also help with the retention of wavering eleven-year-olds, as can an exciting programme with events for boys to look forward to. Boys need to see a goal and purpose for their singing and even in this day and age of family jet travel can still be excited by the prospect of a big choir occasion.

7.2   Outreach and recruitment

Demographic management is one of the most important functions in the direction of boys' choirs. Outreach and recruitment are clearly a fundamental, if not the fundamental tool of demographic management. Some words on the topic need to come somewhere in a book on contemporary choral work with boys. I wish I had a magic formula on recruitment, but I'm afraid I don't. There are a few general principles that can be examined in this chapter. For specifics, however, I can only report on what some successful choir directors have actually done in later chapters . There is no guarantee, unfortunately, that what works for one can simply be copied by another.

To understand the general principles, it is first helpful to analyse what we may be up against. We have already seen that a particularly big obstacle is that of eleven-plus transfer. This need not, of course, prevent us from recruiting boys in primary schools but it may have an effect on retention at a later date. The degree to which primary school boys see older boys who they look to as role models involved is also important. The main points that need to be addressed are boys' inferiority to girls, real and imagined; the synchronisation of singing and sport; relationships and reciprocity; branding; and targetting.

7.2.1 Boys' inferiority to girls, real and imagined

I have written two other books about gender and singing, and do not wish to repeat myself here, even if I had the space. I have managed to steer clear of the vexed question of whether choirs should be mixed or single sex, or even whether girls should be allowed to sing at all in places where once only boys sang. Perhaps there is a clue in the title Contemporary Choral Work with Boys! However, there is something very important that needs to be said in relation to recruitment. Much is written about the alleged 'problem with boys', by which is meant that on average boys perform less well in school examinations than girls, are more likely to be in trouble and behave badly than girls, and generally have a narrower cultural outlook than girls. In the worst case, boys' cultural outlook begins and ends with 'fightin', fuckin' and football'.

These things, for all sorts of reasons, have taken on something of the self-fulfilling prophecy. When you visit a primary school, you will meet children who actually believe not just that only girls *should* sing, but that only girls *can* sing. All sorts of things have encouraged this belief. At the top of my list, however, comes the lack of skilled music teaching and teachers' low expectations. This is not to say that I believe primary school teachers in general a bad lot. There are all sorts of reasons that are outside their control and for which they cannot be held blameworthy for having low expectations of boys with regard to singing. There is some as yet inconclusive evidence (see Chapter 8) that boys, on average, may be inherently slower learners in singing than girls. Whatever may turn out to be the genetic or neurological position, the belief that boys are not good singers combined with the lack of knowledge about how to address this is likely to be the more potent dimension.

The consequent psychology is not that hard to understand. At the risk of generalisation, most boys like to be 'on top' and plenty of research has shown the extent to which boys' surprising fragility and fear of failure relative to girls inhibits performance in all sorts of cultural and academic spheres. This fear of failure, of course, is usually a secret one and commonly concealed by denigration of the activity that is feared. Boys are portrayed as loud, confident and boisterous, whereas this is often only a front to conceal inner insecurity and maintain 'reputation' in the constant struggle for status. You, as the recruiter, have got to remove from boys their fear of failure at singing. This is likely to mean creating an opportunity for them to try out singing in a safe environment and discover that it can be fun and something they are able to do. 'Safe environment' usually means boys only, because the presence of girls may inhibit them for precisely the reasons stated above. Some of my most recent investigations have revealed the extent to which boys fear, or are even terrified of, auditions. If you place such an obstacle in their way, don't be surprised if few turn up. It is far better to hear them as a group in school and pick out the promising ones for some subtle flattery. Most successful recruiters I have observed have done this in one way or another.

7.2.2   The synchronisation of singing and sport

Most boys will enjoy singing to a greater or lesser degree if it is presented in the right way to them. The problem is that they may be even more attracted to sport. On the whole, plenty of boys will play sport and sing. What they are less likely to do is miss sport for singing. You have got to be prepared, as far as reasonably possible, to arrange things so that singing and sport do not coincide. Church and community choirs have the advantage in dealing with the 9–13 problem, but schools are generally better placed to manage the synchronisation of singing and sport. The most successful school choirs that I visit almost invariably contrive to squeeze singing in at times when boys are going to miss something they don't like rather than sport. This is unlikely to be a maths or English lesson, much as many boys would like it to be. However, I have seen a good number of imaginative school choir directors achieve success by getting boys out of something like tutor time. The provision of Jaffa cakes and toast can further enhance the success of such mild subversion. Of course, if there is to be a good concert, boys will have to give up some of their quality time at some stage. Most are quite willing to do this if their loyalty has been won and they can see that they need to work hard to achieve a good result in something worthwhile. They may even miss a Saturday's sport, though I would always check when the cup final is before arranging concert and rehearsal dates!

Church choirs, with their requirement for Sunday attendance, have been hard hit by the rise of Sunday sport for boys. I am not sure that there is an answer to this other than to accept an inevitably large decline in the number and size of parish church boys' choirs. Where there is a choir school, there is perhaps the best of all worlds. The 9–13 problem is solved, there is a safe environment for singing, and sports practices and fixtures can take place around choir commitments. It is possible to mitigate the sport problem to some extent in parish choirs by providing plenty of recreational sport before and after rehearsals. The more enterprising choirs I have seen organise sport and singing fixtures against other choirs, or events such as 'lads and dads' matches. Don't expect, though, to run a thriving boys' choir with heavy rehearsal and service commitments if you have no interest in the social and sporting side of the boys' lives. They are giving you a lot of their time and loyalty. Whilst their musical development and the thrill of a good concert constitutes the major return, it is in my view an abuse of that loyalty to give them no compensation for sport and leisure missed. Aside from this there is the purely practical issue that you won't retain many boys if you don't.

7.2.3   Relationships and reciprocity

There has already been a whole chapter on relationships , but good relationships in all spheres are just so important that it is almost impossible to say too much. Chapter 6 concentrated on the all-important relationship between conductor and boys. If you are recruiting boys from primary schools, though, pause for a moment's thought. Why should a school help you? What have you done for them? The successful Chorister Outreach Programme (COP), run by the cathedrals during the Sing Up era, offered schools a lot—for example, a free music specialist for twelve weeks, repertoire help, visits to assembly by choristers, the chance to join with other schools to perform in the cathedral. An amateur choir is unlikely to be able to match this, but what could you offer? You have (I hope!) musical expertise. I have been quite critical of the lack of this in primary schools, but here is a golden opportunity to help. You may well have a wonderful venue for a concert or music festival you can offer to the school.

The very least that is required is a meeting with the headteacher to explore the question and to show a willingness to enter into reciprocity, the principle upon which relationships are built. This meeting is so important because relationships are absolutely dependent upon face-to-face human contact. Most schools are used to the concept of partnership. They may well have a partnership with their local teacher-training institution. Perhaps they will have a partnership with a local football-coaching scheme. There go your boys! Are you round the table or not? It is ironic that football clubs, which you would think are preaching to the converted, can put more effort into helping schools than choirs. The COP, which was originally dreamed up by Truro Cathedral for all the reasons I have just outlined, like all great ideas, was based on a simple but winning formula.

You also need to think about the parents. If you see parents as an occupational hazard you are definitely in the wrong business running an amateur boys' choir. You absolutely need their support and commitment for a whole host of reasons. The most obvious is in making the boys available, on time and clean, and being the inevitable unpaid taxi service. You may need their help with fundraising, or you may want them to make a financial contribution in some way, which may, for at least some, be quite a sacrifice. A lively social life for the choir is far more possible if parents are willing to help with this. Boys consume cakes by the lorry load and I recently visited a successful county boys' choir where parents almost baked cakes faster than the boys could eat them (almost).

It is all very well printing glossy recruitment leaflets with bold claims about how much choir will help a boy's progress and education, but if you never meet with parents to discuss the progress of individuals or show parents ways they can help their sons, it is largely empty rhetoric. If you can involve dads, you are really in the premier league. My most recent research is beginning to reveal the extent to which male parents, who ought to be role models, are actually disengaged from their sons' singing and musical lives. There is a huge amount of work to be done here by imaginative, enterprising choir managements.

Finally, if yours is a church choir, you are going to have to become wise to the extent church has become an alien concept for the large majority of parents. Long gone are the days when the parish church and its choir were part of the woven social fabric. What percentage of your regular congregation are couples of an age to parent eight-year-old boys? You need to face up to the fact that where once the church was a trusted institution, there is now public revulsion toward priests and others who abuse boys. Do not make the mistake of underestimating the damage done. Trust has to be rebuilt and the only way to do this is through investing in genuine face-to-face relationships. The task is far from impossible and can be hugely rewarding in the long run. Warm relationships can lead to parents supporting your church choir even if they are not and never become religious believers. If it matters to you, some may even convert to your faith through their son's membership of the choir.

7.2.4 Branding and targeting

Like it or not, branding has become important. Part of being 'cool' is being associated with a 'cool' brand. Think like a boy. 'Reputation' matters to boys. How will being in your choir enhance their 'reputation'? Demographic management relies heavily upon retention. As boys grow older, they become more aware of their surroundings and more sophisticated in their analysis of how others judge them. This is when you may start to lose them if you give no thought to the public image of your choir. To give them credit, many boy singers suffer decidedly uncool choir brands because they value things other than the superficiality of big brand culture. But there are limits and 'choir' in general has become a tarnished brand for many young people. This tarnish, however, is as superficial as the brand culture itself. Boys can equally become very proud of their choir membership if you give some thought to your image and appreciate how much you are doing for boys if you give them something to be proud of. Do not feel it beneath your dignity to engage the services of a marketing professional. The one thing you need is a USP (Unique Selling Point) and style of your own. This is the only time in the book I mention Libera!

Closely associated with brand is choice. It is an uncomfortable truth that in the days when parish church choirs regularly had thirty to forty boys in them, there wasn't much else for boys to do. Whatever your views on 'dumbing down' may be, boys today face unprecedented levels of academic pressure and rising expectations for homework. These make their leisure time a more precious commodity than was known by previous more carefree generations. Children today also have a bewildering range of leisure choice like never before. What have you done to make your choir an activity of choice for boys? What friendships does it offer and what opportunities for escape and chilling out? What role models are your choir able to offer? Why would young boys want to become like the established singers in your choir? Is it a choir that any singers would want to join because the choir has a reputation that enhances the reputation of the individual members? If it is, don't under-sell it. What stories run about it in the local media? Who sees them? What 'spin' is put upon them? How many of these stories appeal to children? Think it through. Why would any boy want to join your choir? Why would a musical boy want to join it and prioritise it as an activity of choice?

This last point relates to the important need to target recruitment. Ask any marketing professional about the importance of targeting. Why do websites run cookies? I have stressed the importance of a lively social life, a choir chill-out room with table tennis, a field to play football or just go wild on, pizza feasts after special rehearsals, regular bowling trips, a camping trip . . . There may also be choir pay . It undoubtedly helps to attract and sustain boys' commitment. But all these things are peripherals. They are rewards for those boys who already give the choir their loyalty. They are not the fundamental reason for joining it. Choirs are for singing in and learning about music in. This was my first big lesson from ethnographic research in a boys' choir. If you have recruited the right boys, they will love their singing and want to progress in their musical learning. That trumps any peripheral.

So you have to target musical boys who will actually enjoy using their voices. Where will you find such boys? Any school will have some, but you have to identify and filter them out. We have already talked about a softly, softly approach, based on subtle listening to individuals within groups. You need access to those groups, either through your role as a regular teacher or through initiating their existence through an outreach programme. If you go heavy-handed and haughtily down the audition route, you are in danger of missing this vital nurture stage. If you have good relationships with the parents and community, musical boys might actually be brought to you. You need the widest possible network of relationships with other music professionals, particularly peripatetic teachers of individuals. Good relationships with such colleagues may result in musical boys being recommended to your choir. There is no escaping that it all comes back to the amount of time you invest in networking and relationship-building!

7.3   Fitting voices to parts

Hitherto we have considered only the demographic management of the treble section. If your choir is to consist of lower parts sung by young men whose voices have not settled, demographic management takes on a whole new perspective. The first thing to be clear about is precisely the point that voices have not settled. It is too early to state that a fifteen-year-old is a 'tenor' or a 'bass', although I know plenty of choirs where this is done. Young men need guidance through voice change, probably even more than boys need guidance through their treble stages. Once again, we are reminded that any choir of adolescents inevitably has to some degree a pedagogic function. The pedagogic element is almost certainly greater in later adolescence than early adolescence. The well-developed boy treble voice is capable of supplying the top line in a choir otherwise made up of competent, mature adults. The newly changed voice is finding its way, much at the same time as its owner is finding his way in most other bewildering aspects of life. Young men are in choirs to learn and discover, and very probably to chill out and discover new forms of social interaction. The intense days of the exacting treble line are over.

In my view, this means that the 'rules' for demographic management that apply to trebles have to be relaxed. Voice change, as we have said, is highly unpredictable and idiosyncratic. You cannot therefore plan a concert six months in the future on the basis that you will have six basses and six tenors. You have to prioritise the developmental needs of the young singers and go with what you have. This, of course, can change quite a lot over a six-month period. I suspect also that many choir directors might be amazed to find what their so-called 'tenors' are actually singing! Technology now allows researchers to pick out individual voices during choral singing and analyse what they are up to.

One of the most common phenomena I encounter is young men allocated to tenor lines who cannot actually reach the bottom of the tenor register. This is in fact so common that we are reminded of Duncan McKenzie's (1956) alto-tenor plan. It was devised for a reason! Does this matter? It perhaps depends on how rule-bound you are in your outlook. It depends also on the extent to which the young man is serious about a future singing career and taking individual lessons. Whilst there are many young men singing a vague tenor without being able to reach either extremity of the range, they seem to do so quite happily. Perhaps the 'if there's no harm' rule applies here.

What are the alternatives? We are back to the Schools A, B and C of Chapter 4. If you are an adherent of School C, you will get round the problem by keeping the young man on the treble line for as long as he can get the notes out by whatever means (hopefully without pain to singer or listener). You will then advise that he leave the choir for a rest until he has found a new, settled voice. If you are an adherent of School B, you will be prepared to experiment and move individuals around. You may allow the young man a few months on Swanson's (1977) 'contra-bass' before trying him on a higher part. If you are an adherent of School A, you will probably want to see a nice, neat, pre-dictable progression of your singers through the various stages of cambiata. Whatever approach you take, dealing with young men possessing unsettled voices is not the same as running a choir where your sopranos are sopranos and your tenors are tenors.

For an optimal combination of pedagogical soundness and practicality, I am inclined to opt for the School A policy, though with the caveat of a liberal rather than fundamentalist approach. My reasons are as follows. Various different versions of cambiata have been proposed at different times and by different authors (including the Cambiata Vocal Institute itself). Cooper's original scheme is outlined in Table 6.

Part	Tessitura	Extended
Treble	D_4-D_5	$A\sharp_3-F_5$
Cambiata	A_3-A_4	F_3-C_5
New baritone	D_3-D_4	$A\sharp_2-F_4$

Table 6. Cooper's original cambiata ranges

In this scheme, there is a cambiata tessitura which is about right for boys at the light green phase of puberty. We should recall from Chapter 6 that boys at this phase may have a break to falsetto anywhere between A_4 and C_5, so we do not want a tessitura higher than A_4 as some boys will have frequent and uncomfortable falsetto breaks at the top of the range, or may force the 'chest' upwards producing tension, a strained sound and intonation difficulty. Not all light green boys will get the low F_3 of the extended range, and you will definitely have a problem with your dark blue boys. Should they be treble or cambiata? The biggest drawback in this scheme, however, is that dark green is not catered for. A tessitura of $A_3–A_4$ will be too high for sustained comfort, but not all dark green boys will manage the D_3 of the new baritone tessitura. Certainly they will be left behind if the baritones descend as far as the bottom $A\sharp$ of their extended range. This is a serious drawback.

Barham and Nelson (1991) solve these problems with their TCCB (Treble, Cambiata I, Cambiata II, Baritone) scheme—see Table 7—but create others.

Part	Range
Treble	$A_3–F_5$
Cambiata I	$G_3–C_4$
Cambiata II	$E\flat 3–F_4$
Baritone	$A_2–D_4$

Table 7. Barham and Nelson's TCCB scheme.

The biggest possible objection to this, which applies equally to Cooper's original scheme as well, is that trebles are included. Why should this be a problem? For me, the most critical question has to concern who sings the top line. Treble or cambiata? I once borrowed from 'quite a decent composer' (Beethoven) to create the Cambiata Chorus (see Figure 2). There is no treble line. The 'tune' or melody is in the Cambiata I part, which stays safely below A_4 where some light green shirts might be in danger of forcing their 'chest' voice too high or breaking into falsetto. Cambiata II has the harmony and does not go below E_3. If it did, many dark green shirts would begin to lose tone or depress the larynx as they are not yet tenors and very few will be able to reach C_3. Neither does it go above C_4. If it did, some boys would encounter difficulty with a lower/upper register transition. This is unambiguously cambiata music, written principally with the two categories of 'green shirt' boy in mind. Light greens sing Cambiata I and dark greens sing Cambiata II.

Treble voices are very powerful. As soon as you introduce a treble part, you make the Cambiata I part a harmony part, unless (as I have sometimes attempted) you create some convoluted scheme of melody sharing between parts or attempt to use the trebles solely as a harmony part by writing, in effect, only descants. This is not a purely academic point. The well-developed but unchanged treble voice will have 'ring' harmonics and its intensity in the higher registers increases logarithmically, as anyone who has attempted to record trebles across their whole range will tell you. This is why quite small boys can sing alongside professional adult male singers in cathedral-style choirs. It is not just a question of relative numbers. Once puberty has set in,

Cambiata Chorus

Figure 2: Cambiata Chorus

these upper harmonics are lost and the voice carries less well. Trebles, there-fore, can literally ring out above cambiata boys and are a 'dangerous' resource in a cambiata choir.

My preference here is to keep changing voice choirs and unchanged voice choirs separate. A three-part SSA or TITIITIII boys' choir works very well and can accommodate some green shirt boys as altos. A three-part CCB (Cambiata I, II and Baritone) also works very well and the Cambiata Is are heard singing what can be a uniquely beautiful and mellow top line. Think of Bach's Brandenburg 6 where there are no violins and the violas have the top part. A marriage of the two kinds of choir, however, is seldom as satisfactory. The trebles may ruin the cambiata sound. The issue really revolves around the difference between a Treble and a Cambiata I. Both have somewhere around A_3 as the bottom of their range. The difference is that Cambiata Is do not cross into the full 'head voice' or develop the 'ring' that makes trebles so prominent. I think also that when Barham and Nelson specify A_3 for trebles and G_3 for Cambiata Is they are splitting hairs and attempting to create order where none really exists. Plenty of true, unchanged trebles can reach a clear G_3.

Another problem with Barham and Nelson's scheme is that no distinction is made between tessitura and extended range. Most dark blue shirt boys will manage $A_3–F_5$, so could be trebles. Nearly all will equally well manage $G_3–C_4$, so could also be Cambiata I without difficulty. Light greens, how-ever, whilst being comfortable with G_3 as the bottom of their range, may in some cases get into trouble with the C_4. Of course, some light greens might manage it perfectly well at your first rehearsal in January, but struggle during the concert in March! A bottom note of E_3 or $E\flat_3$ should work well for most dark greens. Some light greens may also produce a good, clear tone as low as this. Quite correctly, boys at this stage can be allocated to Cambiata II because few of them will get below the $E\flat$. They will not be able to hit a good clear tone on C_3, the bottom of the tenor range. At the upper end of the Cambiata II range specified by Barham and Nelson, though, you may well hit problems. Depending on where each individual voice is, from C_4–E_4 a boy may be developing his upper to lower register passagio. This is the notorious black spot of the phonational gap that can hit boys who are used to a treble 'head voice' and have not much exercised or even discovered their new lower register. Similarly, black shirts will be happy with an A_2 bottom, but D_4 will take at least some of them across a register break they may not yet know how to handle.

Part/Phase	Range
Cambiata I, Phase A	A_3–A_4
Cambiata I, Phase B	$F\sharp_3$–$F\sharp_4$
Cambiata II	E_3–E_4
Baritone, Phase A	C_3–D_4
Baritone, Phase B	A_2–C_4

Table 8. Phases suggested by CVIA.

Barham and Nelson's scheme has weaknesses for choral work in my view because it does not distinguish between a tessitura and an extended range. It does not address the possibility that boys with good choral experience will be quite capable of using their whole voice, even during change. It will not work for every voice in your choir if your approach is dogmatic and does not give boys permission to miss notes out. The most recent version I have seen from CVIA attempts to overcome these difficulties by introducing a Phase A and Phase B of development (Table 8):

I do not have too much of a problem here with the bottom notes given, although it is obvious that in some choirs Baritone Phase A might be classified as tenor but without extended upper range. Some Cambiata IIs might still struggle with the C_4–E_4 range, but is there really a significant difference between Cambiata I, Phase B and Cambiata II? I cannot see many six-part arrangements (excluding trebles at that!) in prospect, and this is not really intended. In my view this is another example of attempting to impose order where, in reality, chaos exists. The problem here in my view is confusion

between theory that describes in an abstract and generaliz
what boys' voices do during puberty and a working theory th
may use to allocate real boys to parts actually found in the ch
Why not just resort to Cooksey's scheme as an approximate gu
scheme remains in the view of most experts the most accurate s
sification of male voices at puberty.

So we are back to the big problem of whether boys with changing voices
should or should not be included in conventional SATB choral work. A good
degree of common sense as well as a good understanding of both scientific
and practical theory is therefore needed. Empathy with your singers is also
very necessary. You will need to give different boys 'permission' to miss different notes out at different times. You should have an ongoing dialogue with
your boys as individuals concerning changing parts midway through the year's
session.

Most importantly of all, perhaps, you will need to be prepared to compromise to some extent with regard to where boys sing in relation to their
friends. Remember that the discipline of demographic management of the
treble section has to be relaxed in later adolescence, particularly for boys who
have many things other than choir on their minds. It is no use assuring them
on the one hand that it is normal for puberty to come at different times for
everybody, then making them feel bad about it by enforcing a separation from
boys who may be longstanding best friends but who just happen to have
reached a stage of puberty earlier or later. If, on the other hand, a whole section of your choir does something en masse such as transpose a section down
an octave, you have almost certainly paid insufficient attention to matching
parts to voices. This might be acceptable practice in the school classroom, but
not in more finely tuned, performance-orientated choral work.

So how do you allocate boys to parts in a changing voice choir? One
method was suggested many years ago by Irvine Cooper (1962). I have found
that an Anglicized version of it works very well. Cooper used the tune 'Jingle
Bells'. I have changed it to 'O When the Saints' and have not yet met any
English boys who do not know this or cannot be persuaded to overcome their
inhibitions and sing it lustily.

1.   Have the boys stand up in rows with sufficient spacing to permit
     your circulation amongst them.
2.   Get them all going on 'O When the Saints' in the key of D major.
     When they are all warmed up and reluctant enthusiasm has dis-
     placed shyness, tell them to keep going no matter what.
3.   You will find most probably that they are singing in octaves apart
     according to their degree of pubertal maturity.

4. Move (I nearly said run) between the rows, gently telling the ones singing down the octave to sit down and stop. A tap on the shoulder is OK (though I wouldn't recommend the leg as Cooper did in those halcyon days of innocence!). These seated boys will be your emerging baritones.

5. Now repeat the exercise with those boys still standing, but transposing up a fifth to A major.

6. You should find another octave split. Any boys singing down the octave can be tapped on the shoulder and sat down. These boys will be your cambiati .

7. Any boys still standing because they are singing in the upper octave are trebles. They deserve the heartiest of all the applause—and will probably get it if you are suitably encouraging!

This will give you your starting point for the year's work with the choir. Remember that in a changing voice choir, voices will change! Be prepared then, for some boys to change section during the year. Be alert to this and encourage the boys' interest in their progress. Make sure that all the boys understand that there will be days when certain notes may be difficult or uncomfortable. They should have 'permission' to mime these, but if they or you are aware that there is a permanent shift in which notes are comfortable, it could be time to move.

An alternative means of allocating your boys to parts and keeping track of their progress is through the voice change app. A lot depends on how big your choir is and whether you have the opportunity to see boys individually or in small groups regularly. My strong preference is for an organizational set-up that will allow this so that boys' vocal health can be monitored and, perhaps most importantly, boys can understand better what is happening to their voices and ask questions that there would not be time for, or that might be too embarrassing, in a larger group.

Table 9 suggests how you might use the app as a guide to the demographic management of a changing voice choir:

To end this chapter, here, unedited, is one of my most treasured examples of vocal agency, the boy's own will with regard to his voice and singing. This is a 'School A' situation:

INTERVIEWER: Right, now, you know the Cambiata choir?

BOY: Yeah.

INTERVIEWER: What part do you sing?

BOY: Er, I think I sang Cambiata II but, I sometimes went to the, like EBs, the, is it extended baritones or . . . ?

INTERVIEWER: Emerging baritones.

BOY: Emerging baritones. I find that much easier because I sing tenor.

Shirt colour	Phase
Light blue	This boy is a pre-pubertal treble and likely to remain so for the whole year. On Cooper's system, he would sing in the upper A major octave if he is a trained treble, though he might sing down if he is not. Do you actually want him in a cambiata choir? He could sing Cambiata I, but still has a clear treble voice that might be wasted.
Dark blue/light green	These boys have changing voices. What separates green from blue principally is a break into falsetto somewhere between A_3 and C_4 due to ligament development. This could happen during the year. Once a boy has this falsetto, he has clearly reached the cambiata phase. All boys at this stage could be cambiata, but you might want the ones whose falsetto is good and easy as trebles. Some could move from Cambiata I to Cambiata II during the year. Watch out for a clear, resonant E in the tenor octave and strained tone around middle C and above. Once you have this, they are most comfortable on Cambiata II.
Dark green/black	These boys are at or just past the climax of voice change and will be Cambiata II or Baritone. This change could well happen during the year and the main thing to look out for is whether they can produce a clearly tuned note on Tenor C. Until they can, they are best as Cambiata IIs.

Table 9. [Please provide caption].

INTERVIEWER: You sing tenor?

BOY: Yeh.

INTERVIEWER: Right, OK. Well, I'm going to have to tell you something that you might not totally like to hear.

BOY: Yeah? [long, drawn out, sounds apprehensive]

INTERVIEWER: Your voice is still treble. So the lowest part you should be singing is Cambiata I. Now, [pause] what do you think about that?

BOY: [Sighs and snorts] To be honest … I just, I only really sing high when I'm happy and (pause) … well … well if the lowest part I can sing is cambiata, how come I sing in the tenors at my choir?

INTERVIEWER: Well. I think you can't be singing tenor. Whatever you're singing it isn't proper tenor. We'll do some vocal exercises in a minute . . .

BOY: [indistinct groan-like sound]

INTERVIEWER: . . . that I'll be able to play to you to hear. What part do you think you should sing, we've got a rehearsal day coming up in about a week, what part do you think you should sing then?

BOY: Well, I sang Cambiata II well, all right without a problem. What, I don't see how this is possible.

INTERVIEWER: I see how it's possible. What do you see that's not possible, <n>?

BOY: Well if my voice is Cambiata I, how come I can sing Cambiata II and EBs?

INTERVIEWER: Well, that's what we're going to try to find out. You see, when we look at where your speaking voice is, it's quite high. What we'll do today, we'll check your range very, very carefully, and make sure we've got it right. And if it comes out as Cambiata I would you be happy to sing with the Cambiata Is?

BOY: Eeeeyuh, not really.

INTERVIEWER: Why not?

BOY: Because I've always been comfortable with tenor, well, with what I was singing.

INTERVIEWER: Is it, um, I mean, are there any other things than the voice part that decide where you want to sing? Like, does it matter who you sing with?

BOY: Well, I need to know 'em a bit. I'm not going to sing with a stranger in the street.

INTERVIEWER: Mmmh, no, OK, but . . . well, you know most of the boys in the choir, you're not going to sing with a complete stranger. Would you be happy to sing with the cambiata Is?

BOY: Yeah, but, I'd rather sing Cambiata II.

INTERVIEWER: Why would you rather sing Cambiata II?

BOY: 'cos I'm more comfortable at that pitch. I'm not one of those choristers you test so I'm not based on the high notes.

By contrast, here is an example from School C where the boy, being a cathedral chorister in a performance choir, has his vocal agency strongly reigned in:

INTERVIEWER: And do you say you sing falsetto in choir?

BOY: Yeh.

INTERVIEWER: Is that what you think or is that what somebody's told you?

Boy: Well, Dr <Director> told me to, well, he told me to keep trying to sing, um and falsetto seems to work OK actually at the moment, so I keep doing it.

Interviewer: Mm ...

Boy: I mean it wears my voice out quite quickly so I have to rest it quite often but ...

Interviewer: Mm, it will wear your voice out. It'll dry your vocal folds. Do you drink a lot of water?

Boy: Yeh, I do drink a lot.

References

Barham, T. & Nelson, J. (1991). *The Boy's Changing Voice: New Solutions for Today's Choral Teacher.* New York, NY: Alfred.

Cooper, I. & Wikstrom, T. (1962). Changing Voices. *Music Educators Journal,* 48(4): 148–51. doi:10.2307/3389562

McKenzie, D. (1956). *Training the Boy's Changing Voice.* New Brunswick: Rutgers University Press.

Swanson, F. (1977). *The Male Singing Voice Ages Eight to Eighteen.* Cedar Rapids, LA: Laurance Press.

Further reading

Barham, T. & Nelson, J. (1991). *The Boy's Changing Voice: New Solutions for Today's Choral Teacher.* New York, NY: Alfred.

Williams, J. (2013). *Teaching Singing to Children and Young Adults.* Abingdon, UK: Compton.

Interlude 3: Ben and George

Ben and George are not brothers or in any way related. The common bond between them is that neither is in any way associated with ecclesiastical choirs and both have sung in Cambiata North West (CNW), described in Chapter 9. CNW is not their only singing, but all their choral work has been secular. Both are boys who have participated in my longitudinal study. Ben, at the time of writing, is aged fifteen years and nine months. I have seen him through the entire voice change process, just catching him on the turn from unchanged treble at the age of 12:08. During puberty, Ben's vocal range expanded, and expanded spectacularly to a range of five, yes, five octaves. This he achieved by mastering all four registers of the male voice. He was able to sing down almost to the bottom of the piano keyboard by a quite remarkable tuned vocal fry. He could then sing up through 'chest' and 'head' to a piercing whistle register. I have a recording of Ben singing Sibelius' Finlandia in a cambiata range of a sixth, $G_3–E_4$, and an octave higher as a 'boy soprano'. Both are achieved with ease and no difficulty around lift points, though everyone who has heard the recordings feels that the lower cambiata one is the more 'masculine' and Ben's true vocal identity at that age.

Ben was able to do all this by the intelligent application of theory. During our termly assessment and measurement sessions we discussed such matters as the registers of the male voice. Ben took an interest in his EGG results—not in a 'keen' sense, but clearly absorbing all and presumably experimenting during my absence to show what he could do at the next session. Ben, it has to be said, lacked neither brainpower nor musical ability. He had achieved Grade 8 on the horn by the age of eleven and a place in the National Youth Orchestra by age thirteen. His progress through voice change is shown in Table 10:

This shows clearly that puberty had set in when Ben was twelve, the voice being well into the in-puberty stage by the age of 12:11 and on the cusp of the mutational climax that occurred during the year Ben was thirteen. By the end of that year (age 13:11) the voice had completed mutation (or 'broken' in lay parlance) and the assessments between the

Age (years:months)	EGG
12:08	202
12:11	173
13:04	138
13:09	119
13:11	125
14:04	123
14:08	112
15:06	113

Table 10: Ben's progress through voice change.

135

ages of 13:11 and 15:06 were of how Ben was beginning to work on his 'emerging baritone' with a view to an adult tenor. Ben sang Cambiata II in the CNW concert in 2011 when he was just thirteen . This is well within the current range of normality, though had Ben been a chorister, he would have been one of those boys who would have had to leave before the end of Year 8.

George, on the other hand, would be a boy who could have lasted into Year 9 as a treble. He is, at the time of writing, aged thirteen years and nine months. Many an ecclesiastical choir would be glad to have him as a mature, experienced treble, but this isn't George's scene. Though I had known of him as a volunteer guinea pig for conductor training days, he came to my attention when he took the audience by storm during the 2012 CNW concert where he performed a solo item with his guitar. His song 'It's All About You' could have gone viral on the YouTube 'cute' stakes, but fortunately all concerned had more sense. A year later, he repeated and topped that achievement with another song he had composed, 'This Is My Love Song'. The audience loved it but for the other boys in the choir, it was heroic or 'super-cool'. It is sometimes said that boys can be jealous and I have observed this on a number of occasions. This wasn't one of them. The other boys' admiration and approval was heartfelt, genuine and generous.

Such was the success of this event and the quality of his song that the choir's current conductor spent a day with George creating a three-part Cambiata choral arrangement that is currently being rehearsed by the choir. George is a talented young singer–songwriter who surely has a very promising musical future, but he is not a traditional chorister. He had been singing Cambiata in the Cambiata North West choir and I was looking for a good cambiata voice to record and analyse, much in the same way as I was looking for the good unchanged treble that I found in Max. George agreed to participate and the big discovery we made at our first session was that he was a treble, not a cambiata. To date, I have had only three sessions with George. In Table 11 are the results:

Clearly I had caught George at the cusp of the 'in-puberty' stage. The comparison with Ben at the almost identical age of 13:09 is instructive (119 Hz). In the four months of our time together, he has crossed the crucial 200 Hz boundary from 'light blue' to 'dark blue' shirt. He was unable at the first session to reach the bottom note of the cambiata piece we were recording (F#$_3$) without larynx depression and weak tone. By the time of the third

Age (years:months)	EGG
13:04	210
13:06	202
13:08	197

Table 11: Please provide a caption .

session, it was just about there. George does not habitually use his 'head voice' and became distinctly uncomfortable at the upper passagio point. However, a little work on this soon took him past this into a secure and good-sounding treble, which resulted in a slightly surprised look on his face!

George's circumstances illustrate two important points about treble and cambiata. First, there are a good many boys aged between twelve and fourteen who are capable of singing treble but do not readily identify as trebles. This is a good example of the tendency to exaggerate the secular trend to earlier puberty, or at least confuse it with vocal agency. George does not want to be a treble, all the more so now that increasing numbers of his Year 9 friends are singing lower parts in the cambiata choir. Second, there is a substantial zone where the treble and cambiata ranges are the same anyway. The real difference is that cambiata sing only in the lower register, whilst trebles sing most of their time in the upper register to the extent that some may never really enter or cross a lower passagio. George's lower register is not in any way 'barbaric'. It is both musical and 'boyish'—which after all is what was wanted for the recording! George was also fully capable of a good two-octave treble range and found his 'head voice' quite easily even at the age of thirteen. As with Ben's versatility, it would seem that regular and musical singing opens up a range of exciting possibilities for boys in early to mid-adolescence that are seldom appreciated or exploited.

There must be many boys in the cambiata choir who are exercising vocal agency to be with their friends. George is by no means the only one who cannot reach the bottom notes of the part he has contrived to be with. The boy quoted at the end of the Chapter 7 is another example. There are boys in that choir who could be trebles but choose not to be. Equally there are also boys in the same choir who choose to be trebles when they could be cambiata. I can think of one straightaway who is in Year 8, sings treble in a good all-male church choir and treble in cambiata choir. Only last week I dealt with tears because a boy had been allocated by the conductor to cambiata when he wished to remain a treble. He was, he assured me, a treble. By the time the concert comes six months later, who knows where any of these boys may be? The clue is in the word 'changing'.

Ben has no problem with what is 'cool' or what other boys at school think. As far as other boys are concerned, he will use his voice as he wishes, though he listens carefully to the advice of adults he respects. What I think makes the difference in all these cases is that the boys are musical and positively enjoy singing. It is far more important that we find and give good opportunities to those other musical boys the system has missed than get hung up about whether they are Cambiata I Phase A or Cambiata I Phase B.

Chapter 8: Boys' and children's choirs

This, the first of three chapters that form the final section of the book, is where we look at the work of actual choirs to see how the theoretical issues discussed in the previous two sections (Chapters 1–7) pan out in practice. One of my themes has been an endeavour to bridge any potential gap between the theory created by scientific investigation of the voice in the laboratory situation and the theory created by analysis of what successful and experienced choir directors and their singers do in practice. These chapters are inevitably more concerned with the latter, but I wish to maintain mindfulness of the former too.

The choirs I have chosen for case study are all good ones, as evidenced by their winning competitions, invitations to perform at prestigious venues or events, endorsement by a recognised authority or simply by long-established reputation. I have attempted to find choirs that cover most of the different contexts and genres for boys' choral singing. Beyond that, however, there has been no systematic process of selection. A certain serendipity arising from chance meetings with choir directors at conferences or concerts has inevitably played a part in the building up of the professional network from which the choirs have been selected. I apologise, therefore, if you the reader know of or direct a choir you think should have been included. You can always be in the next book if you get in touch!

8.1   Who or what are 'children'?

Throughout this book, puberty has been a central theme. There are many definitions of childhood and children. More often than not, they are sociological rather than biological. Childhood is often viewed by academics as a socially constructed concept, and a contested one at that. Some would say the concept of childhood as a precious and innocent period of life is but an invention of the nineteenth century. This is a topic I discussed at some length in my previous book, *How High Should Boys Sing?* (2009). Here, my discussion is curtailed in favour of a biological definition. We have seen that the age of seven is the approximate time that a triple laminate structure of the vocal folds appears, and the age of about twelve or thirteen the time when the vocal ligament begins to take on its adult composition. The child voice (for boys) may be said to exist broadly between these two biological markers.

Up to a point, this coincides with the organisation of schooling. In the UK, schooling has been, since the 1988 Education Act, organized into 'key stages'. Key Stage 1 is from age five to seven. For children below that age, the old term 'infants' might still be employed to denote that seven really is the absolute lower limit for choral singing. Cognitive as well as physiological factors might be taken into account here. This is not to say that under-sevens should not sing. This is far from the case but the topic demands a full and detailed treatment in a book other than one on choral singing by boys. Key Stage 2 is from age seven to eleven, and it is during this time, according to John Cooksey (1999), that the boy treble voice reaches its 'pinnacle of development' most commonly by age eleven, before puberty attacks purity and range. It would thus be highly convenient to define 'children' as aged between seven and eleven. Unfortunately, it is not as neat and tidy as this. First, as we have seen, boys who regularly practice choral singing enjoy an 'Indian summer' of treble voice for a good two or three years of puberty. Second, the age of eleven is unusually young for the end of primary schooling. Twelve is more common across the world and might be a better age to define the end of childhood singing. By this age, however, an increasing number of boys will be past the 'pinnacle of development' and a few may even have voices extending into the baritone range. In these chapters (8–10), we shall see real people, conductors and singers, struggling with this problem.

If we retain a strictly biological definition, then the marker of a testicular volume smaller than 3ml defines a boy child better than any chronological birthday. Accompanying this is a clear vocal definition. The speaking voice is likely to have a mean pitch of anywhere between 220 to 250 Hz or above. If well-developed, the child singing range will be from about A3 to F5. The most likely age for this biological stage in most boys is around ten years of age. Here there is another complication that we address in this chapter.

Sexual dimorphism will be relatively slight at this age and stage of development. There will be very little difference between boys' and girls' voices. The pitch ranges and registration transition points will be largely identical, although there is research we shall look at shortly suggesting that outside the elite boys' choirs, girls are likely to have the larger range and to be the more competent singers. I am aware of passionate controversies about whether boys' voices sound different to girls'. I am tempted to say that a boy's voice will be stronger and edgier than a girl's of the same stage of childhood and that this arguably suits choral work better. Any such statement, however, is a hostage to fortune for there are so many differences between individual choirs that may have at least as much an effect as the sex of the singers.

I cannot recall where I first encountered the term 'diamond model of progression' so am unable to give credit to the term's originator. It wasn't me, but I am certainly a firm advocate of the concept. It is a much better way of seeing things than key stages or chronological age. It refers to the observation that there are three broad periods: the first period of childhood is when voices are androgynous and boys and girls can sing together at the same pitch. The second is the time of early adolescence when voices diverge significantly during puberty. This is when single-sex choirs become very necessary and I am inclined to use the term 'boy' rather than 'child (who happens to be male)'. The third is the time of later adolescence when the edges of the diamond re-converge as mixed-gender choirs again become viable. The 'young men' are of course able to take their lower parts unthreatened by the girls.

In this chapter we are going to have to confront the fact that some of the best children's choirs are actually mixed-gender. We are at the point where the diamond originates immediately prior to divergence. When the possible singing range is largely the same, the argument for single-sex choirs reduces to little more than subjective cultural preference. This is not something I wish to express an opinion on. There are, however, important exceptions to this principle that we shall shortly learn about. The first has to do with the reme-diation of young boys' lack of basic musical experience, the second with older boys' continued interest in singing beyond primary school.

8.2   Where might child choral singers be found?

A straightforward answer to the question of where children will be found is 'in school'. Unfortunately, though, if what we are looking for is children engaged in choral singing then the search becomes a great deal harder. Many primary schools have what they like to call 'choirs' but few of these match the definition of choral singing I have given. This, it will be recalled, involves use of the whole voice, a challenging repertoire and strict discipline with regard to unanimity of vowel production and intonation.

It gives me no pleasure at all to have to record that England is almost cer-tainly the worst offender with regard to an acute divide between publicly and privately funded education. If you wish to hear choral singing by children (i.e. seven- to eleven-year-olds) you are far more likely to hear it in the independ-ent, fee-charging schools. How true this may be in other countries I cannot state from a research basis, but I suspect it may apply to some lesser degree in many. This has nothing at all to do with the children or their parents and everything to do with the perceived priorities in the schools. Independent schools are significantly more likely to employ choral specialists than publicly funded schools and to value choral work, including that by boys, as an impor-tant part of the broader curriculum.

There has long been a rhetoric in English primary schools of the 'whole child' and a 'broad and balanced curriculum', but I find this unconvincing. The majority of primary schools in actual practice value only the core 'basic' subjects of English and mathematics and what matters to them is their posi-tion in league tables as determined by the children's test performance in these subjects. It is often argued that these priorities are forced upon the schools by government, but this is again an unconvincing argument. The school leadership determines the school's value. Where the leadership values choral singing, it can be found. Paradoxically, it is quite often found in outstanding primary schools where standards of literacy and numeracy are also better than in schools that more narrowly focus on the 'core'. This has little to do with the social background of the school. Schools with socially 'difficult' intakes of children can produce good choral work, whilst schools with highly motivated, compliant 'middle class' children can be quite content with tuneless shouting in the chest voice, mainly by girls.

Other texts written shortly before the present one may talk optimistically of the lavishly funded government 'Sing Up' strategy for England. Though it had many good features, I do not believe that this programme was an unqualified success. Aside from its failure to tackle the vital question of singing in the lower secondary school (see Chapter 9), the programme failed to learn from research that has demonstrated that a sudden, time-limited burst of large scale funding is not the way to tackle long-standing structural deficits in arts provision. Sing Up has come and gone and the core structural inequalities remain. Lest the reader think I am being unfair, he or she may be sobered up by consideration of the fact that the composer Howard Goodall, who acted as Sing Up's 'national ambassador', was himself a former boy chorister educated at one of the elite Oxford choir schools.

I have nothing against these schools. Without them, we would have precious little good choral singing by boys. One good outcome of the Sing Up programme was the funding to extend the chorister outreach programmes established in cathedrals such as Truro and Bristol to almost every choir school in Britain. Tellingly perhaps, Graham Welch's evaluation (Welch et al, 2009a) of the Sing Up programme appeared to demonstrate that the improvements in primary school singing tended to be greatest when associated with the choral work of a choir school. At the time of writing (February 2014), a fair number of these schemes are endeavouring to continue through charging for their services, but the economic times are hard.

Meanwhile, we have simply to get on with the task of providing the best possible choral opportunities for as many children as it is possible to reach as best as we are able. The reality is that for the majority of children educated outside the independent sector, there are only two real possibilities:

1. The 'postcode lottery' whereby children attend, largely by chance, a primary school led by a visionary headteacher who values the arts and appoints or encourages teachers competent to manage choral work;

2. The tireless efforts of music staff at county or 'hub' level who prioritise the often highly frustrating (but hardly ever thankless) task of running an area boys' choir and persuading schools to publicise this to boys who might benefit.

Of course, various other individual initiatives spring up from time to time and I would like to have been able to say that parish church choirs provide good choral opportunities for boys as they certainly once did. We shall look at the particular issues there in the final chapter. For now I am going to look at an example of an independent junior school, a state maintained primary school and an area boys' choir that illustrate all the above points as well as the theories of choral singing and boys' voices discussed in the first part of the book.

8.3   Truro Prep School Choir

It had not been my original intention to include this choir. I have made a number of trips to the musical county of Cornwall over the years, first to travel with the Truro Cathedral choristers to observe their work in primary schools, more recently to work with the well-developed Cambiata movement in Cornwall (see Chapter 9). A trip to research the Cornwall County Boys Choir yielded a bonus visit to Truro Prep School that is well worth reporting, if only because of the similarities between the work in Truro and the state school work in Huddersfield that I analyse shortly in more depth. The point is that children from almost any background respond equally well to inspired choral teaching. The same principles apply in both private and publicly funded sectors.

The Truro Prep Choir is trained by Angela Renshaw who applies apparently limitless energy to her role as vocal strategy lead for the Cornwall music hub. We meet Angela twice more, in connection with the Cornwall Boys Choir and the Cambiata: The Emerging Voice programme. There are several choirs at Truro Prep, including one for boys only. Every pupil at the school sings in at least one choir. The one I heard was the auditioned school choir that consists of boys and girls up to the age of eleven. Although a good proportion of the choir are boys, there are nevertheless more girls. Angela explained that this is not because boys perceive singing as 'uncool', but because more girls than boys pass her audition. Angela's experience is that 'boy monotone growlers' always significantly outnumber girls with pitching difficulties. I shall return to this very important theme later in the chapter and again in Chapter 9.

The choir sang with unanimity and precision. Intonation was accurate and the tone 'choral' rather than the enthusiastic but obviously childish sound that is more commonly heard from children of this age. I had a lengthy discussion with Angela about how she obtains such a good 'choral' sound, from her boys' choir and also from this choir. For both choirs, Angela spends a lot of time on basic technique, in particular ensuring that the children know what the principal vowel sounds are and how to produce them with unanimity. This came as no surprise given the emphasis I have placed on vowel production and its association with resonance as a key component of choral tone. A lot of time is also spent improving diction through practising the consonant sounds.

Also unsurprising was Angela's admission that when all was said and done about supporting the breath and the correct use of abdominal muscles, 'imitation is very high on the list'. Her main method of teaching vowel production is by getting the children to imitate her. There is a good case here for any aspirant or improving choral director to take singing lessons so that they are able to provide a good model for imitation without the pitfalls of assuming that choral vowels are the same as speech vowels (see Chapter 2). Angela is not a fan of the current fad for 'backing tracks'. She believes that children need to imitate live models. Vocal modelling by the conductor or teacher is clearly important, but Angela extends this to keyboard playing. She does not believe that a pre-recorded accompaniment will produce the same results as a conductor or rehearsal accompanist who can stress to the children what is required in any given bar or at any given moment. No experiment, to my knowledge, has been conducted to demonstrate that this is reliably the case. I can only state from my own experience of rehearsing boys that pre-recorded accompaniments simply get in the way of what I want to show them.

Repertoire itself plays an important part in the production of choral tone. The repertoire of the choir is eclectic and Angela warns that though no particular style or genre is preferred, we should be prepared for surprises. 'They'd enjoy a Benedictus but they'd also enjoy Lady Gaga!' A favourite piece that they had really relished as a guest choir on Aled Jones' Cathedral Tour was John Rutter's 'Celtic Blessing'. At the time of my visit, they were enjoying rehearsing a locally arranged Cornish folk song called 'The Nine Brave Boys'. This was a 'sad song', in marked contrast to the expectation that children's music has always to be happy and upbeat. Angela told me about how she spends quite a lot of time talking to the children about emotion and how music can convey emotions through the telling of stories in song.

An almost taken for granted fact was that the repertoire is such that the choir has to sing in 'head voice' much of the time. This was true of every case study and given the theory discussed earlier, I am confident that choice of repertoire that requires 'head voice' is the most important single factor associated with pleasing choral tone in children's singing. Angela insists that the repertoire must also be challenging. The children enjoy singing in parts and tackling unfamiliar languages. They would be bored with music that was too easy or condescending. She is not keen on 'pop songs that they already know'. Though they will sing these, usually with enjoyment, they provide no challenge. The children already have their own agenda about the songs and do not come with the open mind necessary for learning. Angela also has quite an issue with the language of pop, which she regards as not always appropriate. She raised the same issue when we talked later about the Cambiata choir for older boys, but was quite clear that she 'detests language for older teenagers or adults being used in primary schools.'

I was particularly interested to learn about how Angela recruited children to the choir. She describes singing as a key feature of the curriculum followed by all children at the school. It is how they learn to read notation, develop aural skills and learn musicianship. The choir is auditioned, but over the years, Angela has learned that sticking up choir audition posters is not the way to do it. For one thing, such an approach results in a choir of mainly girls and a few 'odd boys'. Angela desires 'real boys' in her choir. These are the boys who will also play a lot of sport and may not always be the best behaved. Often, though, such boys who would not normally have seen choir as for them turn out to be the better singers.

The method she has evolved is to work gradually towards 'audition' by first singing with the children, then listening to them in big groups that gradually become smaller as the children gain in confidence. When she judges them to be ready, she will hear individuals and when she hears someone good, she 'more or less tells them that they've been selected for the choir.' In a prep school, this is little different to the process of watching boys carefully in PE lessons and telling the promising ones they've been selected for a team. It is part of the ethos and the boys accept it. The choir meets both during and outside school time and this too is part of the way things are done for sport and expected. I asked if any resist being 'picked' for choir. A few protest, in which case they are asked to try it for a month. After this very few drop out and girls are as likely to do so as boys. Why, then, does this process select fewer boys than girls? The Lindley case study gives us an important clue.

8.4   Lindley School Choir and Lindley Boys Choir

I first heard Lindley School Choir when they performed in Leeds Town Hall for the Annual Convention of the Association of British Choral Directors. There were many excellent features of their performance, but I was struck immediately by the quality of tone. It did not sound at all like the 'barbaric' sound so feared by Francis Howard (1895) (see also Chapter 2). It sounded like a well-disciplined choir with beautiful tone and accurate intonation. As with many other children's choirs, the majority of members were girls, but there were a fair number of boys. A particularly intriguing and tantalizing programme note caught my eye, however. It explained how the school also maintained a boy-only choir for 'other' boys. This had to be a case study!

Lindley Junior School is a larger-than-average primary school for Key Stage 2 children (aged seven to eleven). It is situated in a suburb of

Huddersfield. The UK schools inspectorate, Ofsted, describe this as 'an area of relative social advantage', although I would describe the housing in the neighbourhood of the school as fairly modest. Ofsted have rated the school as 'outstanding' over a sustained period and attribute this success primarily to the inspirational leadership of the headteacher. The headteacher and her team are understandably enthusiastic to achieve the best possible results across the whole curriculum. Her support of music, however, is particularly strong and there are three good musicians on the staff. A telling little detail was the headteacher attending the rehearsal to turn pages for the pianist.

The choirs are directed by Alison North, who is undoubtedly passionate about what she does. She was not convinced, though that the children saw it this way. 'Children of this age wouldn't say passion, would they? They'd say "she's nice" (we discourage that!) or maybe, "she's enthusiastic"'. Enthralled at the sight of a 130-strong boys' choir, I asked one of the boys which boys were not in the choir. 'Ones who don't like singing' was his characteristically pragmatic reply. The children's experience is that singing and choir for boys is 'normal'. With approximately 240 boys in the school, this is perhaps a more realistic window into boys' attitudes than those schools conditioned by low expectations and the belief that 'boys don't sing'.

But Alison is passionate. She responded initially to my question simply in body language that conveyed 'very passionate'. We agreed that whatever 'passion' is, it's necessary to have it to take children beyond certain limits with their singing, particularly boys. How can this quality be taught to other people then? Alison didn't think it could be. 'You know, I don't think you can if you're talking about passion.' She continued, though, to uncover an important reality. 'My own passion was dormant until Pat (the headteacher) released it. It could've been squashed like it was before at my last school, for seven whole years'.

There are a number of primary schools I could have selected to demonstrate that where there is a head who values music and appoints teachers enthusiastic to engage the children in singing, boys will usually sing. It is when such leadership is lacking, that a combination of low expectations and the belief that 'boys won't do that' is found. Lindley School takes illustration of this phenomenon to a new level. The head and her staff unashamedly aim for high quality. They are quite clear that 'high quality' does not just mean lots of children participating. It means children striving hard to achieve excellent performance of an often-difficult repertoire. The result of such an approach is not, as some might imagine, elitism and exclusion, but the entire role of 485 children singing at the 'whole-school sing' to a better standard than most school choirs.

My principal reason for visiting Lindley, however, was to understand the programme note about a boys-only choir for 'other boys'. We have already seen that at Truro Prep, girls outnumber boys by virtue of the fact that they are more capable of passing the audition. This suggests that we may be missing something very important if we simply dismiss the gender imbalance as a product of 'uncool for boys'. The same was very much true at Lindley and I have come across a similar issue in cathedrals that offer voice trials for both boys and girls. This takes us to the heart of the debate about whether or not differences in the 'hardwiring' of boys' and girls' brains accounts for the fact that girls, on a broad average, appear to learn music and languages more quickly than boys.

Joanne Rutkowski (1990) in the US, and Graham Welch in the UK, have both produced graded measures of different aspects of singing competency. Usually, when these are employed, girls are shown to have more advanced and better developed singing behaviours than boys. For example, Welch and his colleagues (Welch et al, 2009b) found in their evaluation of five schools participating in the cathedral chorister outreach programme that girls had a statistically higher mean normalized singing assessment rating than boys. An overview of research undertaken by Debra Hedden was unable to decide whether such results are due to the manner in which girls' and boys' brains process information about singing or the attitudes boys have to singing. Graham Welch has tended to the latter view and cites also what he calls a clear 'school effect'. He gives the example of one inner-city school in which all children made progress, regardless of gender. In another school where pupils were from higher socio-economic status backgrounds, relatively few children made progress in singing. The major difference appeared to be teacher expectations. There is clearly a very strong 'school effect' at Lindley.

The story of how the Lindley choirs evolved contributes an interesting and instructive insight. As with almost every choir I have visited, evolution plays an important part. Boys' choirs do not develop because somebody has read the scientific theories of John Cooksey and thought 'I must find some boys and put that into practice.' They evolve because somebody has a passion for choral singing and a passion for boys to participate. That is why theorization of these case studies constitutes, I believe, an important contribution to knowledge.

As the school's newly appointed music teacher, Alison was keen to start up an auditioned choir. The head agreed, but only on condition that another choir was also run for any child who wanted to sing, regardless of ability to pass an audition. Thus was born the Lindley School Choir and the Lindley School Training Choir. Both of these choirs at their inception consisted almost entirely of girls. Alison was entirely clear about the reason for this.

Only four boys out of the whole school could sing sufficiently well in tune to meet her entrance standard.

The gender imbalance in the training choir, however, proved to be even greater. It was almost entirely girls. Boys, it seemed, if rejected by audition, were no longer interested. Alison could not accept this and had one more trick to play. She decided to try a boy-only choir. She made the critical decision to float this choir at a time when it would not compete with demands on boys to engage in other activities, particularly sport. With the full understanding and support of the head, it was decided that the boys' choir would meet during curriculum time between 09:00 and 09:30 every Friday. Boys began to come and the enterprise went from strength to strength. Alison was entirely clear that one thing and one thing only made the difference. 'Boys weren't coming because it was on at lunchtime. Plain and simple.' The boys' choir is now an established part of the school culture. A teacher at the separate site infants' school has started an infant boys' choir and boys join the junior school in Year 3, expecting to sing.

The effect on auditions for the Lindley School Choir has been marked. During the year of my visit, thirteen Year 4 boys reached the audition standard. The item that has most changed, Alison reports, is pitch-matching and the ability to sing in tune. These vital skills, that are clearly deficient in the majority of boys generally, are learned through membership of the boys' choir. In that sense, the choir is offering the remedial work that is necessary in a culture that has come to overestimate worryingly the degree to which boys' inability and unwillingness to sing is a 'hard-wired' or essential biological fact. The experience is highly instructive for research into the neurology of singing competency and research into the social psychology of music equally.

Purely by coincidence, on the day of my first visit to Lindley, the boys' choir was recording a song for the Rugby League World Cup. Two officials from Huddersfield Rugby Club had arrived, complete with a professional camera crew, to record an old song from the Club's archives that the boys were to sing the following year at the stadium. This might be considered a typical 'boy thing'. Indeed, one of the boys was overheard to say 'I'm glad I'm not a girl' as they came into the hall! Nevertheless, we need to be clear that the singing came first. Once you have a good boys' choir, people will take note. The 'gigs' will come, because people like to hear boys sing.

Some 130 boys, aged between eight and eleven, filed into the school hall and behaved with impeccable professionalism. They knew the words and music well and needed only a few admonitions about greater animation and clearer enunciation to work up a performance that was successfully captured in one main take. Though a song about rugby, there was none of the 'barbaric' chest voice shouting that Francis Howard feared so much. The tone was light and clear, and the tuning, even from the youngest boys, remarkably accurate. Potentially difficult intervals were managed with ease. The boys had clearly been taught to access their 'head voice'. I do not have the firm research evidence to confirm this, but I strongly suspect that use of the 'head voice' contributes quite a lot to improving the boys' pitch-matching and intonation skills. It is another of those things that will make an interesting research project when somebody invents a ten-day week!

The story is not all sweetness and light, though. Alison had a bad experience when she felt that she 'ought' to enter the Boys' Choir for the National Festival for Youth Music in Birmingham. Only sixty out of 120 boys actually turned up for the festival. 'Turning out in their own time is the real struggle,' she reflects. The level of support from parents is a large part of the reason for this. A significant number will not even support evening events at the school. Alison states that she and the school are very well aware of the impact demands for choir can have on family life. Here, there is a very important difference between the auditioned and non-auditioned choir. Part of the audition package is an understanding that if you pass the audition you also enter into a higher-level contract of commitment. Generally, she does enjoy this level of commitment equally from both girls and boys in the Lindley Choir. Underpinning such a commitment has to be a cohort of parents who choose to prioritise a musical dimension of their child's development. No boys' choir can really function without such parental backing when boys have football, judo, cubs, swimming and potentially numerous other calls on their time. Finding parents who positively want their sons to be musical has to be part of the process of creating and sustaining a boys' choir.

My own take on this is that the case study illustrates clearly the need for as many schools as possible to follow Lindley's lead and recognize that there is a job to do in the remediation of long years of neglect and subscription to the erroneous belief that boys can't and won't sing. This either means single-sex music classes for children as young as seven or eight, or a very capable teacher who understands a lot about singing competency and gender. The latter is probably necessary however things might be organized.

Alison sees her choirs as fundamentally pedagogic, the boys' choir perhaps more so than the Lindley choir. The primary reason for both choirs' existence is, Alison avers, to teach children to sing. However, she adds the important caveat that the choirs exist, not just to teach children to sing, but to do this well. A high standard of performance results from this aim and this serves to remind us that the two ends of the continuum are far from mutually exclusive. It also raises questions about whether pedagogic choirs ought in any case to exist without the aim of doing the job well. One reason Alison gives for not being a performance choir is simply the lack of performance opportunities.

She says this in spite of the boys' invitation to sing at the Rugby League World Cup and Lindley Choir's invitation to sing at the Association of British Choral Directors (ABCD) Convention. One-off invitations as highlights in the year of a pedagogic choir are perhaps different to the regular performance commitment of a cathedral choir.

It soon became clear that two features of Alison's practice were more than anything else responsible for the good choral tone. In my judgement, both boys and girls were using their whole voice, but singing predominantly in the upper register or 'head voice'. There was also an exceptionally high degree of focus and discipline evident. Alison did not confess to any theoretical knowledge of boys' voices during our conversations but the extent of her practical, professional knowledge was considerable. It is this kind of knowledge, after all, that mostly gets results. We actually found little difference between our two approaches. Alison agreed that the children sang predominantly in 'head voice' and that they learned to do so, moreover, by imitation. She described it in these terms:

> Chest voice is a powerful voice we use here in the lower notes. It disappears higher up when it becomes the head. We use head voice more than anything else. That's what we do. I don't use the terms much. I say this is how I want it and I demonstrate.

Alison's ability to demonstrate was clearly extremely high. There was little doubt that these children were learning to sing by imitation. She could produce at the drop of a hat exactly the sound she wanted from the children and they mirrored her every gesture. The sound she produced, as well as being artistic, skilful and highly expressive, could be described as a light, head tone. Of course, once a choir is on the roll, new children are no longer entirely dependent upon the teacher's voice to imitate. They have the older children who surround them. As we have already seen in previous chapters, this method of learning has been part of choral art probably for centuries, including in some or possibly even all of the best choirs.

If there is a long established tradition of choir sound, younger boys will imitate it regardless of the ability of the conductor to model what is wanted. Without a pre-existing choir sound, though, the question of creating the desired tone becomes much harder. I remember from several decades ago, when I first started a boys' choir from scratch, I was quite unable at the time to get any kind of full-bodied sound from my recruits. They had nothing to imitate and I was unable to supply them with a model. Alison was clearly able to do this. Perhaps at this point we need to address the vexed question of male and female adult voices for imitation. There are two schools of thought on this. One maintains that children will automatically transpose an octave up if sung to by an adult male in full voice. According to this view, male conductors should not use falsetto as to do so presents the children with entirely the wrong method of voice production.

The alternative view maintains that children cannot pitch accurately from a voice that is sounding an octave below the target pitch. A woman's voice is therefore to be preferred, even for boys, but a man might also achieve results if he uses falsetto. My own inclination is much to the former view, though limited use of falsetto can sometimes help boys struggling in the earlier stages to grasp the initial pitch. As a more general rule I cannot see how children can learn to sing well by imitating falsetto sounds that may be not at all like the quality of a properly cultivated voice. Children learn by watching as well as listening and may perhaps develop faulty muscle memory by watching a man struggling to produce falsetto. They may even imitate the actual timbre rather than just the pitch. Strangely, I do not know of any yet published research study that has attempted to settle this question, though there is a lively (and inconclusive) debate on ChoralNet (http://www.choralnet.org>). In Chapter 9, where we look at a male conductor, we see an additional perspective. Meanwhile, there is absolutely no evidence that boys in any way suffer from having a woman's voice to imitate. To the contrary, at Lindley it has clearly helped them find a good 'head voice'.

The extent to which all the children at Lindley mirrored Alison's every move is most definitely worthy of comment. Throughout the rehearsal I observed, I noted 100 per cent psychological flow. 'Flow' is a term used in the psychology of music to denote complete absorption in the activity such that no extraneous thoughts intervene. It is very rare to find this in most pedagogical situations. However, the children sang almost continuously throughout the rehearsal and I can only describe a kind of 'soul connection' between singers and conductor. At no time was there a break in flow such as might be occasioned by an exhortation to the children to 'watch'. If there truly was 'flow' it would mean that no non-musical thought entered a child's consciousness to disrupt concentration on the musical task and this appeared to be the case. A metaphor might be a flock of migrating birds that suddenly changes direction all together for no reason apparent to the observer. Although I scanned the choir frequently I noted no occasion on which any child had lost eye contact with the conductor. Alison had only to take a breath and the children would as one mirror her exact manner of doing it.

I doubt very much that this could ever be achieved over the intrusion of a backing track, so I conclude by reiterating the view of Angela Renshaw from section 8.3 . Truly musical, choral results can only be achieved through the direct human input of the conductor and this has to mean having a voice and/or keyboard readily at hand. Backing tracks, of course, have found much use in situations where a generalist primary teacher is unable or unwilling to sing or play to the children, but I see nothing to be gained from their use in choral training. Lindley School Choir demonstrates just what can be achieved by a teacher who can sing confidently to and with the children.

8.5   The Cornwall Boys Choir

However good a school choir might be, it is unavoidable that it is only the children in that school that are able to sing to that standard. Wherever the postcode lottery operates, a child attending a nearby school may be as able and potentially interested in choral singing as members of a choir such as Lindley, yet may never discover or develop that interest. I put this point to Alison. Should there not be a community choir for boys? Her answer was unexpected. Lindley School is the community. She saw no difference between the school, as servant of its local community, and the community itself. How true this is in an age of ideologically promoted parental choice, I am unable to say. It would certainly be true, however, to state that one would not have to travel far to cross the bounds of the Lindley catchment to reach an area where boys have no opportunity for choral singing—at least, not to anything like the standard at Lindley.

There is another even greater drawback to the situation at Lindley, and one which Alison hugely regrets. When the children leave the school, their opportunities for choral singing cease. This is the case for girls as well as boys. At one of the high schools to which the children progress, there is said to be 'no singing at all'. In Chapter 7 on the subject of demographic management, we devoted an entire section to the 9–13 problem. Here we have a perfect example. Alison has some very capable eleven-year-old boy choral singers whose career will be cut short just as they approach the age at which many boys in cathedral style choirs approach their golden year. This illustrates the need for a coordinated approach at something beyond the individual school level, a theme I consider for the remainder of this chapter and much of Chapter 9.

We move then, in this final section, from the private school with its music specialist and the postcode lottery of publicly funded schooling to the tireless efforts of music staff at county or 'hub' level who prioritise the often highly frustrating (but hardly ever thankless) task of running an area boys' choir and persuading schools to publicise this to boys who might benefit. The creation of networks and infrastructures that enable boys from any school to participate in good choral singing cannot, in my view, be underestimated. This takes us back to Cornwall in this chapter, and to Warwickshire in Chapter 9. My main aim is to highlight the kind of networking that goes on.

The county of Cornwall shares with the country of Wales a deserved reputation as a land of song. Male voice singing is very much part of the Cornish musical scene and the Cornwall International Male Voice Choral Festival is well known. There was some embarrassment therefore, in the year 2007, when the festival began to invite foreign choirs. Boys' choirs came from all over Europe, but Cornwall itself had no boys' choir of its own to enter in the festival. Once again, England was shamed as *Das Land ohne Musik* ('the land without music'). A concerted effort was made, therefore, to recruit and develop a boys' choir and the Cornwall Boys Choir came into existence in 2008. This was a county venture through what has subsequently become the Cornwall Music Education Hub and not to be confused with similar initiatives at Truro Cathedral. Cornwall is a large, rural county and positive effort is required to run satellite groups so that Truro does not end up as the only centre of choral work.

The initial vision had been for a four-part young male choir, but the boys' choir emerged as a trebles-only choir for eight-year-olds up to the age of voice change. Catering for older boys evolved as a separate though related enterprise (see Chapter 9). The question therefore immediately arises of the 9–13 problem and with it, children or boys? When I attended a concert by the Cornwall Boys Choir, I was most impressed by one particular soloist whom I estimated as aged about eleven. On congratulating the boy afterwards I discovered that he was thirteen. Taken off-guard somewhat, I offered him the slightly lame comment, 'Oh, well you have a lot of experience behind you then.' This question of identity is not to be dismissed lightly. For boys aged between about eleven and fourteen, there is a clear tension between biological age and social age that needs sensitive understanding, so I mentally admonished myself.

There is also a Cornwall Children's Choir for Year 2 (ages 6–7) up to Year 4 (ages 8–9) as well as the Cambiata choir for boys of secondary school age that we look at in Chapter 9. The Boys Choir itself sits broadly between the two, spanning the crucial 9–13 age group. Boys move on at voice change when they are ready. Some, like the boy above, are keen to stay whilst others would rather move to the Cambiata or perhaps leave altogether. Angela reports that the Cornwall Boys Choir copes well with the vital task of demographic management. There is a healthy turnover of boys moving on and new younger boys joining. The choir's age demographic peaks around a cluster of Year 5, Year 6 and Year 7 (age span 9–12). This is exactly how it should be according to what we know about puberty (see the analysis of the National Boys Choir of Scotland in Chapter 9). A few thirteen- and even fourteen-year-olds who willingly linger on because they have suitably unchanged voices and wish to remain in the choir is fine.

The Cornwall Children's Choir is mixed-gender. The diamond model is therefore followed although, at the time of writing in February 2014, a planned Cornwall Girls Choir has not yet come into existence. Angela gives an interesting explanation of this. She believes that if you start a boys' choir first, the girls will want one and demand equality. If, however, you start with a girls' choir, very few boys will similarly clamour for equal treatment. There probably never will be a boys' choir and you will end up as *Das Land ohne Knaben* ('the land without boys'). Angela and I have arrived at the same conclusion, she through many years of practical experience and I through many years of academic research. Angela reports a growing understanding of this by schools she works with which are now more willing to entertain single-sex provision of singing than was the case when more simplistic views of gender equity were dominant.

The Children's Choir is divided into three geographical regions to cover the whole county and meets weekly for forty-five-minute sessions at mostly school-based locations. It is also 'open access' (i.e. non-auditioned). It was clear to me that Angela has assembled a talented and committed team of teachers who support the work of the choirs through running area satellite groups in their own schools. These teachers can in turn receive professional development and improve their own choral training skills through association with the enterprise. I am convinced of the necessity of doing this. My main point in this final section of this chapter is to present a case study that illustrates how to get round the postcode lottery issue.

The Cornwall Boys Choir similarly functions through a network of area satellite rehearsal venues. Quite often these are schools, but not always. Angela is again supported by a number of committed assistant conductors. Not only does this kind of networking offer opportunities to boys, but of equal importance are the opportunities offered to teachers who may not be able to sustain an entire boys' choir in their own school.

There is not, at the time of writing, any necessary sequence of progression from the children's choir to the boys' choir because all these ventures are relatively new. Boys are recruited to the Cornwall Boys Choir mainly through a combination of school recommendation and audition. The audition Angela describes as 'not hard'. There are some simple pitch-matching tests, tests of the ability to copy a simple phrase and to read words with clarity. Boys are asked to bring a simple prepared piece that they know. There is obviously not a shortage of boys able to meet this standard, though it cannot be stated whether the Cornwall Children's Choir has an impact on this. There is a fine balance to be struck with auditions. On the one hand, boys can be scared off. On the other hand, if the choir has a reputation, preparing for and passing an audition confirms to the boy that he has achieved something worthwhile. Boys, after all, would not expect to be selected for an elite football team without some trial of ability and aptitude.

Angela has found that the most effective method of recruitment is to ask the schools, through the music hub, to advertise the choir to parents. Again, the fact that schools are prepared to give thought to recommending boys for audition is evidence that the choir has had an impact on the schools' consciousness. Schools are usually inundated with requests and cannot respond to all. Angela has therefore succeeded in getting across the twin messages that the choir has a reputation and is worthy of support, and that in any school there will be a few boys who will enjoy choral singing at a level beyond what is likely to be possible in the school. I know of too many other well-intentioned schemes that have failed to overcome this essential hurdle. Perhaps 'passion' is once again playing its part. Teachers are not, in principle, unwilling. They are just so busy that it takes a real enthusiast to overcome the setbacks of poorly attended meetings in the early phases of launching a new venture.

The approach to networking seems to be successful in recruiting the kinds of parent who will commit to the choir because they feel their son enjoys singing and it is something they want him to do. A very high level of practical parental support for the choir was evident, not least through the industrious mass baking of cakes for the boys' 'cake breaks'. Parents who are willing and able to offer transport clearly are an essential ingredient for success in a rural county. None of this is achieved without a considerable infrastructure of administration and support. Nobody will succeed with a boys' choir unless they are prepared to undertake the substantial and ongoing groundwork necessary to sustain the infrastructure.

Finally, Angela is aware of the need to promote the interest of adult males in supporting boys' choral work. I am only just beginning in my research to discover just what a major issue this is. The concert I attended was the culmination of work Angela had been doing to promote the interest and support of the boys' fathers. I sat next to one father who was quite happy supporting his son passively but would not be seen dead singing himself. For the last item, however, it was announced that the dads would join in. The site of the boys gleefully pushing, shoving, dragging and almost having to gang up and carry their reluctant fathers down the aisle was one I shall never forget! The serious point is that if boys are having to act as male role models for their fathers, contemporary choral work with boys has a long way to go in overcoming a longstanding structural problem that has been allowed to develop in male singing.

References

Ashley, M. (2009). *How High Should Boys Sing? Gender, Authenticity and Credibility in the Young Male Voice*. Aldershot, UK: Ashgate.

Cooksey, J. (1999). *Working With Adolescent Voices*. St Louis, MO: Concordia.

Howard, F. (1895). *The Child-Voice in Singing: Treated from a Physiological and a Practical Standpoint and Especially Adapted to Schools and Boy Choirs*. New York, NY: H.W. Gray/Novello.

Rutkowski, J. (1990). The measurement and evaluation of children's singing voice development. *The Quarterly Journal for Music Teaching and Learning*, 1(1–2):81–95. (Reprinted in *Visions of Research in Music Education*, 16(1).)

Welch, G., Himonides, E., Papageorgi, J., Saunders, T., Rinta, C., Stewart, C., Preti, J., Lani, M.V. & Hill, J. (2009a). The National Singing Programme for primary schools in England: an initial baseline study. *Music Education Research*, 11(1):1–22. doi:10.1080/14613800802699523

Welch, G. Papageorgi, I., Vraka, M., Himonides, E. & Saunders, J. (2009b). *The Chorister Outreach Programme: A Research Evaluation 2008–2009*. London: IMERC/ Institute of Education.

Further reading

Mills, J. (2005). *Music in the School*. Oxford: Oxford University Press.

Tagg, B. (2013). *Before the Singing: Structuring Children's Choirs for Success*. New York, NY: Oxford University Press.

Chapter 9: Boys' and youth choirs

In this chapter we look at the post-11 scene. I have used the word 'youth' to distinguish this age range from the under-12s because one isn't going to call a fourteen-year-old and certainly not an eighteen-year-old a 'child'. However, 'youth' may not be ideally the best word and the concept needs some exploration before we look at the choirs. If you talk to boys and young men about identity, you may well find that they do not like to be called 'youths' and may actually have less of a problem with 'boy'. The term 'youth' has a meaning bordering on the pejorative, as in 'gangs of hooded youths'. The UK, in particular, has suffered in recent years from a phenomenon known as ephebiphobia, which roughly translates as the irrational fear or hatred of youth. The less responsible politicians and media have done much to whip up ephebiphobia amongst an ageing population that has forgotten what it is like to be young. Former Prime Minister Tony Blair's term 'feral youth' has become a classic in the sociology of adolescence.

The choral world, however, ploughs on oblivious to such niceties. 'Youth choir' is the accepted term for a high-quality and usually large choral ensemble of young people. Conceptually, youth choirs have tended to follow in the wake of youth orchestras. If opportunities exist for the very best young instrumentalists to come together in an orchestra, why should not similar opportunities exist for the very best singers? Youth orchestras in the UK tend to operate at county level, though there are, of course, National Youth Orchestras in both England and Scotland. England's National Youth Orchestra aims to 'create performances that astound and inspire musicians and audience alike'. It is a platform for the country's most able young instrumentalists that espouses a clear rhetoric of performance, though there is still a pedagogic function in bringing such musicians together to learn how a professional standard orchestra operates. Any possible objections to the term 'youth' are overcome by the prestige afforded by membership. At county level, the standard is still high. Hertfordshire, for example, requires a Grade 8 standard for audition.

The logic, however, does not apply in as straightforward a way to choral work with boys. An important critique published by Graham Welch and John Cooksey (1998) drew attention to the fact that singing development is not linear. As readers of this book should know only too well by now, a boy chorister currently peaks at around the age of twelve or thirteen before retiring into the relative shade for much of the remainder of his adolescence. An auditioned youth choir at its peak consists of mixed-gender SATB voices aged roughly eighteen to twenty-five. The processes leading up to this are not simple progression through grades and the needs of boys and girls before that age are different.

157

As we saw in Chapter 8, boys and girls can sing together as children when voices are more androgynous. The years of puberty, however, enforce a separation, mainly for vocal reasons, but also social. In this chapter, we have moved firmly into the divergent centre of the diamond model (see Chapter 8). You either accept this or have hardly any boys singing. It is as simple as that. Once the traumas and upheavals of early to middle adolescence are past, however, boys and girls can come together in middle to late adolescence when the girls are soprano and alto and the boys are beginning to develop as respectable tenors and basses. Equally, a good number of boys may wish to remain with an all-male group they have come to enjoy, perhaps until university intervenes.

9.1   NYCoS National Boys Choir

I can think of few better case studies than this excellent choir under its inspirational director, Christopher Bell. The NYCoS National Boys Choir is part of the National Youth Choir of Scotland (NYCoS) and sometimes referred to as the National Boys Choir of Scotland. NYCoS illustrates well my opening point. Scotland had a national youth orchestra, but no choir. NYCoS was founded in 1996 with the vision of raising the standard of singing throughout Scotland through an approach grounded in the Kodály system. Then as now, one of the most impressive features of NYCoS is its system of progression from primary school to national choir through a coordinated network of area choirs. Fifteen such area choirs now cover Scotland and the number is rising, particularly of area boys' choirs. Outreach to and support of schools remains the bedrock of the entire pyramid-shaped enterprise. Primary schools occupy the base of the pyramid, area choirs the middle tiers and the national choirs the apex.

The choir therefore is approached through auditions at the end of a road of progression and the entry standard is high. The choir has some control over the quality of applicants through its pyramid structure and I remain convinced that this is a model to be emulated. Experience of developing NYCoS led Christopher Bell to the inevitable conclusion that single-sex work was necessary, for boys at least. In 2002, over 150 boys applied to join the new NYCoS National Boys Choir after NYCoS itself had performed during half time at an England v Scotland rugby international at Murrayfield. As we saw with the Lindley Boys Choir, performance on the rugby pitch can help, but the development of the National Boys Choir owes by far the most to the excellence of the choral work and singing tuition, building upon the success of outreach that identifies and nurtures musical boys.

Christopher did not at first know quite what to expect. He had been a boy chorister himself at St Anne's Cathedral in Belfast. A different path taken by Scotland at the Reformation has led to a less extensive choral tradition than might be found in England, though a number of Scottish establishments do now maintain similar choirs and services to those south of the border. In Belfast, the choir rehearsed three times weekly but sang only on Sundays. Nevertheless, this experience had given Christopher the mental image of the boy chorister sound associated with English cathedrals. It remained to be seen whether this would be the sound to aim for or achieve with a national boys' choir.

The choir that developed consisted of boys of roughly chorister age (i.e. typically in the early stages of puberty at around age eleven, twelve or thirteen), but the tone they were going to produce had yet to be discovered and evolved. The sound emerged from good individual tuition in the use of the whole voice and exacting demands for accuracy in the choral ensemble. The choir does not meet regularly, but comes together principally each Easter for an annual week of intensive tuition, choral rehearsal and recreation, culminating in a grand public concert.

In 2007 a NYCoS National Girls Choir for girls aged thirteen to fifteen was formed. As well as illustrating perfectly the diamond model, this experience of starting with the boys first echoes that of Angela in Cornwall (see Chapter 8). If you start with boys, you will end up with both a successful boys' choir and a successful girls' choir. If you start with girls, you will in all probability only ever have girls.

Inevitably, it was found that the choir could not be confined to the 'in puberty' stage. First a 'Junior Corps' was formed for younger boys with entirely unchanged voices and then a 'Changed Voices' section for young men completing puberty. Confusingly, perhaps, for readers of this book who may have familiarised themselves with the app, the three sections are distinguished by shirt colour. The National Boys Choir itself wears blue shirts, the Junior Corp white shirts and the Changed Voices (thankfully!) black shirts. All three sections meet for an intensive residential week around Easter, following their own separate courses and repertoire but also coming together to rehearse pieces to be sung by the entire ensemble in the concert. This is also a model that has much to commend it.

I have been a guest twice now at the Easter course, the facility to observe rehearsals and interview boys and staff having contributed much to the writing of this book. During one of these visits, the boys were added to the 1000 voices database. I recorded each individually for later analysis with the following result. The mean age of the 'white shirts' was 10.2 years. Their mean SF_0 was not assessed. The mean age of the 'blue shirts' was 12.3 years with a mean SF_0 of 206.4 Hz (range: 253–184 Hz, SD 38.2 Hz). The mean age of the 'black shirts' was 13.9 years with a mean SF_0 of 140.8 Hz (range: 215–99 Hz,

SD 22.9). This is shown in Figure 3, which makes an interesting comparison with the English cathedral choristers shown in Chapter 4.

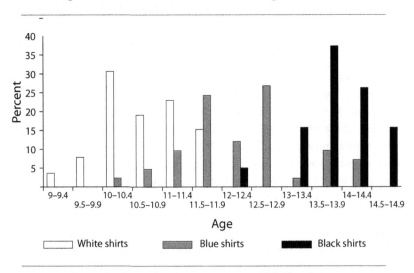

Figure 3. Distribution of boys by age across sections of NYCoS Boys Choirs. .

The overall pattern of pubertal stage is similar to that found in the English cathedrals. There are no unchanged trebles beyond the age of 11.9. The youngest boys with changing voices appear in the 10–11 age group, whilst the 12.5–12.9 age group comprises entirely in-puberty changing voices and represents the age of mutational climax. The first fully changed voices appear in the 12–12.4 age group, which is consistent with the position that Year 8 (12.5–13.5) boys in cathedral choirs may have to leave the treble section. The age of fourteen, or a boy's fifteenth year of life, is now the time at which all boys reach the completing puberty stage. At the beginning of the boys' fifteenth year of life, about one quarter had yet to reach this stage. By the end of the year, all had reached it.

9.2 Cambiata choirs

Choirs specifically for changing voices run along principles such as the Cambiata scheme are not common in Europe. We may possibly be on the cusp of a slow change with regard to this. The National Youth Choirs of Great Britain (NYCGB) now have a well-developed four-part choir for changing voices that is called 'cambiata'. A principal motive for this is an increased concern with vocal health and the need to 'do the right thing' for in-puberty boys. The NYCGB cambiata section is an auditioned choir. Boys first have to audition for NYCGB itself. On arrival at a residential course they will be seen again by a vocal coach and may find themselves in the treble choir as they perhaps expected, or placed in the cambiata choir if it is judged that this is best for their stage of vocal development. However, boys who have sung cambiata for NYCGB not uncommonly re-join the treble sections of their regular choirs on returning in September. Understandably this sometimes causes confusion and occasionally a degree of ill-feeling. It remains to be seen whether similar practice might spread. It seems unlikely to me. 'School C' is too well-embedded in the English psyche and the Cambiata scheme was not in any case designed for the kinds of choir that would be recognised as performance choirs in this book.

I am going to focus then on two choirs that follow Cooper's actual principles for cambiata. These are choirs whose principal aims are to maintain and develop the interest in choral work of boys who might otherwise drift away during puberty. We are not talking about boys who will shed tears if they can no longer sing the high treble of an eight-part renaissance mass. As we saw in Chapter 5, Cooper's cambiata principles were designed specifically with the pedagogical aim of keeping junior high school boys singing during the music class. Cambiata belongs to 'School A', the belief that boys sing in a contracted range that descends in predictable steps during puberty. Boys need to be heard in order to ensure that they are allocated to the right section of the choir, but not as a means of regulating entry to the choir. I would not, therefore, use the word 'audition'. The emphasis is on securing the newly emergent modal voice and avoiding difficulties associated with passagio to unstable regions of the range. This approach is well-suited to boys who may have come through a primary education where the 'head voice' was never developed, who have sung only repertoire pitched too low to develop good choral tone, and probably too loudly. For boys such as this, cambiata can offer a new start in singing at age eleven.

Our first choir is called Cambiata North West and is run by the ABCD North West region. The remit of ABCD is principally the training and development of conductors and Cambiata North West exists very much with this in mind. Its outreach is principally to teachers working in secondary schools who are concerned to be skilled and successful at keeping boys singing across the crucially difficult eleven to fourteen years. Through this, of course, good singing opportunities for boys are created. As with the National Boys Choir of Scotland, however, a certain degree of evolution has been involved in the development of the choir.

It is currently a four-part choir of some 80–100 or so voices ranging in age from ten to sixteen or seventeen. Though following Cooper's main tenets, it has been organised loosely on Barham and Nelson's suggested ranges for

Treble, Cambiata I, Cambiata II and Baritone (see Chapter 7). The name of the choir was suggested by some of the boys. Much effort in the early stages was expended on trying to dream up a 'cool' name that avoided the risky terms of 'choir' and 'youth'. The boys were disarmingly pragmatic and suggested it be called exactly what it is. A Cambiata choir in the north-west! It really does not work when adults try to be 'cool'!

ABCD's North West region had already been running an 'honour choir' for what I have described in this book as 'children'. Much in the way predicted, boys in the North West Honour Choir faced an uncertain choral future on becoming young adolescents. Gill Fourie, an enthusiastic supporter of the Honour Choir, could see the impending need for an initiative to keep boys singing. She arranged two training days on voice change and cambiata for local teachers and conductors. These were attended by a number of teachers working in the region who could see the sense of the training and shared Gill's strong commitment to choral work with boys. What evolved was something rather different and considerably larger than an upward extension for adolescent boys formerly belonging to the Honour Choir. Several of the teachers who attended the original training were committed members of the ABCD and applied themselves to the task of creating cambiata singing groups in their schools. This is probably the key to the success of CNW. It is truly a pedagogical movement, for the boys of course, but equally for their teachers and the growing range of young conductors encouraged by ABCD to learn more about how to manage boys during voice change.

The movement has grown into a successful regional network covering the north-west of England and including, at the time of writing, a school from Northern Ireland. The pattern established is that of three annual workshops spaced six to eight weeks apart and culminating in a public concert on the evening of the final workshop day. In theory at least, the boys learn and practice the repertoire selected for the concert at school, whilst also rehearsing cambiata pieces of their own. The concert each year consists of six to eight items sung by the whole choir, supplemented by performances by some of the individual school cambiata groups and instrumental items by some of the boys.

The result of this approach is that the whole 'choir' only exists three times a year. It is clearly impossible to develop the kinds of relationship or disciplined singing that would be found in a choir meeting at least weekly. The same would be true, of course, for the National Boys Choir of Scotland. In both cases, the quality that is possible when the boys all come together is dependent upon the work in the area choirs in the case of NBCS or the school cambiata groups in the case of Cambiata North West. Gill is very clear that a non-auditioned choir should not be an excuse for poor quality voicing or sloppy musicianship. Indeed it is Gill to whom I am in debt for the term 'just singing'.

Gill defines choral partly by repertoire, which she thinks should be wider-ranging that that attempted by the choir during the year she was interviewed for this book. She is not sure that CNW can truly be called choral because its repertoire has been 'too "poppy"'. She believes that too much 'poppy' material deprives a choir of cohesive substance to work on for vowels. I would have to agree with her on this issue, given the number of times I have stressed the importance of meticulous vowel work for the development of good choral tone. Of course, a pedagogical choir that has its foundations in secondary schools is going to be very much concerned with what is 'cool' and what boys who were not socialized into Palestrina at the age of nine will sing. Cambiata North West has, during its history, performed a reasonably eclectic repertoire, introducing boys to noble melodies such as Sibelius' Finlandia as well as film music and folk music. Karl Jenkins' *Songs of Sanctuary* (Adiemus) worked particularly well for the cambiata voices.

Gill regards the choir as definitely and entirely pedagogical. She goes as far as saying it has no performance element, her justification (in response to my definitions) being that everybody in the audience is a parent, relative or friend of a choir member. She points out, though, that the choir's evolution is taking it more towards being a community choir. The membership has become evenly balanced between boys who are members of school cambiata groups and boys who have started coming on their own without such nurture or support. Gill stresses the role of the choir in providing a safe haven for boys who would otherwise give up singing because of peer pressure.

She feels that the Sing Up national programme for primary schools did some good in that parents could see benefits. This impacts on parents' perceptions as they realize that when their son moves up to secondary school, 'nothing will happen'. This raised expectation in parents was a strength of Sing Up, but of course the fact that the programme never addressed secondary schools in a serious way was also a significant weakness. Arguably the need in secondary schools is and always was greater than in the primary schools. Continuity is certainly vital. Year 6 boys (the final year of English primary school, age eleven) are important to Gill. Any boys' choir, as I argued in Chapter 5 on demographic management, needs constantly to be fed with younger boys. Members of Cambiata North West have 'voted with their feet' by staying on, so the baritone section has grown. To retain its four-part character, the choir can therefore only be in a state of growth, which is probably a good problem to have!

The large majority of Year 6 will be unchanged voices or trebles in early change, capable of either a treble or a Cambiata I part. This fuels an ongoing debate in Cambiata North West. My own view, as I set out in Chapter 9 , is that trebles can spoil the cambiata sound or deprive cambiata boys of singing the top line. However, this is probably trumped by the immediate practical need simply to ensure that Year 6 boys are not lost to singing as so often happens without strong musical leadership in primary schools. The choir caters for a good number of boys who have never developed a 'head voice'. Gill feels that if she were the conductor, she'd perhaps do things differently. She would, she says, choose different repertoire, repertoire that would make them go into 'head voice'. However, she concedes that because they are a large group, there probably isn't the time. There are other priorities to focus on in moving the boys from 'just singing' to choral work. These include, in Gill's view, posture, support, breathing, diction and a disciplined approach. She repeats the need for a repertoire that challenges, stating that 'it needs to be a harder repertoire for it to be choral'. Perhaps the point at this juncture is that there is a limit to the extent to which any boys' choir can lie at one or other extreme of the pedagogy–performance continuum. There is a fine line, Gill states, to be trod with regard to discipline. The choir is not school. Boys do not have to come. On the other hand, a sympathetic audience of parents and friends only is not going to provide the kind of challenge that performance to a 'real' audience would do.

By way of contrast over 300 miles (and a very long train journey) to the South West is to be found Cambiata Cornwall: The Emerging Voice. This initiative is funded by the Cornish arts organisation FEAST and operates as part of the Cornwall Education music hub. It is very much the brainchild of Angela Renshaw, whom we met in Chapter 8 as vocal strategy lead and inspiration behind the Cornwall County Boys Choir. Cambiata Cornwall: The Emerging Voice has similarities with Cambiata North West. It is based on Irvin Cooper's principles and also strongly linked to a network of secondary schools, serving a pedagogical function for boys and teachers. There are also important differences, not the least being an orientation to performance not (at the time of writing) found in the north-west.

Angela cites an 'ace card' that was laid early on in the history of the choir. This was a chance opportunity to substitute for another choir and sing at the Royal Albert Hall. Both the Cornwall Boys Choir and the Cambiata performed together at this event. Another lucky break came not long afterwards with the opening of the Heartlands Innovation Centre in Cornwall. This received high-level royal endorsement because the event was attended by Prince Charles and his wife in their capacity as Duke and Duchess of Cornwall. Both were said to be most impressed with the choir's singing.

Angela describes events such as these as the 'total reason for those boys to sing'. She feels that there is a difference working with boys in this respect.

They respond well to targets that are challenging, short-term and achievable. Boys in a choir need to and do have a lot of fun, but when the chips are down, Angela says, they work hard. The Cambiata has become a 'beast of its own' since those early breaks, but Angela is never short of ideas to maintain the boys' enthusiasm and the choir's profile. In Angela's experience, a steady supply of events to work for is necessary to prevent boys drifting away with a 'what's the point?' attitude. One that particularly caught my attention was Boys on a Bus. One hundred boys on two buses travelled the length of the county disembarking in most of the major towns to give impromptu performances in the street. It was, says Angela:

> an amazing event and one of the best I've ever done. Complete stran-
> gers gathered round and wanted to offer them money. Men in the street
> joined in and there was an instant, magic camaraderie. On returning to
> Truro, they were completely surrounded.

Angela thus sees a significant performance element to the choir's work. Having high-profile events to work for motivates the boys to accept the discipline necessary for something more than 'just singing'. Providing an ongoing programme of such events, however, demands a large amount of energy as well as imagination. There are also questions about the extent to which competitive festivals might be part of a boys' choir diary, given that it is not uncommon to have only one entry in the boys' section. The choir is not then competing like for like and may be disadvantaged if the cambiata voice is unfamiliar to the judges, as is often the case.

In spite of this, Angela's perception is that, more than the Cornwall Boys Choir, the Cambiata attracts quite a few unknown people to the audience. She reports that there seems to be a genuine interest in discovering what changing-voice boys sound like, and a reservoir of public good will to the enterprise. As I have suggested many times, people like to hear boys sing. It is a reassuring aspect of young masculinity. According to Angela, 'You get the feeling that the audience want it, that they feel it's filling something missing.' Cornwall is a musical county with a stronger tradition of male singing than most, but it has still been my own experience that a boys' choir can make people sit up and take note, wherever it may be.

Like its counterpart in the north-west, this choir sings in three parts—Cambiata I, Cambiata II and Baritone. There are no trebles. The Cambiata and the Boys Choir can and do join together if a full four-part ensemble is required. Angela feels that three part arrangements work the best for boys with changing voices. The Cambiata I therefore sing the top line. In terms of tone production, Angela agreed that my analogy of the violas on the top line in Bach's Brandenburg 6 was a 'nice way of putting it'. The tone, though

still that of boys' 'unbroken' voices, is mellow and lacks the shrill sound of trebles. Much as the died-in-the-wool choral enthusiast delights to the ringing
sound of high treble voices, we need to appreciate that many young people
find this distinctly off-putting. This applies at least as much to girls as to boys.
Here is the reason given by a focus group of Year 7 (twelve-year-old) girls for
not liking choir: 'It's too high-pitched. It gives you a headache.'

It is a point to bear in mind! If a good, mellow 'viola-like' sound is to be
produced by cambiata boys, I cannot stress too strongly the need for discipline in the creation of arrangements. The arranger has a safe tessitura of only
a sixth to play with and ignores this at his or her peril. You cannot just take a
song you like and pitch it at roughly the right starting point for the voice part.
There is a great deal more to arranging for cambiata than mere transposition.
A classic example of how not to do it can be found in the song 'You Raise Me
Up'. I have in my library a dreadful recording of this and I will spare embarrassment or the end of a good friendship by giving any clues as to where it
was made. Suffice to say, the boys are cambiati. They start off well with, if you
like, a good 'viola' tone. The key is B flat major, so the starting note is F_3. 'Each
restless heart' reaches F_4, and begins to sound strained with loss of intonation
accuracy because the boys have exceeded their safe tessitura and do not know
how to manage registration. 'But when you come' which takes the song to
its full range of a twelfth brings tears to my eyes for quite the wrong reason.

Angela believes that a good choral sound is one that is consistent and
uniform in any style of song. In choral work, unanimity of vowel production
and tuning is essential in any genre, not just 'classical'. I asked whether pop
songs could make good choral arrangements. Angela felt that some could and
cited a mash-up mix of different riffs by the National Youth Choirs of Great
Britain. The exuberant and youthful style of this singing is not dissimilar to
the performance given by the Boys Choir and Cambiata at the Albert Hall.
Angela's view is one I entirely concur with.

I asked Angela to suggest the three most important elements of making
Cambiata a success. She had no hesitation in placing repertoire at the top of
her list. This was for three reasons. The first was the technical one of choosing
arrangements that the boys will sing well because mistakes such as putting
choice of favourite song above tessitura location are not made. The second
was the pedagogical one of opening boys' minds to other challenges than an
endless diet of rehashed pop. The third, closely related to this, was the need
to create a good balanced concert programme. This was clearly important to
Angela. Part of her definition of good choral sound included something that
feels right for the audience and draws them in. She suggested the following
as a good balance for her Albert Hall programme:

- A ballad
- A mash-up
- Some traditional Cornish songs
- A formal hymn-like song with organ accompaniment to finish on.

The second and third elements on Angela's list were the way rehearsals are conducted and looking after the boys. Angela described her rehearsals as 'not over-familiar, quite regimented'. I think we can be clear that boys like fun, but they also appreciate a professional approach to the job in hand. They also like a brisk, purposeful pace. Angela described the importance of not letting things drift, either in the short-term of an individual rehearsal or over the long-term of a whole series of sessions. It is very necessary to maintain energy with a clear focus and end game when working with boys of this age. When first asked to nominate her top three elements, Angela instinctively said 'cake' as the second and then told me not to write that down. I have ignored this instruction, though, because I invariably advise schools that want to attract boys to singing to give them cake! Angela's more considered reaction was that building relationships with boys through good teaching skills and genuinely looking after them actually came equal top with repertoire. There is thus clear endorsement here of my own position on the primacy of relationships (see Chapter 6). The 'cake break', during which the boys consume the considerable volume of cake baked for them by their parents, is a way of caring about the boys, and a seriously and genuinely necessary one in my view.

9.3   Warwickshire Choristers

I have chosen the Warwickshire Choristers, under their director Garry Jones, as the final case study in this chapter for a variety of reasons other than their undoubted excellence. They are an example of a secular boys' choir situated comfortably toward the performance end of the continuum. It is a choir that meets regularly and exists entirely in its own right, rather than as the result of gathering together school or area choirs for a course week or singing day. It answers questions of the pedagogy or performance 'why do we do it?' type. It successfully manages the changing voice without recourse to a system such as cambiata. It raises interesting questions about performance and music festivals. Finally, it illustrates in the best possible way all that I have said about relationships.

There are actually three choirs within the organization. Boys begin as County Boys and are expected to progress towards membership of the County Choristers. County Choristers and County Boys sing together for at least three major concerts a year, at which they are advertised as the full County Boys Choir. Then there is the County Male Voices, for young men with changed voices. The County Male Voices do not exist, as I erroneously but understandably imagined, because the need arose to have somewhere for ex-choristers to go. They exist because, Garry says, 'I thought they ought to'. He is clearly fiercely proud of them, and with every justification. About eighty per cent of them are ex-County Choristers, nevertheless. There are over eighty singers in the County Choristers and over fifty in the County Male Voices and very high standards are achieved. The Choristers have appeared in the final of 'Choir of the Year' and sing in up to four parts. Both groups have regularly appeared and won awards in the Music for Youth National Festival, and both have achieved awards at the Cornwall International Male Voice Festival.

Garry is not convinced of the need for something like cambiata. He suspects that if this had been offered to ex-choristers, they might have left. His reasoning is that the Male Voices 'have learned the ethos of singing and performance'. They do not, in other words, have to be gently enticed by promises that they won't be embarrassed by cracking voices or have to sing like girls. They are young men who know and value what they are doing and for whom being in a performing choir is second nature. Garry made an interesting comment about relationships that have developed between the boys. 'The precious have ceased to be precious and the brutal have ceased to be brutal.' This is a positive result of regular meeting. Young people discover what choir membership means socially and are moulded by their experience. This is unlikely to happen in choirs that come together only occasionally and do not progress beyond the 'honeymoon stage' of relationships.

The Warwickshire choirs developed out of Garry's former experience as County Music Inspector. He also directed the County Youth Chorale and realised the need for a much more strategic approach to the development of boys' and young men's voices. Recruitment to the Choristers is through a letter to the primary schools pointing out that the time for voice trials to join the famous county choir has come round again. The letter asks schools to select boys they think would benefit and stresses that there is no audition. The voice trials are simply to gauge the boy's experience and indicate his development needs and initial place in the choir. The choir's logo is used and Garry was clear, in response to my asking, that promoting the choir's reputation and status is a significant factor. Without this, he speculates, the response would be weaker. If a school does not respond, a follow-up letter is sent to the headteacher, pointing out that the school is one of those that do not have a boy in the choir. This often does the trick. With music services in Warwickshire and elsewhere becoming less linked to Local Authorities and with the promotion of Creative Hubs, Garry believes that an increasing variety of effective promotional strategies of this kind needs to be developed in order to ensure that the opportunity to sing is offered to as many boys as possible, whatever their background.

The experience underlines the point I made in Chapter 6. The reputation and status of a choir is important if boys are to be persuaded to make it an activity of choice. Concerning my other key issue of synchronising singing and sport, Garry has a canny solution. There are two rehearsals of the choir per week, one in the centre of the county and the other in the north (or three in the case of the Male Voices). Boys normally attend the one nearer to their homes, but can and do attend the other one if they have to miss the one at their normal venue, as often as not for a sports fixture. The whole choir meets roughly twice a term in a central place and this will be at a weekend. Give and take here pays dividends. Boys can sometimes turn up some way into the rehearsal muddy and dressed in sports kit. If they ask to miss a rehearsal altogether for a match, Garry may say no, unless they score a goal or a try! This mutual understanding cements the boys' loyalty and evidences my suggestion that boys will be prepared to miss sport for choir if there is give and take on both sides and the choir clearly has a priority concert coming up.

At the beginning stage, Garry does not like the term 'training choir'. Hence the term 'County Boys' is used in preference. Nevertheless, there is a need for boys to progress through a series of standards before they are ready to cope with life in the County Choristers. They do this at their own pace when they are ready. A boy will need, for example, to be able to pick out one note from a chord of three to cope with life as a County Chorister. Garry sees this as an event in an individual's progress, not a hurdle to overcome. He achieves all that he does without the obstacle of an audition. 'I do not and will not have auditions,' he says. 'I don't see the necessity for it when kids are growing.' Boys are heard individually because of the need to know them, not because of an obsession to test them for testing's sake.

Here, the inevitable pedagogical and pastoral dimensions of work in a successful boys' performing choir shines through. Midway through our interview, Garry's mobile phone pinged and he excused himself to look briefly at it. It was a text to inform him that one of his choristers had just won a National Under-12 kayak championship. The boy will 'get applause at the next choir rehearsal'. The fact that the boys' parents would want to text Garry about this success speaks volumes about the quality of relationships. This is a choir that exists, not to serve its conductor's vanity (see Chapter 6), but quite genuinely for the musical life and personal welfare of every boy that belongs.

Garry's own past experience includes a time as a counter-tenor choral scholar. He finds this helpful in developing the boys' abilities. I put to him the experience of Alison North (see Chapter 8) who had found that, without the opportunity to teach almost at remedial level basic pitch-matching skills in a non-auditioned boys choir, far fewer boys than girls met the standards for her auditioned choir. I was keen to discover his views on why boys appear to be deficient in the rate of musical learning relative to girls. Did he feel that he needed to undertake work to remedy shortcomings in primary music education before boys were able to begin choral work?

Garry was not sure that he agreed with my point about pitch-matching. He agreed that something like fifty per cent of boys that come to him cannot pitch match to the piano. However, they are more likely to pitch match to his voice. If they struggle with matching just a single note, Garry sings a tune to them and in most cases they have the pitch a few moments later. Garry finds it more effective to sing at boy pitch through his counter-tenor voice and believes that boys find it easier to pitch to this than his tenor or bass voice an octave lower. This, of course, remains an ongoing controversy. My own view has been that children (boys and girls) automatically transpose up an octave and that what matters more is the demonstration of a good singing voice. We were able to agree that a good tenor or bass voice is probably a lesser evil than singing to boys in falsetto if one is not a trained counter-tenor. As far as I know, this is a topic that is ripe for research (see also the views of David Flood in Chapter 10).

Garry is clear that a successful boys' choir is one that is unapologetic for its belief that boys can enjoy choral work for its own sake and will value music making intrinsically. During our interview, we exchanged 'epiphany moments'. As I have related elsewhere, my own epiphany moment occurred during my ethnographic study of the choir of St Mary Redcliffe, Bristol, back in 2000. I discovered that I had been wrong for many years in thinking that swimming trips, camping trips, bowling trips, football games and pizza feasts come before the music in the life of a boys' choir. Boys are committed to good choirs, I discovered, because they 'love' the music and choral singing. Garry's equivalent experience was of a project called Action Aloud, and then his experiences in the early stages of establishing the Warwickshire Choristers.

In his inspector's position he had understandably sought to make things attractive to boys. With County Music Service funding he established a project based on the aloud/allowed pun. Fifty boys were taken on adventure activities such as kayaking and climbing, and were introduced to some choral work at the same time. Action Aloud lasted about eighteen months but eventually foundered because its foundations were what Garry now describes as a 'gimmick'. 'If you believe that singing is for boys,' he says, 'then it is singing you must do. They will soon see through any subterfuge.'

Garry was right, though, to recognize that boys need a challenge. On his retirement, with a grant from Youth Music, he set up a singing day for interested boys and from this created a group more focused on achievement in singing as an end result in itself. The singing challenge came unexpectedly early in this process through a personal acquaintance with Edward Higginbottom, director of Oxford's world-class New College Choir. 'Why don't you bring some of the boys to sing evensong with us?' Garry was initially awed by the idea, but eventually chose twenty boys from his new group purely by the criterion of age as a surrogate for experience. He seated them round the piano to go through the Walmisley in D minor canticles and Panis Angelicus. He reported 'two long hours of bliss'. 'I'm good at this,' he thought to himself. 'I know how to get top notes, and I know what to say to them.' The boys were good at it too. Children do not have the prejudice about 'cool' that is so often ascribed to them by adults who are convinced they will only like 'pop'. If you 'know what to say to them' and 'know how to get top notes', they will, as I have stated on numerous occasions, sing anything, eventually coming to disdain what they call 'cheesy' music.

The repertoire of both choirs is eclectic and Garry spends many hours searching for new pieces that he hopes the boys will enjoy. He speaks repeatedly of the Spooky Men's Chorale as inspirational (see <http://www.spookymen.com>). It is never easy to predict what will be a hit with the boys, but to confine their repertoire to 'pop' or show music as is so often done is clearly wrong. The Choristers particularly enjoyed Britten's Corpus Christi carol for example. Garry played me a video of the Male Voices performing Pitoni's well-known motet *Cantate Domino*. This was simply stunning in its accuracy, energy and the enthusiasm and commitment of the young men.

The all-important approach to puberty and voice change is one that greatly interests me. Garry is not precious about fitting voices to stages that require special parts. The pre-mutational boys sing in three or more parts much in the Germanic tradition of SSA . Perhaps it is my prejudice but I feel that there should be more of this in the UK, which I sometimes think has hang-ups over boys singing only the top line whilst adults sing the other parts. As with Westminster Cathedral choir (see Chapter 10), boys can sing first or second treble or alto, through Garry tends to use the term 'third treble' in preference to alto. He described an eight-year-old with a naturally low voice who has learned to sing third. He is careful to say 'sing third, it's the best part!' as boys might otherwise assume that, as in sport, the third team is somewhat inferior to the first team. More frequently, however, it is not unnaturally the older boys who are to be found in the seconds and thirds. Garry describes a 'lovely rich bottom tone' and I know exactly what he means. These are boys using their whole voices, not just the emasculated upper portion above D_4 as in the School C approach.

Garry recognizes voice change as the time when boys cease to be able to control this whole voice comfortably. It is time then for them to be offered the opportunity to join County Male Voices. The majority are keen for this to happen and see it as a desired increase in social status. I find myself much in agreement with Garry's point that older boys need the same voice care as younger ones. He listens carefully to individuals in the Male Voices and a new entrant may well be put on the top tenor part where he can readily be heard. This is, perhaps, another version of alto-tenor. The change between third treble in the County Boys and first tenor in the County Male Voices is a subtle one that can bridge the gap and cater for the alto-tenor stage.

Can Garry's instinctive 'know what to say to them' be taught? Garry, like Alison in Chapter 8, thinks this is not easy. Certain technical and musical aspects can of course be taught. Observing others at work can pick up metaphors that work with boys. Ultimately, though, it is difficult to avoid the conclusion that there is a magic ingredient somewhere. This can be recognized. He agrees that empathy is important in choral work with boys and feels that this quality can be recognized in the way people talk to boys. Are they able to pitch their speech at the right level without condescension? The recruitment and development of future conductors who will be able to continue work such as Garry's therefore requires an alertness to recognizing the necessary qualities in young musicians and refining them. It requires an opportunity for boys to develop the instinct from an early age. Work to provide boys with this opportunity is vital if choral work is to survive and prosper.

References

Cooksey, J. & Welch, G. (1998) Adolescence, singing development and national curricula design. *British Journal of Music Education*, 15(1):99–119. doi:10.1017/S026505170000379X

Chapter 10: Choirs of boys and men

It will be clear from any study of the preceding nine chapters that choral work with boys revolves around the treble voice. I have covered other voice parts sung by 'young men', but pride of place has gone to the treble voice because it is in that voice that boys make their unique contribution to choral work. To make sense of this, I have described and analysed choirs along a pedagogy to performance continuum. Any boys' choir is to an extent pedagogical because its members, by virtue of their status as children or school students, are learning about choral singing. Some boys' choirs, however, fully satisfy my definition of performance choirs in that a potentially large, anonymous audience will pay to hear them sing. This is not because they are parents and friends, but because highly trained boys' treble voices are a recognised musical resource.

Perhaps the clinching argument is that there are choirs where boy trebles sing with professional adult men singers, the boys supplying the treble line, the men the other parts. This phenomenon is almost unique. I can think of few other instances apart from perhaps the acting profession where children perform alongside adults to the same professional standard. Even that falls short of choral work, however, because child actors play the parts of children. The treble lines in our best professional choirs are not there because it is desired to portray children. They are there largely on their own merit and through their own intrinsic musical value.

The context in which this happens is also all but unique. It is confined to England and those few places in the world where the 'English choral tradition' is emulated. I can think of few main situations other than the cathedrals and collegiate chapels of England where such choirs of boys and men exist. There are, of course, some excellent choirs in Germany where boys have to prepare music for church services to exacting standards that can be called professional, but these differ significantly in that professional adults are seldom employed and older boys or 'young men' sing the alto, tenor and bass parts.

I cannot and do not intend to give a complete account of the English cathedral choir in one chapter. Other books, particularly the excellent and painstakingly researched history by Alan Mould (2007), satisfy that need. My own contribution to knowledge about this topic has been to understand better the relationship between choral work with young males and puberty, including changes in the timing of puberty. Closely allied to this endeavour is the desire to address properly boys' welfare and vocal health. Attitudes to such matters have changed enormously in recent times. I hope I have established in earlier chapters that, though there probably is a small secular trend to earlier puberty in boys, it is changes in welfare, vocal health and cultural taste that have the larger part to play in what makes contemporary choral work with boys contemporary.

I wish, therefore, to conclude my survey of contemporary choral work with a look at the way boys are taught to perform alongside professional adult male singers and the particular demands this makes upon them intellectually and vocally. This will include the impact of possible changes in the timing of puberty on the actual sound of the professional boys' choir, and on the treatment of the boys themselves. This chapter is informed by the research I am currently undertaking. I hope what I have to say may be of value to the teachers and conductors of such choirs. However, one very important role that is played by any professional performing organisation is to set the standards of aspiration for amateur organisations operating in the same field. In the first main section of this chapter, therefore, I intend to address a few remarks in the direction of amateur choirs of boys and men.

10.1   Professional and amateur choirs

The professional status of the English-style cathedral or collegiate chapel choir derives from what is sometimes referred to as the *opus dei*. This literally means 'work of God' and refers to the requirement to maintain the daily 'offices' or ordered round of services. Any parish priest will say these at least twice daily, usually on his or her own. This is part of the 'job description'—some would say the most important part. It is therefore in that sense professional work. Prior to the reformation it was thought fit to embellish the daily offices with elaborate music and professional singers, or lay clerks, were employed to assist the ordained clerks in the *opus dei*. Boys were employed to sing the highest parts, as well as to perform various rounds of menial duties necessary to the functioning of the establishments.

For reasons too complex to elaborate here, this tradition adapted to and survived the reformation in England and recovered at the restoration of the monarchy after a brief (though violent and destructive) loss during Oliver Cromwell's short-lived Commonwealth after the English civil war. It continues today and it is necessary, in the context of pedagogy and performance, to understand that this is why an English cathedral choir is 'professional'. It is not professional in the same way as a touring concert choir that broadcasts, records and performs at prestigious concert halls. Some cathedral and collegiate choirs do of course tour and record and the distinction has become increasingly blurred, but this is not their reason for being. It is not necessary for a large, or indeed any, congregation to be present at cathedral evensong for the *opus dei* to take place.

The work of teachers in schools who direct pedagogical choirs is also professional. It is not strictly necessary for school students to perform to audiences in order for this professional teaching and learning work to take place. Of course, an appreciative audience of parents, friends and supporters of the school gives the young people something to work for and makes the learning of choral singing rather different to the learning of mathematics or geography. Boy choristers in cathedrals will also sing to appreciative family members as well as the *opus dei* and the anonymous worshippers and music-lovers who have come to hear them. No categorisation is watertight and neither would we want to make it so. It is as important for boy choristers as any other children to be loved and appreciated by their families.

Outside these two clear definitions of professionalism, however, fall the truly amateur choirs. The word 'amateur' sometimes has a pejorative meaning, but to do something for love has also been regarded as a higher calling than to do it for financial reward. Amateur choirs do not have to be 'amateurish' in the derogatory sense and some are indeed excellent. However, the only amateur choirs of boys and men known to me are those that exist in parish churches and here I do think there is a problem. There was a time when such choirs regularly provided good choral singing opportunities for many boys who, for whatever reason, would never have become cathedral choristers. Parish choirs have declined catastrophically, both in overall numbers and in numbers of singers per choir. Whilst there are still some very good ones, others struggle at the threshold of viability and this is not a healthy situation for their young members.

An organisation calling itself Treble Line was set up quite recently with the intention of supporting the few choirs that remained. Treble Line carried out a thorough and professionally executed survey that makes depressing reading for any supporter of the parish church men and boys choir. According to this survey, 'about sixty such choirs are thought to remain in the UK, perhaps only a quarter of the numbers in the early 1980s.' The survey used as its baseline a survey conducted by the Royal School of Church Music in 1992, which identified 144 such choirs. Averaged over the twenty years between 1992 and 2012, this represents a loss of 4.2 choirs per year, clearly an unsustainable haemorrhage. Perhaps the decline will slow down and find a natural new level, but if the median choir membership is seventeen boys (as quoted by the survey) the total estimate of just over 1000 boys makes it difficult to believe that the amateur parish choir constitutes any real part of the future of choral work with boys.

Many reasons are, of course, given for this. Prominent amongst these are the decline in church attendance and religious commitment generally, the ageing of church congregations, split families, unwillingness of primary schools to support choirs that do not offer equality of opportunity for girls (rightly so!), increased leisure opportunities, 'uncool', adverse publicity about paedophilia and, of course, competition from Sunday sport. At least some of these problems also beset secular choirs, though the relative inability of church choirs to reach compromises over the timing of sport and singing is a particular handicap. However, I think all these miss what I have come to believe is the real point. This is that in all but a few exceptional parishes the Church of England no longer wants parish choirs of men and boys performing choral music.

Such choirs cling on in the few parishes that see value in cathedral-like services characterised by a non-participatory role for the congregation in most of the music. This is fine if it is what is genuinely wanted and supported by the congregation and clergy. Where the only people who see the value in choral singing are the choir themselves, trouble is usually not far round the corner. Some honest reflection on the nature of amateur singing is perhaps called for. Amateur choirs exist at least in part because their members enjoy participating in choral singing as a hobby. If the quality level obtained is somewhat less than that set by the professional choirs, it is fine for the choir to sing for its own purposes, but to inflict it weekly on a congregation that would rather explore other more participatory ways of worship can be perhaps the root cause of much ill-feeling.

This has certainly been the clinching factor in almost all choir extinctions that I have witnessed, including two in the last year alone. The choir is simply told that its services are no longer required. I have seen first-hand the considerable and heartfelt upset caused when boys who really cannot be expected to understand church politics, but who have given loyal service, are suddenly 'sacked'. It really is important that planning and forethought goes into the avoidance of such situations. Perhaps if there is doubt about boys' continuity of service an adult choir that can sing the occasional full choral evensong is the better option. Amateur choirs also need to reflect on the pedagogical dimension of their work. I have seen recruiting leaflets that make bold claims about this, but the rhetoric is less often matched by the reality.

Wherever circumstances do remain favourable to an amateur choir of men and boys continuing, there are certain contemporary lessons to be learned from the professional choirs. These are, I would suggest, mainly in the fields of outreach, demographic management and vocal health. The question of demographic management was discussed in Chapter 7. The point to add here is that it is often parish church choirs that are the worst offenders with regard to faulty demographics. The problem is closely related to the problem of outreach. It is hard to recruit new younger boys, therefore there is an understandable temptation to retain the older boys for too long in a fraught attempt to make the numbers look better. This problem is often compounded by a diminishing overall number of trebles.

It is sometimes forgotten (or perhaps never known by the younger generation) that in their heyday, parish choirs commonly contained between thirty and forty boys and seldom fewer than twenty-five. I can still count forty in the black and white photograph of the choir I was fortunate to accompany during the 1970s! These boys, however, had somewhat less powerful voices than their professional counterparts. This was really brought home to me not that many years ago when I took part in a joint evensong with a cathedral and parish choir. It was a good job it was not a rugby match because one cathedral boy was equal to at least three parish boys in power output! Boys who sing intensively in a professional context simply develop more powerful voices than boys who sing only at weekends. The power comes from regular conditioning, not forcing.

When the number of boys in a parish choir falls from the thirties to the low teens or fewer and the boys are exhorted mercilessly to make themselves heard above other sections of the choir, the result can come perilously close to the 'hoarse and oversung' that perhaps afflicted J.S. Bach (see Chapter 5). This is not at all conducive to good vocal health and I am led, frankly, to question whether it should happen at all. To some extent the situation is self-compensating through the lesser power of the men. Most amateur adult singers have nothing like the power and projection in their voices of the professional lay clerk. The question of balance, nevertheless, is one that needs to be looked at carefully.

This is related to the question of what to do with the boys when they are finally finished as trebles. In the professional choirs, it is accepted that the boy's time in the choir has simply come to an end. This can be a heart-wrenching time for tears and sadness, but I know of very few young men who have taken to a life of depressive alcoholism as a result. In spite of the extreme sensitivity some writers show to the phrase 'broken voice', professional choristers usually bounce back and become highly successful in their careers, musical or otherwise. The contention that boys are lost permanently to singing because they have been told that their voices have 'broken' is simply not borne out by the very encouraging number of highly successful professional vocal groups such as Voces8—all of whose male members are ex-choristers.

In the amateur singing world, a rather curious paradox exists. Many church choirs struggle to find enough men, or any men at all in some cases. Composers are even writing anthems for upper voices with an additional part that can be sung if any men happen to be present. Where the choir is all-male, in contrast, the problem can be that of too many men! This has to say something important about gender and choral singing and requires a whole book to do the topic justice. Should boys with changed voices simply continue to sing without break in an amateur men and boys' choir?

There is much to be said on the pastoral and social side for this, but there are dangers with regard to the singing. The boy may end up on the wrong part and he may well oversing in an attempt to sound like the men. These matters should already be adequately covered in Chapter 5, but it is worth reiterating the advice that young men with newly changed voices should be heard regularly and should sing gently in the lower region of whatever voice they have at the time. Keeping boys singing through voice change assumes that this will be done. If it is not, resting the voice, as advised by the old school of ecclesiastical choir training, may in fact be a preferable alternative to having boys sing tenor or alto too soon. The second danger is that, if the recruitment of younger boys is insufficient, the demographic balance of the choir will be too far out of kilter. The choir might even look wrong, with overflowing back rows and a few forlorn little trebles looking very small in an otherwise empty front row.

The best way of avoiding nearly all of these difficulties is to maintain high numbers in the choir. There is little point in reiterating the comments made in Chapter 7 about demographic management, save to point out how hard it really is. It has become very difficult for the well-intentioned but loan amateur running a men and boys' choir. Any choirs that survive and prosper are likely to be those that are truly wanted by clergy and congregations willing to demonstrate their commitment through imaginative, professional approaches to outreach, recruitment and retention. This can become too big a job for one person. It requires a team with a professional approach even if it is done for love rather than financial reward.

10.2   The choir director and the voice coach

My studies over the years have led to an increasing interest in the role of the voice coach or singing teacher. As we have just discussed, voice coaches have in recent decades become part of the team in professional choirs of men and boys, but have yet to become as accepted more generally. It is still possible to meet people who believe that children, unlike adults, have a 'natural voice' and that this will be spoiled or even damaged by singing lessons taken too early. I would like to know exactly what a child's 'natural voice' is! Is it a 'head voice' (as some argue vehemently) or a 'chest voice' (as others argue with equal vehemence). Is it a voice that sings accurately in tune or a voice that sings with more enthusiasm than aural awareness? Are we destroying children's 'natural voices' if we require them to sound vowels or articulate consonants in a particular way?

My view is that when we start asking questions such as this the idea of a 'natural voice' does not make a great deal of sense. We become guilty of the 'naturalistic fallacy'—the belief that whatever is found in raw nature is 'right'. Choirs are not found 'in nature' at all. As we have seen, the very act of singing is counter to nature. The larynx evolved as a valve to protect the lungs and one of the biggest problems in singing is remaining relaxed when 'nature' dictates muscular tension. If boys have a 'natural state', it is probably one of tree climbing in the rain forest. This does not require synchronisation of yells to the demands of a composer and I cannot actually imagine a choir of 'natural voices'. The concept is just incoherent. However, various claims have been made over the years about what are the more 'natural' ways of choral singing for boys. In Chapter 2 I referred to the work of George Malcolm at Westminster Cathedral. Malcolm, as well as being an early exponent of authenticity in the construction of musical instruments, believed that a more 'natural' sound would be produced if boys were not taught to produce an 'uncharacteristic quality of tone'. This has long fascinated me, so I made a trip to Westminster Cathedral to meet the boys and their current director, Martin Baker. I also arranged an interview with their singing teacher, Anita Morrison.

It is important, of course, to remind ourselves that Westminster Cathedral, being the premier Roman Catholic cathedral of England, is not really representative of the English Choral Tradition as defined by the Anglican evensong. The repertoire is 'continental' in that it reflects the Catholic liturgy, features frequently the music of such composers as Palestrina and Vittoria, employs a large amount of Gregorian plain chant, and considerably more Latin than would be found in the more typical Anglican cathedral. This, as we shall see, is of considerable significance.

Martin Baker is acutely aware of his position as inheritor of the George Malcolm tradition. He sees his role as honouring that tradition whilst adapting it to the present age without dogmatism. He is quite clear that the choir is a performance choir. 'We exist,' he says in reference to my concept of the greater anonymous audience, 'one hundred per cent for the people out there.' My own impression was that, though that might be so, the boys were learning a great deal through the daily practice of performance. The standards I observed being required were unremittingly demanding whilst also extremely musical. It was an interesting take on pedagogy and performance.

Martin shares some of my scepticism concerning the term 'continental tone' itself. The sound of the choir is not the robust tone of the Tölzer, though it clearly does have something of the incisive, cutting edginess that some listeners probably would call 'continental'. He also points out that 'these are Catholic boys singing mass in a long building'. The boys' normal performance position is an elevated one in the Eastern apse behind the high altar. A powerful sound must indeed be projected some distance down a voluminous space. Martin regards this as a 'high-risk' production that is 'more vulnerable to tiredness and off-days' than the more traditional, softer Anglican tone.

He sees technique as a means to an end and his role as defining that end. It is Anita's role more to define the how. Each boy has an individual fifteen-minute lesson with Anita on two out of every three weeks and all the boys have a weekly session with her on Saturday morning. The boys obviously spend a great deal more of their time rehearsing and performing with Martin than they do undergoing technical instruction with Anita. As we have discussed in earlier chapters, repertoire, performance conditions and acoustic environment do so much to condition the voice. What the boys actually do on a daily basis is therefore almost certainly the larger influence on the way they sing. Martin sees the process beginning with the actual selection of boys. 'Ideally you get a boy who speaks and sounds like it to start with. Some boys' voices just won't go there.'

He agrees very much that boys learn to sing primarily by imitation. One of the boys was able to articulate this in an interesting way: 'Our voices don't change over the years, it's the choir sound.' There is, of course, more to it than just imitation and daily rehearsal. Martin was clear that his main contribution to creating tone was the critical work he did on vowel production. The choir spends much time on the five pure Latin vowels, with attention also to pitched consonants. Accuracy and unanimity of vowel production plays a key role in creating the choir's tone. A sustained legato is really important to Martin with well-connected vowels not interrupted by clipped consonants. He described how he had come to refine his work in this area, paying increased attention to the pitched consonants. That, he says, has resulted in further improvement in the vowel sounds.

Anita elaborated on the importance of Martin's work on vowels. She is quite clear that the choir's brightness derives from resonance, not muscle tone. She preferred the term 'Italianate brightness' to the word 'steely' I used, though she conceded that 'I suppose there is a slight edge that makes the boys sound hearty'. She supports Martin's work on vowels by helping the boys develop resonance, a process that begins with the youngest who spend quite a lot of time on primal sounds such as whooping. This can result in the harder sound, even from young probationers. Anita felt that development as the boys grew older was more in agility than hardness of tone. During my visit, each year group of boys sang on their own to me, which certainly confirmed this to be the case. The unanimity of vowel production and pitch-matching I witnessed are, of course, the aims of disciplined choral singing by boys whatever the hoped-for tone. It is a matter of good, practical musicianship and professionalism.

Martin does not talk much about registration. 'Head voice? I leave that to Anita'. However, when pushed, he is confident that his boys use their whole voice. 'Anita wouldn't want me to use the George Malcolm term of shout and push things up.' Anita in fact is very clear that the boys use, and with some understanding, their whole voices. She dismisses the possibility that any boys at the Cathedral ever could have sung only in 'chest voice'. This is simply an urban myth. 'There's no way they would be able to [push chest voice to the top of the range]. They couldn't get above D[5]. It's impossible.' Equally, she says that she has never worked with boys who sing only in 'head voice'. I was reassured by what Anita had to say on this topic as it confirms my contention that Kenneth Phillips overstates the case in his description of the 'English choirboy school' (see Chapter 2).

According to Anita, 'It's how much they mix down. Down towards E[4] it'll become very breathy because the folds just won't phonate properly [in thin configuration/cricothyroid action].' As far as I am aware, Westminster is unique amongst English cathedrals in having boy altos. There are also adult counter-tenors, but these are more strongly represented at weekends. The boy altos hold much of the part during the week. This makes the choir in some ways more like a Germanic choir where SSA voicing is the norm rather than the English 'boys on the top line only' tradition.

The boy altos are not former trebles with changing voices. They are boys who have naturally slightly lower unchanged voices. I do not understand why boy altos are so rare outside the Germanic tradition. Place any three twelve-year-olds next to each other and you will observe probably significant differences in height. The same is true of their laryngeal dimensions. The range of SF_0 for boys in pre or early puberty is so great as to render any mean quite misleading. The situation I found in the choir, though, was one of somewhat more versatility than I had imagined after my first conversation with Martin on the phone. Boys can and do change from treble to alto and back as Martin experiments during the year whilst Anita 'keeps an eye on what is happening'. Most of the boys will have a little go at some stage, though for some it is 'no way'. This can only be possible if the boys are used to using their whole voices.

Benjamin Britten, who is said greatly to have liked the sound of Malcolm's boys, wrote his *Missa Brevis in D* for this choir. I really did want to hear how the boys coped with the large range of this piece, particularly the third treble part. The boys obliged and sang the Gloria from memory for me! I listened intently to hear how they tackled the low F sharp minor chord in bar 18. Martin goaded them with an obvious confidence in what they could do. 'He thinks you won't be able to sing that low'. Boys love a challenge! The F♯ itself is within a tone of the bottom of the alto range and midway between the bottom of the Cambiata I and II ranges. The tone was clear, not loud or forced, and of the quality of an unchanged voice. Some of the boys were keen to show me that they could reach below this F$\sharp$ and did manage a clear tone on the bottom note of the Cambiata II range (E3). These same boys, however, had no difficulty in reaching C6.

Anita was confident that, perhaps unlike some German choirs, the boys do nothing to increase 'chestiness' through attempting to enlarge the vocal tract by larynx depression: 'That just isn't good singing'. I was taken by a remark Martin made to them during the rehearsal, 'You're getting a little bit yobbish down on the low notes. Can we lighten up a bit?' Anita's take on 'natural' is that 'I just want to get the boys to sing free and easy, to get the best sound and not interfere. I don't fiddle and get in the way of their voices and the way each naturally wants to work.' She says that she applies quite a lot of Alexander technique and it was very clear from our conversation that a primary objective was to ensure that the boys were relaxed—tongues free, jaws free, breath and bodies well grounded.

In spite of the 'free and easy' approach, the boys were quite knowledgeable about singing technique. Anita described how she showed them YouTube videos of the vocal folds. 'It's important for them to have an image in their minds'. They had been particularly interested in looking at vowels on YouTube. Whether an actual knowledge of tract shape helps them to produce the resonance patterns that are asked for when particular vowel sounds are demanded would make an interesting research project. Anita believes that the boys know the consequences of folds thinning higher up the register and that they know when they are ready to transition to a different part of their voice: 'They know they'll get a clunk if they take thin folds too low or thick folds too high.'

On the subject of puberty, Anita felt that sometimes the older boys' falsetto is very beautiful. She thinks that they know their range and can be sensible. 'They will know if they have to mime above E5'. Martin reported that he regularly experienced all three classic patterns of voice change. During the current year, he had lost two out of five of his top year (Year 8, age 12.5–13.5) boys to pubertal change. Another Year 8 boy was said to be 'developing a falsetto'. We tested his voice with the app and found a SF$_0$ of 198 Hz, which would render this probably an accurate observation. These results are very much in line with those reported in Chapter 4 for the seven cathedral choirs assessed during my 2011–12 study. They provide some confirmation that the picture given there may be fairly general and they are perhaps a warning to amateur choirs that they should not be keeping more than about two-fifths of their Year 8 boys as trebles.

There is, however, one very important caveat to all of this. One would not pick Westminster Cathedral to be the most typical representation of the 'English choirboy' for the reasons already stated. Largely for this reason, I made a trip to the premier Anglican cathedral of the country. Canterbury Cathedral has a choral establishment of eighteen boys and twelve men. By today's standards, the workload is quite intense with choral services every day of the week, the boys singing all but one of them. At the time of writing, no girls' choir had been established to share this load, though that was in the process of changing. The Cathedral was venturing into a choir for girls at local schools that would sing occasionally.

The boys all attend nearby St Edmund's School, which serves as the choir school, though they also function together as a unit through Choir House, where they all board in the Cathedral precincts. The choir has had a voice coach for the last eight years. The choir's director is Dr David Flood, who has held the position since 1988, having once been assistant to Allan Wicks. David sees the choir in similar 'performance' terms to Martin Baker. 'We're definitely performing every day to different audiences. The boys are taught to sing as well, of course.' The notion of a pedagogical choir was one that David did not easily connect with. 'When I was at school your performances were to show off what you'd learnt, but at the higher end they do or should become performances in their own right.'

David readily agreed that the primary professional purpose of the Cathedral choir was the *opus dei* as I had described it. He prided himself on his responsibility for the choice of a wide, eclectic repertoire, partly necessitated by the diversity of the choir's audience and congregation—wide because of Canterbury Cathedral's role in the world. 'If you put on a concert of all Poulenc, not many would come.' David felt that it was much easier to teach great music to boys: 'Give them something like Brahms and they'll take to it straight away.' I asked him what he felt amateur choirs might learn from the professionals. His answer was in terms of inspiration and aspiration. A number of technical matters emerged during the discussion, however.

Concerning the necessity or otherwise of a voice coach/singing teacher, David had managed without such help for fifteen or so years and the relationship was one that needed to evolve. Kate, the current voice coach, described the relationship as at first one of 'him and me' but that has now developed into a much more integrated, professional teamwork approach. The boys' singing lessons are actually paid for by the school and Kate spends time on a different, secular repertoire with them, though also occasionally helping with the preparation of solos for the Cathedral.

Boys might take Associated Board singing exams with Kate. Grade 5 is set as the default standard. However, Kate does not regard this as a priority and is not that keen to encourage the practice. 'It's not what I'm here for.' What is Kate's role? As with Anita, it is not to change the sound of the choir. David sees her role as to 'produce good habits which I support' and help him achieve the end he is aiming for. The relationship in this sense is similar to the one between Anita and Martin at Westminster. The choir director remains in control and responsible for the ways the boys sing overall. The help of a second pair of knowledgeable eyes that can watch out for individual problems and bad habits helps prevent the faults that inevitably occur in individuals. It is hard to give much individual attention to boys within a busy choir with exacting demands and schedules.

Kate sees each boy for twenty minutes per week. She compares this with the two hours David sees them for on six days a week and agrees strongly with my contention that it is through imitation within an intense musical environment that the boys learn most of what they can do. It was Kate's suggestion that a particular choir sound evolves over the years through a process akin to natural selection, or at least selective breeding! The choir director praises the sounds he likes that just happen to be made by certain boys. Other boys then imitate the sound that is praised. I can think of no better explanation of the mysterious way in which a particular 'choir sound' evolves over the years.

I spent a day with Kate observing her teaching individual boys. I was struck by the very basic nature of the instruction relative to what might be done with adult students. Unsurprisingly, the boys arrived at their lessons far in advance of most non-choristers in their ability to sing the piece they chose accurately and musically (Howard Goodall's 'The Lord is my Shepherd'—the theme tune to TV's *Vicar of Dibley*—seemed the most popular choice!). Technical instruction though was mainly the reinforcement of very basic matters such as correct posture and, above all, breathing. Remembering to breathe at all, let alone in a certain way was on the agenda for several of the boys that came. A large amount of time was spent on ensuring that the boys were able to control tension in their bodies, but through such simple reminders as 'floppy shoulders' and 'are your knees locked again?' There was no attempt to steal from the boys the childish purity and naivety of tone that is so precious to those who value boys' choirs. I am as confident as I can be that this is in any case largely impossible through the direct instruction of young boys. In my experience, if one wants boys to lose their childish purity, the way to do it is through more indirect methods such as maintaining a soprano voice up to and beyond the completion of puberty.

Kate's teaching style was a gentle one that facilitated awareness and reflection in her pupils. She engaged one Year 7 boy in lengthy dialogue about where he needed a breath and whether he had enough in reserve for the phrase. The boy's own views were carefully considered and challenged where necessary. Tension in the jaw was also addressed. The boy was asked how his jaw was on the top note, replying that he thought it was 'fine'. 'What's more important? What you feel or what I see? You have to know what you feel and notice what you're doing.' She also picked up an articulation fault that required a different tongue placing to sound a clear 'd'. These are all small but very important features of a singing style that flows freely and easily, which is what both Kate and David want much as do Anita and Martin at Westminster. One particularly good feature of practice at Canterbury is Kate's weekly attendance at one of the morning rehearsals where she moves freely amongst the boys, gently correcting postural defects and noting points to discuss with David.

There is also a regular twice-termly meeting of choir director, singing teacher and house parent where each boy is discussed individually. Both Kate and David reported the usefulness of these meetings for identifying issues that might be resulting in tension. It cannot be repeated often enough that singing is not a 'natural' activity at all. What is 'natural' is for the larynx and airways to tense up ready for fight or flight. When one sings, one actually in that sense goes against nature, so vigilance against tension in boys (or any singers) must be constant.

One of Kate's important duties, of course, is to monitor the boys' progress through puberty. This she does quite discreetly and in a low key. She belongs very much to the 'as and when they need to know' school of thought, although will explain very clearly about the 'larynx growing' when questions are asked. She feels that, while information should be accurate, available and honest, the subject can provoke a 'mass hysteria' spreading through the choir if not carefully managed. This really does require careful reflection. Boys cannot be so stupid as not to know that they will lose their treble voice one day. They are, after all, surrounded by men and older boys, and they know that there are no boys beyond Year 8 in the choir. In my experience of choristers, if there is to be any 'mass hysteria' it is indeed more likely to be over losing treble voices than keeping them. I have heard anecdotal reports of 'vocal contagion' that is sometimes said to occur when one boy's voice really does change and all his peers then want to leave as well. I have, though, never been able formally to capture such an occurrence in research.

An important part of Kate's practice is being careful to obtain the SF_0 of each new boy on joining the choir as a probationer. In this way, she is able to detect any significant pubertal changes and discriminate between the boys whose voices are naturally low and the boys whose voices are beginning to change fast enough for a review of whether they should remain in the choir. The importance of this longitudinal approach was discussed in Chapter 3, so it was good to see it happening at Canterbury. I asked David if he felt he was losing boys to earlier puberty. He felt that he was, though it varied greatly from year to year. In 2008 he kept all his Year 8s in the choir until July. Since that exceptionally good year he had been losing two or three a year, but the 2012–13 year was a bad one. All the Year 8 boys had gone by March, the month of the enthronement of the new Archbishop! While unfortunate for the choir, this pattern conforms almost perfectly to that predicted by the seven cathedrals research I reported in Chapter 4. Also in agreement with those research findings was David's belief that 'Year 7 is the golden year'. There is little doubt that the age of twelve is the time most boys peak as trebles.

I was very keen to explore with David my contention that the bottom register of a boy's voice is under-used. His first reaction to the question was simply to affirm that a boy's whole voice should be used. The problem he perceived was that it was the higher register that was generally the neglected one. Many of the points he made are ones well-rehearsed throughout my writing. For example, most children never use their whole voice because the music for primary schools is generally pitched too low. Boys are used to hearing a lot of shouted tone. Boys are told that they sound 'girly' by their peers. Also in agreement with research findings, though, was the more positive 'When we sing to St Edmunds, their peers are mightily impressed with what they can do. They knock people flat.' Although all this is known and related elsewhere, it was good to have it confirmed again by as experienced a practitioner as David Flood. Perhaps the most important point here is not to give in to pressures of 'uncool'. When boys see or hear real ability and real quality, they recognise it and forget about what the media tells them is 'cool'.

Assuming that boys are using their upper register, though, what of the lower register and those neglected notes below E4? David agreed with me that the boys do not often encounter that part of their register, but that he would use the whole voice when the music called for it. 'An exception might be when we do Ceremony of Carols. Then I select the boys who can comfortably reach that range. I discourage them from pushing their voices down.' David felt that it was not necessarily always the older ones that had the lower reach. 'There are some boys for whom low A is easy and strong. You could get a boy aged eight who could get there.' Nevertheless, it was the case that for most boys in the choir, the bottom range increased with maturity and this could lead in some cases to pitching difficulties across the passagio for the older ones. I met the current head chorister in his singing lesson and he was able to talk to me about how he negotiated this difficulty through vowel modification.

What then about boy altos? David felt that quite young boys could be alto, but that it would be wrong to use them where they are only required for the treble line. Unlike some of the smaller cathedrals, he experienced no shortage of good counter-tenors. He encountered increasing numbers of fifteen- and sixteen-year-old ex-choristers who came to him looking for opportunities to re-join the choir in some way. The most important criterion for re-admission was less often vocal than the need to pass a DBS (formerly CRB) check on attaining the age of sixteen. Surely, I suggested, their voices would not be mature by that age? He agreed that maturity of course seldom came before the age of twenty, but felt that the voices could still be usable. He says:

> Kate is in touch and she will say if it's wrong. They don't have as much power but they have great clarity and the owner of the voice is desperate to demonstrate it. It also keeps up their reading skills and I will only use a voice when it is ready to be used.

In this way, he had had two strong altos in recent years.

Another question I was anxious to put to David was about balance and the ratio of boys to men. He felt that his own eighteen boys to twelve men was a good balance that allowed all parts to sing fully. I described to him the problem in some parish choirs where there are more men than boys. When I described a situation of ten boys against over twenty men his face visibly contorted with horror. 'Ten boys against twenty men? I would never allow the boys to oversing in such a way. It would be ugly and unhealthy.' He did not always have the full eighteen boys present due to circumstances such as sickness, but professional lay clerks, he felt, knew automatically how to moderate their voices to match the available power of the boys. There had been some good services with as few as fourteen boys against twelve men. David did see a role for muscle tone in creating the power that a cathedral chorister will have relative to a boy in an amateur choir: 'It's because we do it every day.' However, he was also in agreement with Anita's point that fully developed resonance and, of course, accurate unanimous vowel production played a very important part.

David had some interesting views on singing falsetto with boys in rehearsal. He was one of several interviewees who have finally persuaded me to change my position on the vexed question of the octave transposition mechanism. He felt that it was difficult for inexperienced seven- and eight-year-olds to understand that the sound they have to make is an octave higher than a male voice, though by the age of nine they should have grasped this. It was not a problem with many of the US choirs he had worked with where the directors had been female. His own practice now was to use a falsetto voice 'only for pitch-matching.' Rarely did he use an alto voice in rehearsal: 'I will demonstrate their line in a tenor voice.' This seems to me to define best practice (see also Warwickshire Choristers in Chapter 9.) The choir director's falsetto voice should be used sparingly when needed to assist pitch-matching. Good technique and musical interpretation of the part is demonstrated by the choir director's true singing voice.

On the subject of recruitment, the interview took a slightly depressing turn. The issue was with the primary schools where David felt the situation was getting steadily worse. He would ask at schools, 'Who looks after the music?' and would receive more and more often the reply, 'Nobody does.' Sing Up, then, appears to have had little longer-term impact, in Kent schools at least. 'It's not seen as an important thing anymore.' I put the inevitable question about backing tracks. He did not think they were a good way to teach singing because 'there's no interaction, no ebb and flow, no human relationship.' Nevertheless, he did feel that anything to open a door to children singing had to be better than nothing at all: 'So many adults come to me with stories that they had been told at the age of thirteen that they couldn't sing.'

For the Cathedral itself, there had not been any real difficulties in recruiting. 'We have good PR, the Cathedral's always being reported. The package we offer is good and the reputation is high.' Nevertheless, David had taken to 'pre-electing' six-year-olds. 'If I see outstanding six-year-olds in Year 2, I'll pre-elect them.' He felt that this was a risky strategy in that he might not then have a place for an even better boy who came later, but it does underline my point that choirs really do have to think younger these days. David agreed that many parents today do not know what an evensong is (see 10.3) and he has to 'unwrap' frankly for them what choristership entails. 'Most are delighted when they understand. Some have even moved house to be closer to the Cathedral.'

David spends a lot of time working with young children and clearly enjoys doing so. Indeed, he was heading off to the United States the day after our interview to run some children's choir workshops. I explored the inevitable question about fear. Was it fear that held so many teachers back from singing with children? How does one deal with this apparently insurmountable barrier of personality in getting children to sing? David felt a lot of it is built upon an instinctive trust. A child's attitude was, 'I will do it for you if I understand what you're doing.' He illustrated his point with a story I found fascinating because of the research interest I have in boys' judgements of conductors. He had been involved with the appointment of his successor at Lincoln Cathedral and a chorister he knew well made a poor job of singing for one of the candidates in the demonstration rehearsal. On questioning the boy afterwards, he received the reply, 'Of course I can do it. I wouldn't do it for him though.'

10.3   Puberty and the sound of the choir

The final case study is based on what has been my 'local' during the period of research for this book. Blackburn is one of England's smaller cathedrals, but also one of its more enterprising. I am very grateful to Sam Hudson, the present director of music, and to his predecessors on the music staff, Richard Tanner and James Davey, for the opportunity to study the boys closely, making full annual assessments of their growth and development and conducting various experiments on them. Sam's interest in my research on the boys' development and his anxiety to provide the best vocal care and development for them are gratifying. The most recent of my experiments is described shortly. First, I describe Sam's perspectives on some of the other issues discussed in this chapter.

Blackburn Cathedral is ambitious for its music and affords local boys the opportunity to engage in a high standard of choral work. The choir has managed for many years without a choir school but recently a decision has been made that all the boys will attend the same secondary school. Blackburn's chorister outreach programme, in my estimation, is one of the best in the country. At the time of writing, chorister outreach is as healthy as ever in spite of the ending of Sing Up funding. This does not make recruitment for the choir easy, though. Sam reports that fewer and fewer families come with much knowledge of the Christian faith and that they are not generally getting parents who understand what a cathedral is. He spoke of one boy who was halfway through his time in the choir, whose parents were now 100 per cent supportive, but only after they had come to see the benefits for themselves. This had been difficult to achieve at the outset. Sam feels that it is probably very difficult now for a parish church. He feels that there is a certain amount of prestige involved with the Cathedral and this helps: 'The guys like to say we sing in a cathedral.'

Sam feels that the choir does not fit entirely into either category of pedagogy or performance. As a performance choir, it is primarily a servant of the liturgy. In other words, its primary role is indeed the *opus dei* and Sam sees this as granting a degree of freedom from the demands of paying audiences. Alongside this primary role, Sam acknowledges a clear pedagogical function. Part of this is spiritual. Unlike Westminster, where boys must be practising Catholics to gain entry to the choir, a good many boys come to confirmation as a result of their contact with the Cathedral.

Sam thinks carefully about the music the choir sings, looking for opportunities to teach the boys about its history. The boys have a regular weekly theory lesson, but Sam is not convinced that there is much knowledge transfer. He aims for a marriage of practical and theoretical study during a rehearsal. Sam agrees with me that boys learn to sing primarily by imitation, and feels that they learn a lot from each other. However, he is anxious to take them beyond this stage as quickly as possible. He feels that any boy who comes to the Cathedral will already be able to sing and pitch notes. It is far less common for them to have any understanding of theory or notation. 'It's musically plausible that a young boy will learn a piece purely by copying. I can spot that happening and I try to steer their attention to the score.'

Blackburn Cathedral employs two vocal coaches and Sam finds their help invaluable for a variety of reasons. He believes that good choral tone is something that is clear, focused and blended as a group. Unity of vowel sound is very important. Good vocal coaching, Sam thinks, can contribute quite a lot to blend quality. Individual training in technique, he thinks, goes some way to achieving unity of blend when the boys sing together. 'Then there's the whole "breathy" word. I guess I aim for "not too breathy"'. The vocal coaches can help with this too and Sam believes in a 'dual approach': 'If I've identified a locked jaw or pitching difficulty the vocal coaches can work on it. A vocal coach can also say to me, 'I've found this problem.' Sam thinks the opportunity for choristers to have more individual and small group attention is really important. Younger and less confident boys gain a lot from a smaller group approach and 'if a boy has a solo coming up, work with a vocal coach saves a lot of rehearsal time.'

What is the impact on boy trebles of being in this choir when the other three parts are sung by men? Sam thinks there's a different atmosphere at rehearsal when the men are present. 'They think, this is it, now.' The boys are being encouraged to perform on a par with professional singers. They are challenged to get a job done and to sing at a volume that will balance the men. This is not, I would stress, done by forcing tone. It is done by having a sufficient number of boys with well-conditioned voices to do the job.

Of course, the boys are no more able to look forwards to moving into the men's section at voice change in this than any other English cathedral choir. I asked Sam to reflect on the quotation from Bairstow in Chapter 5 (that it is no use boys with changing voices bothering to sing). He was keen to stress that his responsibilities as director of music extend beyond the main cathedral choir. 'I have to make sure I use every musical resource available. I can't send anybody away. It's partly the times, partly the part of the country.' Sam explained that if they wanted to play the organ they could, or they could sing in one of the other choirs. 'It's important to keep them involved in the wider musical scene.'

The Cathedral maintains a Young People's Choir (YPC) for older girls, some girls from the girls' choir and teenage boys up to college age. Most of them are ex-choristers, but they don't have to be. There are, for example, some young men who have moved to Blackburn for sixth form study. The choir sings a full choral Eucharist every month and on other important occasions such as Christmas morning, Remembrance Sunday and a 'very early' dawn Eucharist on Easter Day. I put it to Sam that in spite of this, the YPC would not be as good as the cathedral choir itself. Was it not a comedown for ex-choristers? It turned out that Sam is a believer in the diamond model. There is merit in progression from a men and boys choir to a mixed-gender choir of young adults: 'The YPC is far enough away from the cathedral choir for them to accept things. It's a different director, changed repertoire, but most importantly it's more informal and a chance for them to develop as young adults.'

This points, I believe, to an important lesson for parish churches. A men and boys' choir in contemporary choral work is more likely to thrive as one part of the total musical scene. The diamond model applies. If there is a boys-only choir, only a very hard line would take the view that discrimination against girls is acceptable. If there are separate boys' and girls' choirs and these are both successful, there is probably a need for something like a mixed-gender young adult choir too, perhaps to operate as a buffer between voice change and leaving home. This is perhaps a better place for young men whose developing voices can be regularly assessed and properly cared for. Social integration of young adults now matters where previously the need was to allow vocal development to proceed unhindered by the complexities of sex dimorphism or gender construction. At the other end of the diamond, if you are recruiting from primary schools, there is no disadvantage in running a mixed-gender nursery choir for seven to eight year olds. A factor common to Blackburn as a smaller cathedral and some of the greater parish churches is success in keeping a men and boys' choir through having other choirs as well.

10.4   Puberty and choral tone at Blackburn: some final words

I am going to close with a final look at the main theme of the book—puberty and choral tone. My particular interest in the topic at this juncture concerns the challenges thrown up by the secular trend. We have seen that there is a long-standing tightrope to be walked between musical maturity and physical maturity. We have also seen that there is much more concern with boys' vocal health in contemporary choral work. These two concerns potentially act against each other. Another area of tension concerns how much falsetto tone a choir will tolerate. Researchers such as Denis Striny (2007) and John Wayman (2009) have demonstrated that voices that sound clearly falsetto when heard individually became quite elusive within the choral blend. The majority of English singing teachers quoted in this book see no harm in limited use of falsetto in boys' choirs, taking the view that boys in their early teens are quite capable of sensible self-management. The falsetto tone of some boys can also be quite beautiful.

Given the secular trend I had hypothesized that if the age demographics of choirs remained constant but the average timing of puberty advanced, the proportion of falsetto voices might increase. I had also found in my study of seven cathedrals that younger boys (typically those under the age of ten) could not sing intervals completely accurately when tested on their own. Yet this inaccurate singing also disappeared within the mysterious black box of the choral blend. The opportunity to assess the Blackburn boys in some depth on a regular basis has allowed some useful insights that go beyond what was possible in the earlier cross-sectional study of seven cathedrals. Contact with boys in a cross-sectional study does not offer the opportunity to follow up developments or assess the onset of puberty by noting changes.

Investigation of the choral blend is notoriously difficult. There are good grounds to believe that the singing behaviour of a boy might differ in chorus from what may be heard when the boy is tested on his own in a more clinical setting. There are two basic approaches to investigating individual voices in a chorus, which we may call the analytic and the synthetic. The analytic method requires that each singer in a choir be individually fitted with a radio microphone, and recorded as a separate track on a multi-channel recording system whilst the whole choir is singing. Harold Jers (Jers & Ternström, 2005) has pioneered such work with adult choirs in Germany. In Sweden, Svenker Zadig (2011) conducted a similar style study with a young person's choir, entitled The individual voice in the choral voice. These studies have shown that voices in chorus are milliseconds apart in their timing and that it is possible to identify 'leaders' and 'followers' within the choral blend.

The synthetic method works the other way round. Singers are recorded individually and then mixed together to create a 'virtual choir'. This might be considered a radical if not bizarre thing to do in conventional choral circles, but the technique is very much part and parcel of everyday work in the modern recording studio. Virtual choirs have started to grow in popularity as a cultural phenomenon. The one created by Eric Whitacre (see http://ericwhitacre.com/the-virtual-choir>) is a particularly notable example. I once experimented with a virtual cambiata choir. As each boy left the real choir on voice change, I added his voice to the virtual choir, creating a chorus of boys in the immediately ex-treble stage but several years apart in age. It would have been impossible for them to sing together in real life. It was part curiosity and part fun, but I did learn that a chorus effect seems to be created by the artificial mixing of individual voices.

As far as I know, nobody has yet attempted to create a virtual cathedral choir in a serious attempt to investigate how the overall choral tone relates to the individual voices that happen to make up the choir. I set out, therefore, thinking I might create a resource that would allow different versions of the choir to be created by different mixes as well as hearing the voices individually. In this way, the number of falsetto voices heard in the chorus might be regulated, indeed the entire age demographic of the choir could readily be manipulated at the mixing desk. The secondary aim of the study was actually to compare the sound of the whole choir when recorded conventionally with that of the same choir on the same day synthesized from individual voices. I was not entirely sure what to expect here, but felt intuitively, as would any curious scientist, that it ought to be done.

The test piece chosen was Vaughan Williams' setting of 'This is the Truth Sent from Above'. Using Logic Pro software, a piano accompaniment guide track was first laid down, with a one bar click track to assist starting. (An organ track was also laid down, but in the end not used.) Starting with the head and deputy head chorister, each boy came one at a time in descending order of seniority to lay down his individual track. The boy wore one pair of headphones and I another so that I could 'conduct' him. Each boy rehearsed his part before recording, receiving the same instructions about where to breathe, how long to hold notes at ends of phrases and how to enunciate key consonants, etc. Once the more senior boys had laid the first few tracks, it became possible to offer the younger boys the option of singing either with the piano accompaniment, or with the voices of their older peers. Interestingly, all of them expressed a preference for singing with the piano. In the event two tracks were laid by each younger boy, one to the piano accompaniment and one to the assembled voices of the older boys.

Finally the whole choir took up their normal places in the choir stalls in the cathedral and performed the piece as they normally would with their regular conductor. An artificial acoustic with the same properties of resonance and decay was added to the virtual choir mix. Almost all listeners, including Sam Hudson himself, report that the virtual choir is quite convincing. The chorus effect is certainly heard and the tone is indistinguishable from that of the real choir. Indeed, if only one recording is played and this is the virtual choir, listeners almost invariably state that it is the real choir. The differences are often only detected when both recordings are played. Listeners then identify that the boys are slightly less well together in the virtual choir, and their tuning less unanimous.

Manipulation of the balance and age demographic has some surprising effects. Reduction in the amount of falsetto tone has little perceptual effect, suggesting that choral blend is indeed quite resilient against invasion by some degree of falsetto. However, none of the older boys individually had an unpleasant falsetto tone. In contrast, the younger boys appear to sing louder in the virtual choir and appeared to be mainly responsible for the less unanimous tuning. When their voices are faded down in the mix, the real and virtual choirs sound more alike. A counter-intuitive finding was that the younger boys' intonation was less accurate when singing with other voices than when singing with the piano, though in both cases it was the younger boys who were mainly responsible for tuning faults.

This accords with the cross-sectional study where younger boys judged the key intervals of a fifth and an octave somewhat less accurately than boys aged eleven and over. This is hardly a surprise, but what was perhaps more surprising was that the younger boys at Blackburn all preferred to sing with the piano. Perhaps they felt that this was a moment to show off their voices uninhibited by the older boys. When singing normally with the real choir, they tend to take a more subordinate role. I am unable to say whether the more unanimous singing in the real choir was due to the boys all watching the conductor carefully, listening to each other more carefully, or simply the less accurate singers taking a more subordinate role.

In a separate investigation with another parish church choir, I placed an individual radio microphone on one of the boys in my longitudinal study. I knew for a fact that this boy had reached the 'dark green shirt' stage of puberty and was technically no longer a treble. In one to one clinical testing, it was very clear that he had two pronounced register breaks and a falsetto only reducing top register. He experienced considerable difficulties in control of notes occurring within his passagio. This was not audible when listening to the choir as a whole. I wanted to find out whether some mysterious adrenalin factor came into play when singing with the choir. The answer was that it did not. The same difficulties in passagio were clearly heard when the voice was picked out by the radio microphone. I could not, however, hear these faults in the singing of the whole choir. Perception seems to play a big role in what is heard from a choir. Either the more accurate singing of the best voices dominates, or listener perception moulds an accurate choral sound out of a mixture of inaccuracies occurring at different places.

This particular line of research is at quite an early stage and it may take some years before robust conclusions can finally be drawn. I have included it as a suitable ending to the book, however, for what it says about puberty and age demographics. The secular trend may not be as serious a threat to choirs as is sometimes feared.

References

Jers, H. & Ternström, S. (2005). Intonation analysis of a multi-channel choir recording. *Speech, Music and Hearing: Quarterly Progress and Status Report*, 47(1):1–6.

Mould, A. (2007). *The English Chorister*. London: Hambledon/Continuum.

Striny, D. (2007). *Head First: The Language of the Head Voice*. Lanham MD: Hamilton Books.

Wayman, J. (2009). Identification of the adolescent male voice: unchanged vs. falsetto. MME thesis, Texas Technical University.

Zadig, S., (2011). The single voice in the choral voice: how does the role of informal leaders in the choral voice affect the other singers? In U. Geisler & K Johansson (eds.), *Choir in Focus 2011*. Malmo: Kör Centrum Syd.

Index

Lightning Source UK Ltd.
Milton Keynes UK
UKOW05f0123151016

285266UK00002B/147/P